Lecture Notes in Computer Sci

Commenced Publication in 1973
Founding and Former Series Editors:
Gerhard Goos, Juris Hartmanis, and Jan van Leeuwen

Willem Jonker   Milan Petković (Eds.)

Secure
Data Management

9th VLDB Workshop, SDM 2012
Istanbul, Turkey, August 27, 2012
Proceedings

 Springer

Volume Editors

Willem Jonker
University of Twente, EIT ICT Labs
Faculty of Electronical Engineering, Mathematics and Computer Science
P.O. Box 217, 7500 AE Enschede, The Netherlands
E-mail: willem.jonker@ictlabs.eu

Milan Petković
Philips Research Europe, Technical University Eindhoven
High Tech Campus 34, 5656 AE Eindhoven, The Netherlands
E-mail: milan.petkovic@philips.com

ISSN 0302-9743   e-ISSN 1611-3349
ISBN 978-3-642-32872-5   e-ISBN 978-3-642-32873-2
DOI 10.1007/978-3-642-32873-2
Springer Heidelberg Dordrecht London New York

Library of Congress Control Number: 2012944556

CR Subject Classification (1998): H.2.7-8, K.6.5, H.3, H.4, E.3, C.2

LNCS Sublibrary: SL 3 – Information Systems and Application, incl. Internet/Web
and HCI

Typesetting: Camera-ready by author, data conversion by Scientific Publishing Services, Chennai, India

Printed on acid-free paper

Springer is part of Springer Science+Business Media (www.springer.com)

Preface

This year was the ninth edition of the VLDB Secure Data Management Workshop. The topic of data security remains an important area of research especially with the ever-growing amounts of data in numerous application areas and on the World-Wide Web.

We received 22 submissions of which the Program Committee selected 10 full papers and 2 position papers to be presented at the workshop and included in the proceedings (approx. 50% acceptance rate). We hope the papers collected in this volume will stimulate your research in this area.

The regular papers in the proceeding are grouped into four sections. Privacy and access control remain central topics in secure data management, especially where new applications keep posing new and often increasing requirements. Therefore the first two sections focus on privacy protection and access control. With the fast growth of the cloud for applications and data storage the need for security solutions for applications storing data in the cloud is also growing. Therefore, the third section focuses on secure storage on the cloud. Finally, the topic of trust is receiving more and more attention and gaining concreteness in recent research activities. Thus, the fourth and final section focuses on trust on the Web.

We wish to thank all the authors of submitted papers for their high-quality submissions. We would also like to thank the Program Committee members as well as additional referees for doing an excellent review job. Finally, we acknowledge Christoph Bösch who helped in the technical preparation of the proceedings.

August 2012

Willem Jonker
Milan Petković

Organization

Workshop Organizers

Willem Jonker   EIT ICT Labs/University of Twente,
     The Netherlands

Milan Petković   Philips Research/Eindhoven University of
     Technology, The Netherlands

Program Committee

Gerrit Bleumer	Francotyp-Postalia, Germany
Ljiljana Brankovic	University of Newcastle, Australia
Sabrina De Capitani di Vimercati	University of Milan, Italy
Ernesto Damiani	University of Milan, Italy
Eric Diehl	Techicolor, France
Jeroen Doumen	Irdeto, The Netherlands
Csilla Farkas	University of South Carolina, USA
Elena Ferrari	Università degli Studi dell'Insubria, Italy
Simone Fischer-Hubner	Karlstad University, Sweden
Tyrone Grandison	IBM Research, USA
Dieter Gollmann	Technische Universität Hamburg-Harburg, Germany
Marit Hansen	Independent Centre for Privacy Protection, Germany
Min-Shiang Hwang	National Chung Hsing University, Taiwan
Mizuho Iwaihara	Waseda University, Japan
Sushil Jajodia	George Mason University, USA
Ton Kalker	Huawei, USA
Marc Langheinrich	University of Lugano (USI), Switzerland
Nguyen Manh Tho	Vienna University of Technology, Austria
Sharad Mehrotra	University of California at Irvine, USA
Stig Frode Mjolsnes	Norwegian University of Science and Technology, Norway
Eiji Okamoto	University of Tsukuba, Japan
Sylvia Osborn	University of Western Ontario, Canada
Günther Pernul	University of Regensburg, Germany
Bart Preneel	KU Leuven, Belgium
Kai Rannenberg	Goethe University Frankfurt, Germany

David G. Rosado   Universidad de Castilla-La Mancha, Spain
Ahmad-Reza Sadeghi   Darmstadt University, Germany
Andreas Schaad   SAP Labs, France
Jason Smith   Queensland University of Technology, Australia
Morton Swimmer   Forward-looking Threat Research, Trend
                                   Micro, Germany
Clark Thomborson   University of Auckland, New Zealand
Nicola Zannone   TU/e, The Netherlands

Table of Contents

Trust on the Web

Tradeoff Analysis of Relational Database Storage of Privacy Preferences

Md. Sadim Mahmud and Sylvia L. Osborn

Department of Computer Science,
The University of Western Ontario,
London, ON, Canada
mmahmud4@alumni.uwo.ca, sylvia@csd.uwo.ca

Abstract. When data providers are allowed to specify the privacy purposes for the data they enter into a database, this information must be stored in the database and dealt with by database operators. We introduce four storage designs incorporating sets of intended privacy purposes in a table in a relational database, and perform experiments to study their performance when executing select, insert, update and delete using the storage designs. A thorough discussion of the tradeoffs exposed is given.

1 Introduction

In a business, person-specific data are collected from customers, also known as data providers, as part of service requirements. For example, an on-line company would have data concerning its inventory, personnel and customers. The inventory data would be stored in a relational database in the usual format. However, the company may allow customers to label the individual attributes of their personal data for different business purposes, which we call *privacy purposes*. These privacy labels would vary from one customer to another, and can be changed at the whim of the data provider.

We distinguish between *data providers* and *users*, the former being the people whose personal information's privacy is to be protected, the latter being anyone who accesses the database in the course of business operations - this includes company employees and data providers. We assume several interfaces which we will not elaborate on. These include an interface which allows the data providers to insert, examine and update their personal data and their privacy preferences. There are also possibly many business applications which allow users to place orders, update inventory, ship purchases to customers, etc. These applications are assumed to be able to specify the access purpose when privacy-labeled data is being accessed (we assume that it is a single privacy purpose for each access), and it is assumed that data labeled with privacy preferences is filtered appropriately before being returned to users. Byun and Li [4] contains a good discussion of how to determine access purpose and also how to set default privacy preferences for data providers conforming to certain laws and best practise. Since there is a set

W. Jonker and M. Petković (Eds.): SDM 2012, LNCS 7482, pp. 1–13, 2012.

of possible privacy purposes, the labels we are dealing with are sets of purposes. We assume that these labels can be applied to any of the attributes in a table in a relational database, except the primary key attribute(s).

We motivate this discussion by briefly introducing two scenarios. The first is an on-line catalog business, where customers register and give personal information, order merchandise, pay for it and have it shipped to them. Data providers are allowed to specify purposes (e.g. SHIPPING, FINANCE) to restrict access to some attributes in their personal information to only applications being run for that purpose. Insertion of new customers would be a frequently executed operation, as are queries to locate the customer information, and queries relating to the shipping of and payment for orders. Data providers may update their information and privacy settings occasionally. The second scenario is a social media website, where new data providers and their information is inserted with some frequency, data providers frequently update their personal information and, less frequently, their privacy settings. Their information is selected frequently by their friends. In both of these scenarios, database operations select, insert and update are important. Deletion of the tuple concerning a data provider is also required, although it is not frequently done.

The purpose of this paper is to examine different storage schemes for data with privacy labels on all non-key attributes in a relation containing personal information given by data providers, when relational database operations select, insert, update and delete are performed. Byun and Li [4] have considered a single storage design only for the select operation, but with several labeling granularities. We examine 4 different storage schemes, and show their performance under the four operations listed above. We do not assume a purpose hierarchy, but simply a set of purposes from which the data provider can chose as many as he or she wishes for each attribute (not including the primary key) of their personal data.

We begin in Section 2 with related work. This is followed by Section 3 where our 4 designs are described. Section 4 presents the results of our experiments, a discussion of the tradeoffs exposed, and a brief discussion of possible extensions. We conclude and discuss future work in Section 5.

2   Related Work

Recently, work has been done on adding privacy preferences to data supplied by data providers. This complements work on k-anonymity [10,13], which seeks to preserve privacy of individuals by always grouping them with $k - 1$ others in an answer to a query. Such anonymity is not suitable for the kind of applications we have in mind, where a data provider's data must be used to carry out the business, to ship goods to them or charge them for goods, for example. Privacy has been considered together with role-based access control [3,7]. The work closest to ours is by Byun and Li [4], who consider privacy labels at different granularities.

In their work, labels are applied to every attribute value in a relation, which they call element-level labeling, to every row, or to whole tables. They also consider a purpose tree of privacy labels; in the example in Figure 1, the nodes higher in the tree are considered more general than their descendants. They also allow positive (allowed intended purposes) statements about privacy preferences and negative (prohibited intended purposes) ones. Our work focuses on element-level labeling and initially we do not assume a privacy tree. We assume only allowed (positive) intended purposes are provided.

Fig. 1. Sample Purpose Tree

Labels have been applied to relational databases in the past. For Mandatory Access Control (MAC), labels are taken from a lattice [11], and typically have values like top-secret, confidential, etc. When one combines two pieces of information with different labels, the combination is labeled by the least upper bound (LUB), which, because the labels are in a lattice, is unique; the LUB is the security level at which this combination must be treated. Labels were also studied for time values in a database [9]. Different kinds of time can be considered: valid time - the time during which a certain value is valid (e.g. your salary from 2010/1/1 to 2010/12/31), and transaction time - the time the value was recorded in the database. For time, there is a fixed number of values that make up the label (e.g. valid start and end time, and transaction time). For MAC, since the labels come from a lattice, a single LUB can be assigned to each combination of values, so only a single-valued label is ever needed for a database attribute value or tuple. One storage scheme proposed for MAC, for the purpose of security, was to partition the data into that part visible at each security level and store the partitions in separate physical locations under control of a secure operating system, also labeled and treated as appropriate for that security level [8]. This was to prevent a user being able to see data they were not cleared for by stumbling into the file where it is stored. This physical partitioning of the database to satisfy MAC security policies contains a lot of redundant data, as users cleared to a high level can see data at lower levels, and the lower-level data is therefore duplicated in all the containers labeled at higher security levels [5,6].

While privacy labels may be arranged in a tree or hierarchy [4], this hierarchy should not be treated as a lattice. Suppose we have a tree of purpose labels as in

Figure 1, in which MARKETING is the parent of MAIL, EMAIL and PHONE. If a data provider has labeled a data item with {MAIL, EMAIL}, it is not correct to replace this label with {MARKETING} because the customer did not wish this information to be used for PHONE marketing. So the first difference we have with these old models is that we might have *sets* of privacy labels which are subsets of a given set of possible labels. In other words, we cannot reduce the members of such a set to their LUB as we could in a lattice-based system. We should point out that although it is not correct to change the label in the database consisting of {MAIL, EMAIL} to {MARKETING}, when a user with an access purpose {EMAIL} wishes to access data, and the data is labeled {MARKETING}, this access is allowed.

The second difference between privacy labels and MAC or time labels concerns the uniformity of the labeling. For MAC databases, solutions have been discussed where every attribute value is labeled with a single label [5,6], or each key value and each row is labeled [12]. The time-based labels can be per attribute, but only some attributes would have them (e.g. salary), or the whole tuple would be labeled once if the relevant attributes have been fragmented out. There would be a small number of values in a label (say two for valid start/end, and one for transaction time) and all tuples in a relational table would have the same label pattern. For the privacy labels, if there are p possible labels, all 2^p patterns of these labels are possible. Some data providers might not care about the privacy of some of their information (e.g. their name or address), so that some values in a column can have labels, and others not (or have a DON'T CARE label or the empty set). Not only can the labels vary from row to row in a table, but updates by the data provider can change the labels, e.g. from {PHONE, EMAIL} to {MAIL}.

The third issue is frequency and format of updates. MAC labels are fairly static. Updates to time labels could be frequent but the format of the label would not change. Updates to privacy labels are at the whim of the data provider, so they could be very frequent. They could also change from no label to an arbitrary set, or from one arbitrary set to another. Thus it is essential that any storage scheme be able to accommodate updates to privacy label sets in a fairly efficient manner.

The labeling required for relational data when privacy purposes are to be recorded is, then, clearly different from labeling schemes previously studied. Byun and Li [4] have only studied one version of storage of such data for element-level labeling. They have only looked at the select operation. This paper considers 4 different storage designs for element-level labeling and considers 4 relational operations: select, insert, update and delete.

3   Designs

We tested four storage designs for labeling relations in a relational database with privacy labels, which we will call basic, partitioned, partitioned mask, and single mask. Briefly, in System A, the *basic design*, each attribute in the table may have a set of labels stored in an adjacent column; in System B, the *partitioned design*, the table is partitioned into multiple tables, one for each purpose; System C, the *partitioned mask design,* has a data table with no labels, and a mask table for each purpose showing which corresponding data item is visible for that purpose; and System D, the *single mask design* has a data table and one mask table. Each design is discussed in some detail, with an example, in the following paragraphs.

We illustrate each design with a sample of the customer information data which is used for the experiments described in the next section. For System A, the *basic design,* each attribute of the table has a set of labels from a predefined set. We do not assume a purpose hierarchy. We do, however have an ADMIN purpose which represents database system administration, and we assume that ADMIN can see everything. The purposes which data providers can choose are MARKETING, FINANCE, SHIPPING, and PURCHASING, denoted by M, F, S, and P in Table 1. Note that the ADMIN purpose (A) is in all purpose sets. If the original relation has n attributes, including one key attribute, then the basic design has $2n - 1$ attributes, where the $n - 1$ additional attributes consist of sets of privacy labels.

Table 1. System A, Basic Design for the Customer Information Table

UserID	Title	L_Title	FirstName	L_FirstName	LastName	L_LastName
4	Mr	{A,M,F}	Gustavo	{A,S}	Achong	{A,M,F}
5	Ms.	{A,M,F}	Catherine	{A,P}	Abel	{A,M,F}
6	Ms.	{A,M}	Kim	{A,S}	Abercrombie	{A,M}
7	Sr.	{A,S}	Humberto	{A,M,F}	Acevedo	{A,S}
8	Sra	{A,P}	Pilar	{A,M,F}	Ackerman	{A,P}
9	Ms.	{A,S}	Frances	{A,M}	Adams	{A,S}

For System B, called the *partitioned design,* we partition the data into separate data tables to show what is visible to users having each purpose. Since the ADMIN purpose makes everything available, it acts as a table where all the data is visible, as shown in Table 2. The other tables show a null value if that attribute for that data provider is not to be visible for that purpose; Table 3 shows the data visible for the FINANCE purpose. The other purposes have a similar treatment. Even if none of the data is visible for a purpose, as is the case for UserIDs 6 and 9 in Table 3, we leave a row of all nulls to facilitate quick update of purpose choices by the data provider. If there are p purposes (including the ADMIN purpose), the partitioned design stores p tables, each having the n data attributes of the original database relation. This design is inspired by the separate storage of data in some MAC databases. Clearly, with this design, to do a relational database select with a single purpose, only one table needs to be accessed. If the relation has n attributes and there are p purposes, the partitioned design stores p relations with n data attributes, or takes $O(pn)$ storage of data values or nulls.

Table 2. System B, Partitioned Design, ADMIN Purpose (Also Data Table for Systems C and D)

UserID	Title	FirstName	LastName
4	Mr	Gustavo	Achong
5	Ms.	Catherine	Abel
6	Ms.	Kim	Abercrombie
7	Sr.	Humberto	Acevedo
8	Sra	Pilar	Ackerman
9	Ms.	Frances	Adams

Table 3. System B, Partitioned Design, FINANCE Purpose

UserID	Title	FirstName	LastName
4	Mr	NULL	Achong
5	Ms.	NULL	Abel
6	NULL	NULL	NULL
7	NULL	Humberto	NULL
8	NULL	Pilar	NULL
9	NULL	NULL	NULL

The partitioned design can have a lot of data redundancy, so in System C, called the *partitioned mask design*, we have a data table which contains all the data attributes, but no labels, exactly as shown in Table 2, and store separate mask tables for the non-ADMIN purposes, each having a primary key attribute(s) and then showing a 1 in another data column if the data provider has allowed access for this purpose, and a 0 if not. Table 4 shows the mask for the FINANCE purpose. The other purposes are treated in a similar fashion. The partitioned mask approach, then, has one data table with the original n attributes, and $p-1$ mask tables each storing the primary key and $n-1$ columns of 1's and 0's.

Table 4. System C, Partitioned Mask Design, Mask for the FINANCE Purpose

UserID	Title	FirstName	LastName
4	1	0	1
5	1	0	1
6	0	0	0
7	0	1	0
8	0	1	0
9	0	0	0

The final approach, System D, which we call the *single mask design*, has a data table as shown in Table 2, and one mask table, as shown in Table 5. The single mask table has the primary key of the underlying relation, $n-1$ columns of 1's and 0's and a final column giving the purpose for which the data provider has specified these choices of 1 (allow) and 0 (don't allow). Given an original relation with one key attribute and $n-1$ data attributes, this design has a data table containing the original data, and a single mask table with a primary key attribute, $n-1$ column's of 1's and 0's, and a final column indicating the purpose. It has slightly more data storage than the partitioned mask approach, but only one mask table as opposed to $p-1$ mask tables. It should be mentioned that the single mask design would take up less disc storage to store the schema information for one mask table vs. the $p-1$ schema entries for mask tables required by the partitioned mask design.

Table 5. System D, Single Mask Design, Mask Table

UserID	Title	FirstName	LastName	Purpose
4	1	0	1	F
5	1	0	1	F
6	0	0	0	F
7	0	1	0	F
8	0	1	0	F
9	0	0	0	F
4	1	0	1	M
5	1	0	1	M
6	1	0	1	M
7	0	1	0	M
8	0	1	0	M
9	0	1	0	M
4	0	0	0	P
5	0	1	0	P
6	0	0	0	P
7	0	0	0	P
8	1	0	1	P
9	0	0	0	P
4	0	1	0	S
5	0	0	0	S
6	0	1	0	S
7	1	0	1	S
8	0	0	0	S
9	1	0	1	S

4 Performance Results

4.1 Testing

A number of experiments were run to compare the four storage designs. For these experiments, we used SQL Server on a Windows 7 machine with an Intel Core i5 CPU 660, 4 CPUs, 4GB of ram and a 500 GB hard drive. We used a Customer Information relation containing 35 attributes, including 1 key attribute, based on the Adventureworks database [2]; the relation had 360,000 tuples. We used 5 privacy purposes: ADMIN, FINANCE, MARKETING, PURCHASING and SHIPPING, where the ADMIN purpose is always selected for every attribute. In the basic design, the purposes are stored as a string b#b#b#b where the b's are 1 or 0 depending representing whether the corresponding purpose is selected (only the non-ADMIN purposes are so coded, as ADMIN is assumed for all data). All of the commands are implemented as stored procedures. Each experiment was repeated 10 times. Two sets of experiments were run: the first with one user, varying the number of data items handled, the second with a fixed number of data items, with multiple users. We used a tool called Benchmark Factory [1] to facilitate the experiments.

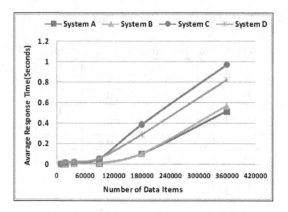

Fig. 2. Response Time for Select, ADMIN Purpose, One User

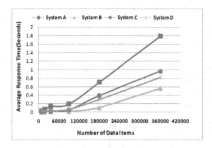

Fig. 3. Response Time for Select, FI-
NANCE Purpose, One User

Fig. 4. Response Time for Select,
MARKETING Purpose, One User

Figure 2 shows the results of testing the select operation for the ADMIN purpose, comparing the four storage designs, for one user with different numbers of
tuples being selected. Figures 3-6 show the results for the select operation, with
one user, for the other purposes.

Figures 7-10 show the results for the SHIPPING purpose selecting different
numbers of tuples when there are multiple users.

Our system assumes insert is done without purposes, and then the purposes
are added/adjusted by update operations. Figure 11 shows the performance of
our four storage designs for insert operations with one user. Figures 12-15 show
the results of inserting various numbers of tuples, for multiple users.

Figure 16 shows the results of the update operation. Here, we test the update
operation for different numbers of users with different numbers of data items.
The average response times of Systems A, C and D are almost the same, so in
the figure they are almost superimposed. For System B, we have shown separately the response times for updating data and updating purposes, as well as
an average response time incorporating both.

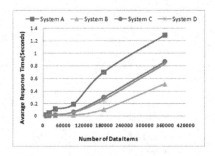

Fig. 5. Response Time for Select, PURCHASING Purpose, One User

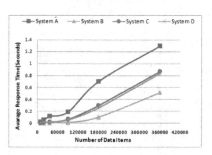

Fig. 6. Response Time for Select, SHIPPING Purpose, One User

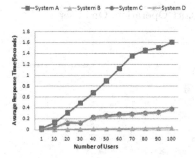

Fig. 7. Response Time Selecting 9000 Data Items, Multiple Users

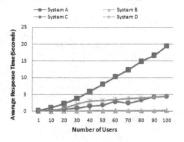

Fig. 8. Response Time Selecting 18000 Data Items, Multiple Users

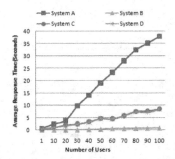

Fig. 9. Response Time Selecting 180000 Data Items, Multiple Users

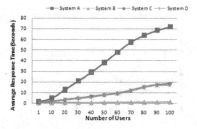

Fig. 10. Response Time Selecting 360000 Data Items, Multiple Users

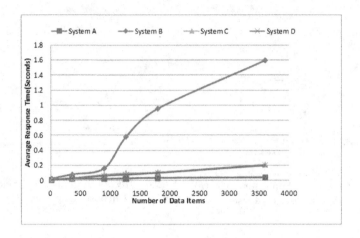

Fig. 11. Response Time for the INSERT Operation, One User

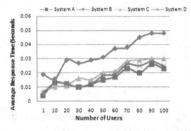

Fig. 12. Response Time Inserting 18 Data Items, Multiple Users

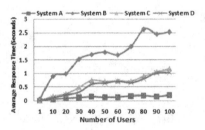

Fig. 13. Response Time Inserting 360 Data Items, Multiple Users

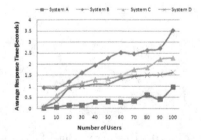

Fig. 14. Response Time Inserting 1800 Data Items, Multiple Users

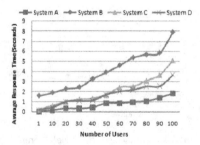

Fig. 15. Response Time Selecting 3600 Data Items, Multiple Users

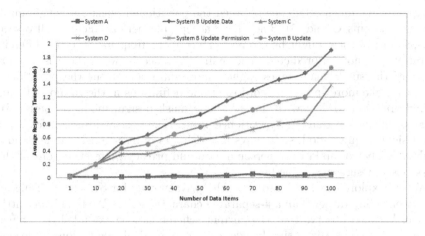

Fig. 16. Results for the Update Operations

Finally, we measured the response time for deletion. These results are shown in Table 6. Here we observe that the deletion from System B, Partitioned Design, takes a great deal more time than the other three designs.

Table 6. Response time of delete operation

System Name	SQL operation	Average Response time (Seconds)
A (Basic)	Delete	0.001
B (Partitioned)	Delete	0.283
C (Partitioned Mask)	Delete	0.002
D (Single Mask)	Delete	0.004

4.2   Discussion

The results presented show a clear tradeoff between the different storage designs. If there are many select operations, and very little updating or deleting, then the partitioned design (System B) performs much better than the others. This might be the case for a web site or business where data providers are assumed not to be concerned enough about their privacy preferences to ever change them, and customer data is seldom deleted. The price to pay for this is increased storage and increased time to insert new customers. If, on the other hand, data providers will be constantly changing information or their preferences, then the basic design, System A, is the best choice. Here the storage cost is much less, but the cost of the Select operation is highest. For the two scenarios discussed in the introduction, select, insert and update are all important, so we should conclude that the basic design and the partitioned design are not suitable for these environments.

There is not much difference between the partitioned mask and single mask designs (Systems C and D). They have acceptable performance on all operations, so one of them might be the best choice if the frequencies of the different operations cannot be predicted. The main difference between them is in storage cost: the single mask takes slightly more data space, but the partitioned mask will take more space to record the table definitions in the catalog. Having a single relation to deal with, in the single mask design, might be better for query optimization than the partitioned mask. The cost of insertion for these two designs is quite good, so in a system with lots of insertions, searches and a modest number of updates of personal data and privacy preferences, one of the mask-based designs would be best.

We did explore other ways to store the privacy code for System A, using an integer encoding rather than a #-separated character string. We found very little change. We also observe that the current scheme can be extended to a much larger set of purposes very simply, whereas the numerical calculations to decode purposes from an integer encoding might be more costly.

A minor point is the assumption above that the primary key is not labeled. If the natural primary key in the data is a number such as a credit card number, which the data provider might be sensitive about, then a system-generated customerID can be used instead to play the role of primary key in the relations. This attribute can be assumed to be visible for everything, as it does not reveal any data supplied by the data provider (this is similar to [4], where the customer ID attribute is given the most general treatment).

4.3 Extension to a Privacy Tree

In [4], to accommodate a privacy tree, the tree is preprocessed so that when a data provider chooses a non-leaf purpose in the tree, the system, using metadata, automatically substitutes the purpose and all its descendants (they also calculate the prohibited intended purposes, but we do not consider those in this paper). This could easily be added to our schemes for both insertion and update. Using the privacy tree shown in Figure 1, if the data provider specifies MARKETING, the system would record MARKETING, EMAIL, PHONE, MAIL as intended purposes in the database. Note that the select operation is assumed to have only one access purpose, so once these purposes are in the database, select based on, say, the EMAIL purpose would be allowed for this data provider's data. The preprocessing should have the same cost for all 4 of our schemes. The testing of this claim is left to further research.

5   Conclusions and Future Work

We have presented 4 storage designs to hold relational data which has sets of privacy purposes labeling all non-key attributes. The 4 designs have been tested for the operations of select, insert, update and delete. Tests have been run both varying the amount of data handled and the number of concurrent users. The results extend some of the ideas presented in [4], where only one storage design resembling our System A, has been tested, and only for select operations. It is interesting to note that System A could be considered the poorest choice among the 4 designs we tested. If all four tested operations are expected with some frequency, the single mask, or System D, gives the best choice for reasons discussed above.

We consider this to be preliminary work on this topic. As future work, we will consider other storage designs. We would like to explore the effect of various indexes on the storage schemes. Perhaps the appropriate indexes would narrow the gaps we found in our experiments. We would like to compare commercial database systems for the different designs - one of them might optimize certain queries better than others. We also plan to consider how the join operation is defined on relations with privacy labels, and how it performs with various storage designs.

References

1. Benchmark Factory for Databases, http://www.quest.com/benchmark-factory/ (last accessed August 2011)
2. Samples and Sample Databases (SQL.90).aspx, http://technet.microsoft.com/en-us/library/ms124501SQL.90.aspx (last accessed September 2011)
3. Al-Harbi, A.L., Osborn, S.L.: Mixing privacy with role-based access control. In: Proceedings of the Fourth International C* Conference on Computer Science & Software Engineering, C3S2E 2011, Montreal, Quebec, Canada, May 16-18, pp. 1-7 (2011)
4. Byun, J.-W., Li, N.: Purpose based access control for privacy protection in relational database systems. VLDB J. 17(4), 603-619 (2008)
5. Jajodia, S., Sandhu, R.S.: Towards a multilevel secure relational data model. In: Proceedings of the 1991 ACM SIGMOD International Conference on Management of Data, Denver, Colorado, May 29-31, pp. 50-59 (1991)
6. Lunt, T.F., Denning, D.E., Schell, R.R., Heckman, M., Shockley, W.R.: The SeaView security model. IEEE Trans. Softw. Eng. 16, 593-607 (1990)
7. Ni, Q., Trombetta, A., Bertino, E., Lobo, J.: Privacy-aware role based access control. In: Proceedings ACM SACMAT, pp. 41-50 (2007)
8. Notargiacomo, L.: Architectures for mls database management systems. In: Information Security: An Integrated Collection of Essays, pp. 439-459. IEEE Computer Society Press (1995)
9. Özsoyoglu, G., Snodgrass, R.T.: Temporal and real-time databases: A survey. IEEE Trans. Knowl. Data Eng. 7(4), 513-532 (1995)
10. Samarati, P., Sweeney, L.: Generalizing data to provide anonymity when disclosing information (abstract). In: Proceedings of the Seventeenth ACM SIGACT-SIGMOD-SIGART Symposium on Principles of Database Systems, Seattle, Washington, June 1-3, p. 188. ACM Press (1998)
11. Sandhu, R.: Lattice-based access control models. IEEE Computer 26, 9-19 (1993)
12. Smith, K., Winslett, M.: Entity modeling in the MLS relational model. In: Yuan, L.-Y. (ed.) 18th International Conference on Very Large Data Bases, August 23-27, pp. 199-210. Morgan Kaufmann (1992)
13. Sweeney, L.: Achieving k-anonymity privacy protection using generalization and suppression. International Journal of Uncertainty, Fuzziness and Knowledge-Based Systems 10(5), 571-588 (2002)

Differential Privacy in Practice

Maryam Shoaran, Alex Thomo, and Jens Weber

University of Victoria, Victoria, Canada
{maryam,thomo}@cs.uvic.ca, jens@uvic.ca

Abstract. Differential privacy (DP) has attracted considerable attention as the method of choice for releasing aggregate query results making it hard to infer information about individual records in the database. The most common way to achieve DP is to add noise following Laplace distribution. In this paper, we study differential privacy from a utility point of view for single and multiple queries. We examine the relationship between the cumulative probability of noise and the privacy degree. Using this analysis and the notion of relative error, we show *when* for a given problem it is *reasonable* to employ a differentially private algorithm without losing a certain level of utility. For the case of multiple queries, we introduce a simple DP method called *Differential* (*DIFF*) that adds noise proportional to a query index used to express our preferences for having different noise scales for different queries. We also introduce an equation capturing when *DIFF* satisfies a user-given relative error threshold.

Keywords: Statistical Databases, Differetial Privacy, Utility.

1 Introduction

Publishing analysis results of massive data collections, while providing substantial potential for research and public advantage, brings up the matter of privacy. Protecting sensitive information about participants has become one of the fundamental problems in society. For example, consider databases of medical records. Public release of statistical information over such data is prone to disclosing sensitive details about the health of individuals.

In recent years, ϵ-differential privacy [5] (DP for short) has become one of the foremost methods to protect information contained in individual records. DP guarantees that the privacy of an individual or a group is highly unlikely to be breached by participating in the computation of the aggregate results. The most common approach to achieve DP is by adding random noise with Laplace distribution to query answers, where the scale of noise is calibrated by the sensitivity of queries (the maximum difference in query answers on two databases differing by one tuple).

In this paper, we analyze when it is "reasonable" to use DP. We quantify *reasonable* in terms of the *relative error*, which is the ratio of the noise to the true query answer. The notion of relative error is important. For example, adding a noise of 60 to a query answer of 30 obviously is not reasonable from a utility point of view.

W. Jonker and M. Petković (Eds.): SDM 2012, LNCS 7482, pp. 14–24, 2012.

We examine the relationship between the cumulative probability of noise and the privacy degree. For single queries, we analyze when it is reasonable to employ DP without losing a certain level of utility.

Turning to the case of multiple queries, when using the method of [5], the scale of noise is the same for all the queries. To see the problem with this approach, consider two count queries, the *small* and the *big*, with answers 30 and 30,000, respectively. Having the same amount of noise, suppose 30, added to the answers of each query with the same probability will cause different "harm" to each query. While *big* easily tolerates this amount of noise without significantly affecting the utility of the answer, adding this amount of noise to *small* makes the released answer quite useless.

In order to alleviate this problem, we introduce a simple method called *Differential* that adds noise guided by a "query index," which is a set of numbers used to express our preferences for the noise scales to each query. For instance, in the above example the query index can be $\{1, 1000\}$. We show that Differential satisfies DP.

Our contributions are as follows.

1. We analyze the relationship between the cumulative probability of noise, the sensitivity, and the privacy degree (Section 3).
2. We examine when employing DP does not harm the utility beyond a certain level. We perform the analysis for two categories, single query (Section 4) and multiple queries (Section 5).
3. We propose *Differential*, a mechanism that, for the case of multiple queries, achieves DP while adding noise guided by a query index. Also, we analyze when Differential satisfies a user-given relative error threshold. (Section 6).

Related Work. There are several works that aim at controlling noise produced by DP mechanisms ([1,8,7,2]). These works study different settings from ours. They focus on reducing absolute error (not relative) and have consistency constraints (e.g. marginals that add up to some specific number).

A method, similar to our Differential, is introduced by Xiao et al. [11]. Their method called *Proportional* computes for a set of queries a set of noise scales that are proportional to the magnitude of query answers on the databases they are applied to. Proportional is shown to not satisfy DP. Another approach that [11] introduces is called *iReduct*. The latter is an iterative algorithm using a sophisticated procedure to minimize relative errors with respect to a database.

On the other hand, here we are interested in minimizing the relative error based on a query index. These preference weights might reflect the proportion of magnitudes of query answers on some static database[1], but this is not necessary.

---

[1] For example if we are to privately release mortality counts for different diseases for a hospital serving a big city, we can set the index to reflect the proportions of mortality rates of diseases in the city or country where the hospital is located. Certainly, such an index will approximately match the disease mortality proportions in the hospital, but this is public information, not a privately sensitive aspect of the data in the hospital database.

In fact, we can have different weights even if the magnitudes of the queries are the same. In such a case we release a more accurate answer to some query at the expense of less accurate answers to other queries in the set.

2   Background

Let q be an aggregate query. For example, q can be a count or a sum query on database D. Such a query can also be considered as a function $q : \mathbf{D} \to \mathbb{R}$, where $\mathbf{D}$ is the set of all databases. Thus, we use the terms query and function interchangeably. We denote by $q(D)$ the true answer of q on database D.

The definition of *differential privacy* (DP) uses the notion of *neighboring databases*. Two databases D_1 and D_2 are called *neighbors* if one of them can be obtained from the other by adding or removing at most one record.

Definition 1. (Differential Privacy [5]) A randomized algorithm $\mathcal{M}$ satisfies ϵ-differential privacy (ϵ-DP) if and only if for any two neighboring databases D_1 and D_2, and for any subset $S \in Range(\mathcal{M})$,

$$Pr[\mathcal{M}(D_1) \in S] \leq \exp(\epsilon) \cdot Pr[\mathcal{M}(D_2) \in S].$$

Dwork et al. showed in [5] that ϵ-DP can be achieved by adding appropriately chosen random noise to the true query answer $q(D)$. Specifically, noise follows a Laplace distribution with probability density function

$$f(x) = \tfrac{1}{2\lambda} e^{-|x|/\lambda} \tag{1}$$

denoted as $Lap(\lambda)$, where λ is called *noise scale*.

Definition 2. (Sensitivity [5]) For $q : \mathbf{D} \to \mathbb{R}$, the sensitivity of q is

$$\Delta(q) = \max_{D_1, D_2} |q(D_1) - q(D_2)|$$

for all neighboring databases D_1 and D_2.

Dwork et al. prove that an algorithm that sets the noise scale to be $\lambda = \Delta(q)/\epsilon$ enjoys ϵ-DP. Namely, when a query q is posed to database D, the output of the randomized algorithm $\mathcal{M}$ will be

$$q(D) + Lap(\Delta(q)/\epsilon).$$

The parameter ϵ is the privacy degree and one can think of it typically as 0.01 or 0.1.

The ϵ-DP can also be obtained for any sequence of queries $q_1, q_2, \ldots, q_m$ on a single database by running the algorithm $\mathcal{M}$ with noise distribution

$$Lap\left(\sum_i \frac{\Delta(q_i)}{\epsilon}\right)$$

on each computation [5].

In [4] Dwork et al. address the matter of overall privacy when the privatized output of multiple queries are released together.

Theorem 1. ([4]) A sequence of m computations over a database D, each providing ϵ_i-DP, satisfies $(\sum_i \epsilon_i)$-DP.

This is also called *sequential composition* in the literature (cf. [9]).

3 Noise and Utility

It is clear that the scale of the noise added to $q(D)$ is independent of the real magnitude of $q(D)$. Note that sensitivity is a characteristic of the computation (query) and does not depend on the database (cf. [3]).

To illustrate, for a count query q, whether $q(D)$ is for example 30 or 30,000 does not have any influence on the value of noise scale. This is because sensitivity is equal to 1 for any *count* query. Thus, for a given ϵ, the noise scale will be $\lambda = 1/\epsilon$. Therefore, an amount of noise, say 69 (a plausible value as we will show), might be added to the answer of the query with the same probability regardless of the magnitude of the true answer. While a noise value of 69 does not affect significantly the "utility" of the query answer of 30,000 magnitude, it renders the privatized answer of the query of 30 magnitude almost useless.

Therefore, we analyze in this section the practicality of differential privacy from a utility point of view.

Let $q(D)$ be the true answer and p be the released privatized answer to query q. We can evaluate the utility of the released answer using *relative error* as follows.

$$RE = \frac{|p - q(D)|}{q(D)} \tag{2}$$

This is similar to the definition of relative error in [6,10]. Practically, we can think of acceptable values of RE as 10% or 15%.

The cumulative distribution function of Laplace distribution in an interval $[-z, z]$ can be computed by the following integral.

$$Pr(-z \le x \le z) = \int_{-z}^{z} \frac{1}{2\lambda} e^{\frac{-|x|}{\lambda}} \, dx = 1 - e^{\frac{-z}{\lambda}}.$$

Therefore,

$$Pr(|x| \geq z) = e^{\frac{-z}{\lambda}}. \tag{3}$$

Let $pr = Pr(|x| \geq z)$. Value z for a specified cumulative probability pr can be calculated using equation (3) as

$$z = -\lambda \cdot \ln(pr),$$

and with $\lambda = \Delta(q)/\epsilon$ we have

$$z = -\frac{\Delta(q)}{\epsilon} \cdot \ln(pr). \tag{4}$$

Fig. 1 illustrates the minimum absolute noise z as a function of cumulative probability pr for three different values of ϵ when $\Delta(q) = 1$. Each point (pr, z) on the curve for a given ϵ means that

> pr percent of the time the random noise has an absolute value of at least z.

For example, for $\epsilon = 0.01$, we have that 50% of the time the absolute value of noise is at least 69, and 30% of the time it is at least 120. This means that the query answer needs to be considerably higher than 69, or even 120, in order for the privatized (released) answer to have some utility.

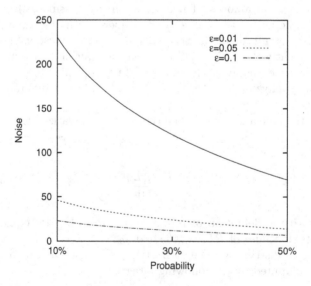

Fig. 1. Noise vs Probability ($\Delta(q) = 1$)

Next, we introduce measures to study the utility of the privatized (released) answers.

4   Single Query

Let q be a query with a single numerical output. Using Equations (2) and (4) we can compute the *minimum true (query) answer* (MTA), such that, with probability $1 - pr$, RE is below a threshold re.

The RE formula (Equation (2)) can be written as

$$RE = \frac{|z|}{q(D)}, \tag{5}$$

where z is the amount of noise added to the true answer of query q on database D. In order for RE to be below a threshold re, by Equation (4), we should have

$$q(D) \geq \frac{|z|}{re}$$
$$= -\frac{\Delta(q) \cdot \ln(pr)}{\epsilon \cdot re}.$$

Thus,

$$MTA = -\frac{\Delta(q) \cdot \ln(pr)}{\epsilon \cdot re}. \tag{6}$$

Example 1. Let q be a count query, and let $\epsilon = 0.01$. Let us consider $pr = 10\%$, i.e. we want to be $1 - pr = 90\%$ sure about the relative error statements.

Recall that the sensitivity for any count *query is 1. From Equation (4), we have that*

$$z = -\frac{1}{0.01} \ln(10\%) \simeq 230.$$

That is, 10% of the time the absolute value of the random noise of scale $\lambda = \frac{1}{0.01} = 100$ is at least 230. Using Equation (6), for an application specific RE threshold $re = 10\%$, we get

$$MTA = \frac{230}{10\%} = 2300.$$

In plain language, the query answer should have a magnitude of at least 2300 in order for the privatized answer to have an acceptable utility (RE $\leq 10\%$) 90% of the time.

Fig. 2 illustrates MTA as a function of ϵ for three different values of pr when $re = 10\%$. Each point (ϵ, mta) on the curve for a given pr shows that:

> The query answer should have a magnitude at least mta, in order for the relative error to not be higher than 10%, $1 - pr$ of the time under noise of scale $\lambda = 1/\epsilon$.

If we substitute re for ϵ in the x-axis of Fig. 2 we get MTA as a function of relative error, with ϵ fixed to 0.1. Each point (re, mta) on the curve of a given probability pr will show that:

If a query answer is at least mta, adding random noise of scale $\lambda = 1/0.1 = 10$ ($\epsilon = 0.1$) will satisfy $1 - pr$ of the time the requirement of having relative error at most re.

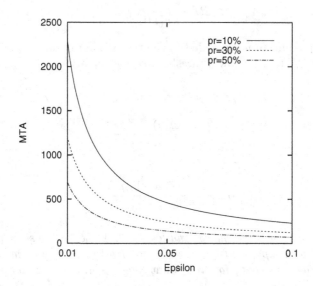

Fig. 2. MTA vs Epsilon ($re = 10\%$). We can substitute re for ϵ and get MTA as a function of relative error threshold.

5   Multiple Queries

In the case of two or more queries on a single database, a randomized algorithm satisfying ϵ-DP adds Laplace noise with scale $\lambda = \sum_i \Delta(q_i)/\epsilon$ (see Section 2). The MTA in this case will be possibly larger than what it would be if only one of the query answers were to be released. This is because the noise scale, being equal to $\lambda = \sum_i \Delta(q_i)/\epsilon$, is larger.

For example, in the case of two count queries, if a record affects both counts (at most by one), then λ will be double, $\lambda = \frac{\Delta(q_1)+\Delta(q_2)}{\epsilon} = \frac{1}{\epsilon} + \frac{1}{\epsilon}$. However, applying noise with *identical* scale to both may distort one of the answers a lot more than the other.

Example 2. Let $\epsilon = 0.01$. Suppose $q_1(D) = 3000$ and $q_2(D) = 30,000$ are the true answers to two count queries on a database D. We have $\Delta(q_1) + \Delta(q_2) = 2$, and $\lambda = \frac{2}{0.01} = 200$. Based on Equation (4), with probability 10%, the absolute noise will be at least

$$z = -200 \cdot \ln(10\%) \simeq 460.$$

Observe that each query answer is distorted twice than if they were considered in isolation. If the threshold on relative error is set to 10%, then the MTA for each query needs to be at least 4600.

Now, adding noise 460 to the true query answers, we have

$$RE_1 = \frac{460}{3000} \simeq 0.15$$
$$RE_2 = \frac{460}{30000} \simeq 0.015.$$

This example shows that whereas adding this amount of noise to the answer of q_2 is reasonable for threshold $re = 10\%$, it distorts the answer of q_1 too much, thus failing to satisfy threshold re.

Differential Noise Problem. Can we find an algorithm for a set of queries that satisfies DP by adding noise that has different scales for different queries?

In the sequel, we introduce a simple method called *Differential (DIFF)*. *DIFF* satisfies DP and adds noise to each query answer guided by a "(differential) query index". A query index is a set of numbers, one for each query, used to express our preference for the scale of noise used for each query.

We note here that Xiao et al. have also proposed a method in [11], called Proportional, which is similar to what we propose here. However, in their method, the noise scales depend on each database that the randomized algorithm is applied to. They show that Proportional does not satisfy DP.

6   Differential

Let $\{q_1, \ldots, q_m\}$ be m queries. Also, let ϵ be the privacy degree we seek for the query set. In the DP mechanism of [5] (analyzed in Section 5), all queries in the set will have the same noise scale λ. Another way to view this mechanism is as follows.

If we denote $\frac{\Delta(q_i)}{\lambda}$ by ϵ_i, for $i \in [1, m]$, we have

$$\epsilon = \frac{\sum_{i=1}^{m} \Delta(q_i)}{\lambda} = \sum_{i=1}^{m} \epsilon_i.$$

Thus, query q_i, for $i \in [1, m]$, bears weight ϵ_i toward achieving overall degree of privacy ϵ.

Here we propose *Differential (DIFF)* which assigns each query its own noise scale λ_i. Let $\Gamma = \{\gamma_1, \ldots, \gamma_m\}$ be the query index (a set of numbers, one for each query). *DIFF* sets each λ_i to be proportional to the corresponding γ_i value. That is,

$$\lambda_i = \alpha \cdot \gamma_i \qquad (7)$$

where $i \in [1, m]$, and α is some constant.

Now, query q_i, for $i \in [1, m]$, bears weight $\epsilon_i = \frac{\Delta(q_i)}{\lambda_i}$ toward achieving overall degree of privacy $\epsilon = \sum_{i=1}^{m} \epsilon_i$.

Constant α can be computed by substituting (7) in equation $\epsilon = \sum_{i=1}^{m} \frac{\Delta(q_i)}{\lambda_i}$. We get

$$\alpha = \frac{1}{\epsilon} \sum_{i \in [1,m]} \frac{\Delta(q_i)}{\gamma_i} \tag{8}$$

and then each λ_i is computed using Expression (7).

A randomized algorithm with λ_i's thus computed will satisfy ϵ-DP. To verify this, let D_1 and D_2 be two such databases. The following equation shows that privatized answers p_i's for queries q_i's are almost as likely on D_1 as on D_2 with DP privacy degree of ϵ. Namely, we have

$$\frac{Pr[p_1, \ldots, p_m \text{ on } D_1]}{Pr[p_1, \ldots, p_m \text{ on } D_2]}$$

$$= \frac{\prod_{i=1}^{m} \exp(-|p_i - q_i(D_1)|/\lambda_i)}{\prod_{i=1}^{m} \exp(-|p_i - q_i(D_2)|/\lambda_i)}$$

$$= \prod_{i=1}^{m} \exp\left(\frac{-z_{i,1}}{\lambda_i} + \frac{z_{i,2}}{\lambda_i}\right)$$

$$\leq \prod_{i=1}^{m} \exp\left(\frac{-z_i}{\lambda_i} + \frac{z_i + \Delta(q_i)}{\lambda_i}\right)$$

$$= \exp\left(\sum_{i=1}^{m} \frac{\Delta(q_i)}{\lambda_i}\right)$$

$$= \exp(\epsilon)$$

where $z_{i,j}$ is the noise added to the true answer $q_i(D_j)$, and the last step is based on equation $\epsilon = \sum_{i=1}^{m} \frac{\Delta(q_i)}{\lambda_i}$. Note that α is *not* a user defined constant and depends on ϵ, on the sensitivity of the queries, and on the query index.

One might be interested in knowing whether using indexed noise as above can satisfy for each query a *user given* relative error threshold re with a cumulative probability pr on database D.

From Equations (4), (5), (7), and (8) we have

$$RE_i = \frac{-\lambda_i \cdot \ln(pr)}{q_i(D)}$$

$$= \frac{-\alpha \cdot \gamma_i \cdot \ln(pr)}{q_i(D)}$$

$$= -\left(\frac{1}{\epsilon} \sum_{i=1}^{m} \frac{\Delta(q_i)}{\gamma_i}\right) \cdot \frac{\gamma_i \cdot \ln(pr)}{q_i(D)}$$

Thus, it can be inferred that if the equation

$$\sum_{i=1}^{m} \frac{\Delta(q_i)}{\gamma_i} \leq -\frac{re_i}{\gamma_i} \cdot \frac{\epsilon \cdot q_i(D)}{\ln(pr)} \tag{9}$$

is true for a set of m queries on a database D, then at least $1 - pr$ percent of the time $DIFF$ satisfies a user given relative error threshold re_i for q_i. From this we derive the MTAs for each query q_i to be

$$MTA_i = -\frac{\gamma_i \cdot \sum_{i=1}^{m} \frac{\Delta(q_i)}{\gamma_i} \cdot \ln(pr)}{\epsilon \cdot re_i}. \tag{10}$$

Observe that in the case of one query, the above becomes the same as Equation (6).

Example 3. Consider again Example 2. Let $\Gamma = \{1, 10\}$ be the query index for the two count queries. From (10), we have

$$MTA_1 = -\frac{1 \cdot (1/1 + 1/10) \cdot \ln(10\%)}{0.01 \cdot 0.10} \simeq 2533$$

$$MTA_2 = -\frac{10 \cdot (1/1 + 1/10) \cdot \ln(10\%)}{0.01 \cdot 0.10} \simeq 25328.$$

Since the answers of q_1 and q_2 are greater than their respective MTAs, we can satisfy the relative error threshold by using mechanism DIFF.

Specifically, we set $\lambda_1 = \alpha$ and $\lambda_2 = 10\alpha$. Using Equations (8) we have $\alpha = \frac{1}{\epsilon}(\frac{1}{1} + \frac{1}{10}) = 110$ ($\epsilon = 0.01$) and from Equation (7), $\lambda_1 = 110$ and $\lambda_2 = 1100$.

Using Equation (4) we have that 10% of the time the noise added to the true answers of q_1 and q_2 has an absolute value of at least 253.3 and 2532.8, respectively (compare these values to noise value of 460 for both queries in Example 2). Now the noise added will not violate the error threshold of 10%.

7   Conclusions

We have analyzed differential privacy from a utility perspective. We studied the connection between the cumulative probability of noise, and the privacy degree. Using the concept of relative error we explored the practicality of DP algorithms for single and multiple queries. Namely, we analyzed the circumstances when DP can be used reasonably without exceeding a given threshold for relative error. For multiple queries, we proposed the Differential (*DIFF*) method that adds noise with scales guided by a query index. We showed that *DIFF* satisfies DP.

References

1. Barak, B., Chaudhuri, K., Dwork, C., Kale, S., McSherry, F., Talwar, K.: Privacy, accuracy, and consistency too: a holistic solution to contingency table release. In: PODS, pp. 273–282 (2007)
2. Ding, B., Winslett, M., Han, J., Li, Z.: Differentially private data cubes: optimizing noise sources and consistency. In: SIGMOD Conference, pp. 217–228 (2011)

3. Dwork, C.: Differential Privacy: A Survey of Results. In: Agrawal, M., Du, D.-Z., Duan, Z., Li, A. (eds.) TAMC 2008. LNCS, vol. 4978, pp. 1–19. Springer, Heidelberg (2008)
4. Dwork, C., Kenthapadi, K., McSherry, F., Mironov, I., Naor, M.: Our Data, Ourselves: Privacy Via Distributed Noise Generation. In: Vaudenay, S. (ed.) EUROCRYPT 2006. LNCS, vol. 4004, pp. 486–503. Springer, Heidelberg (2006)
5. Dwork, C., McSherry, F., Nissim, K., Smith, A.: Calibrating Noise to Sensitivity in Private Data Analysis. In: Halevi, S., Rabin, T. (eds.) TCC 2006. LNCS, vol. 3876, pp. 265–284. Springer, Heidelberg (2006)
6. Garofalakis, M.N., Kumar, A.: Wavelet synopses for general error metrics. ACM Trans. Database Syst. 30(4), 888–928 (2005)
7. Hay, M., Rastogi, V., Miklau, G., Suciu, D.: Boosting the accuracy of differentially private histograms through consistency. PVLDB 3(1), 1021–1032 (2010)
8. Li, C., Hay, M., Rastogi, V., Miklau, G., McGregor, A.: Optimizing linear counting queries under differential privacy. In: PODS, pp. 123–134 (2010)
9. McSherry, F.: Privacy integrated queries: an extensible platform for privacy-preserving data analysis. In: SIGMOD Conference, pp. 19–30 (2009)
10. Vitter, J.S., Wang, M.: Approximate computation of multidimensional aggregates of sparse data using wavelets. In: SIGMOD Conference, pp. 193–204 (1999)
11. Xiao, X., Bender, G., Hay, M., Gehrke, J.: ireduct: differential privacy with reduced relative errors. In: SIGMOD Conference, pp. 229–240 (2011)

A Model for Quantifying Information Leakage

Steven Euijong Whang and Hector Garcia-Molina

Computer Science Department, Stanford University
353 Serra Mall, Stanford, CA 94305, USA
{swhang,hector}@cs.stanford.edu

Abstract. We study data privacy in the context of information leakage. As more of our sensitive data gets exposed to merchants, health care providers, employers, social sites and so on, there is a higher chance that an adversary can "connect the dots" and piece together a lot of our information. The more complete the integrated information, the more our privacy is compromised. We present a model that captures this privacy loss (information leakage) relative to a target person, on a continuous scale from 0 (no information about the target is known by the adversary) to 1 (adversary knows everything about the target). The model takes into account the confidence the adversary has for the gathered information (leakage is less if the adversary is not confident), as well as incorrect information (leakage is less if the gathered information does not match the target's). We compare our information leakage model with existing privacy models, and we propose several interesting problems that can be formulated with our model. We also propose efficient algorithms for computing information leakage and evaluate their performance and scalability.

Keywords: Information Leakage, Measure, Privacy.

1 Introduction

In practice we are continually giving out sensitive information: we need to give out our credit card data in order to purchase something; we need to tell our drug store what drugs we need; we need to give our employer (and many others) our social security number; our airline needs our passport number, and so on. Each bit of information we release represents a loss of privacy, and we never know who may end up getting our information. For instance, our store may share our information with some advertiser; or our airline may give our passport number to some governments.

The separate information losses can become much more serious if some adversary is able to gather and piece together our information. Our goal is to quantify how leakage can increase (or decrease) as information is pieced together. We do not wish to view privacy as all-or-nothing; rather, we wish to view it as a continuous measure that can represent the severity of our information loss. And once we can quantify leakage, we can study strategies for reducing leakage (or increasing it if one wants to take the point of view of a law-enforcement "adversary" trying to learn about possible criminals).

W. Jonker and M. Petković (Eds.): SDM 2012, LNCS 7482, pp. 25–44, 2012.

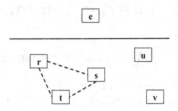

Fig. 1. Information Leakage with Entity Resolution

As a motivating example, suppose that Alice has the following information: her name is Alice, her address is 123 Main, her phone number is 555, her credit card number is 999, her social security number is 000. We represent Alice's information as the record: $e = \{\langle N, Alice\rangle, \langle A, 123\ Main\rangle, \langle P, 555\rangle, \langle C, 999\rangle, \langle S, 000\rangle\}$. Suppose now that Alice buys something on the Web and gives the vendor a subset of her information, say $r = \{\langle N, Alice\rangle, \langle A, 123\ Main\rangle, \langle C, 999\rangle\}$. By doing so, Alice has already partially compromised her privacy.

We can quantify the information leakage by measuring how correct and complete the information in r is against e. In our example, 3 out of 3 of r's attributes were correct while 3 out of 5 of e's attributes were found in r. Uncertain and incorrect information are also important factors in measuring information leakage. If an adversary Eve is not sure about Alice's information, then although the information itself is correct, the leakage should be considered less than when Eve is absolutely confident about the data. Moreover, if Eve is absolutely sure about some incorrect information about Alice, then the information leakage should decrease in proportion to Eve's confidence. Returning to our example above, suppose that Alice also gives the same vendor the following information (through another purchase): $\{\langle N, Alice\rangle, \langle A, 777\ Main\rangle, \langle C, 999\rangle, \langle X, 111\rangle\}$. As a result, the vendor may only be half certain about Alice's address. In addition, if $\langle X, 111\rangle$ contains false information, the vendor now has an incorrect attribute X. Both errors should be factored in when computing the leakage.

The information leakage may also be affected by any data analysis performed by adversary Eve. For example, Eve may run an entity resolution (ER) operation to identify which pieces of information refer to the same person. To illustrate, Figure 1 shows the records of five people: $r = \{\langle N, Alice\rangle, \langle P, 123\rangle\}$, $s = \{\langle N, Alice\rangle, \langle C, 999\rangle\}$, $t = \{\langle N, Alice\rangle, \langle P, 987\rangle\}$, $u = \{\langle N, Bob\rangle, \langle P, 333\rangle\}$, and $v = \{\langle N, Carol\rangle, \langle S, 000\rangle\}$. The record e above the line represents Alice's full information. Assuming that the name is a strong identifier for people, Eve may conclude that r, s, and t refer to the same person and merge their contents into $r + s + t = \{\langle N, Alice\rangle, \langle P, 123\rangle, \langle C, 999\rangle, \langle P, 987\rangle\}$ (denoted as the dotted lines connecting r, s, and t). As a result, Eve may obtain better information about Alice. However, the analysis itself may be costly if the data to resolve is very large and Eve does not have sufficient resources to perform the analysis.

In summary, our contributions in this paper are as follows:

- We formalize information leakage as a general measure of privacy. Our measure reflects the following factors: the correctness and completeness of the leaked data, the adversary's confidence on the data, and the adversary's analysis on the data (Section 2).

- We compare our information leakage model with two related privacy models in data publishing: k-anonymity and l-diversity (Section 3).
- We formulate various problems for managing information leakage that can be solved using our framework (Section 4).
- We describe efficient exact and approximate algorithms for computing information leakage and summarize experimental results (Section 5).

2   Information Leakage Measure

We consider a scenario where the adversary Eve has one record r pertaining to Alice, which could be a piece of information collected from a social network profile, a homepage, or even a tweet. Record r contains a set of attributes, and each attribute consists of a label and value. We do not assume a fixed schema to be able to represent data from different sources. As an example, the following record may represent Alice:

$$r = \{\langle N, \text{Alice}\rangle, \langle A, 20\rangle, \langle A, 30\rangle, \langle Z, 94305\rangle\}$$

Each attribute $a \in r$ is surrounded by angle brackets and consists of one label $a.l$ and one value $a.v$. Notice that there are two ages for Alice. We consider $\langle A, 20\rangle$ and $\langle A, 30\rangle$ to be two separate pieces of information, even if they have the same label. Multiple label-value pairs with identical labels can occur when two records merge and the label-value pairs are simply collected. In our example, Alice may have reported her age to be 20 in one case, but 30 in another. (Equivalently, year of birth can be used instead of age.) Although we cannot express the fact that Alice has only one age (either 20 or 30), the confidences we introduce in Section 2.3 can be used to indicate the likelihood of each value.

In addition, each attribute label l has an weight w_l that reflects the relative importance of an attribute with label l. These weights will be used below to compute leakage, so that attributes with highly weighted labels will contribute more than those with lower weights. In our example, we may give the credit card label C a weight of $w_C = 3$ and the zip code label a weight of $w_Z = 1$, to reflect that Alice considers her credit card number three times more important than her zip code. The absolute values of the weights are not important, only their relative sizes. Thus, if there are only three labels, giving them the weights 1, 2, and 3 is equivalent to giving them the weights 2, 4, and 6. The values of the weights are application specific, and our model provides the flexibility to define the weights based on one's privacy valuation (see reference [19] for more details). We emphasize that the weights are assigned to labels and not on the individual attributes. We believe this simplification is useful, since giving weights to every possible attribute is not practical.

In our model we assume that different attributes are *not* correlated. However, in some cases the values for some attributes may depend on each other, and certain attributes may be inferred from other attributes. For example, the birth date of a person depends on the age of a person because the birth date can be used to compute the age. In this case, if both the date of birth and the age are discovered by Eve, we do not want to account for the loss twice. We get around this problem by simply assuming that our model contains only one of the dependent attributes, e.g., either date of birth or age. In other cases, attributes may be correlated, but not equivalent. For example, phone number and address may be correlated: if we know the phone number we may be able to narrow down the possible addresses, and vice versa. We can model this situation by assuming there are three attributes: J contains the "joint information," A contains the remaining address information, and P the remaining phone information. If Eve discovers Alice's phone number, she has values for J and P; if she discovers the address, she gets J and A, and if she has both address and phone, Eve has J, A and P. Now we can provide weights for the J, A and P labels, and not double count the correlated knowledge.

We also assume a reference record e that contains Alice's complete information. An interesting question is how much of Alice's information has been revealed by exposing the record r? One might say that even if one attribute is leaked, a privacy breach has occurred, so Alice has no privacy. On the other extreme, however, one may say that, since not all of Alice's information has been leaked, the privacy has not been breached. In order to capture the amount of information that has been leaked, we define the *record leakage* of the record r as its similarity against the reference record e (see Definition 1). Also given a database R (which is a set of records), we define the *information leakage* of R to be its similarity against e after the "data analysis" of the adversary (see Definition 2).

In the following sections, we discuss the main components of our measure and formally define record leakage and information leakage.

2.1   Correctness

The correctness measure of a record r reflects the portion of r's information that is correct according to e. We adapt the definition of precision from the information retrieval literature [10] to define correctness. The precision of the record r against the reference e is defined as follows:

$$Pr(r, e) = \frac{\Sigma_{a \in r \cap e} w_{a.l}}{\Sigma_{a \in r} w_{a.l}}$$

If $\Sigma_{a \in r} w_{a.l} = 0$, we define Pr to be 0. Suppose that $e = \{\langle N, Alice \rangle, \langle A, 20 \rangle, \langle P, 123 \rangle, \langle Z, 94305 \rangle\}$ and $r = \{\langle N, Alice \rangle, \langle A, 20 \rangle, \langle P, 111 \rangle\}$. Also say that $w_N = 2$ while the weights for all other labels are 1. Then the precision of r against e is $\frac{2+1}{2+1+1} = \frac{3}{4}$.

There are several ways to extend our definition of Pr. First, we can reflect the degree of error in computing information leakage where more correct information implies more leakage. For example, suppose that Alice is 30 years old. Then the information leakage when Eve guesses that Alice is 31 years old should be higher than the leakage when Eve suspects Alice is 80 years old. Second, we can take into account the statistical background knowledge of the adversary when measuring the leakage. For instance, if knowing that someone has an average age may be less leakage than knowing that someone has an exceptional age. We do not consider these extensions in this paper due to space limitations.

2.2 Completeness

Even if the correctness of r is very high, r may not be significant if only a small fraction of e has been discovered. Hence, we also define the notion of how much of e is found by r, which we call the completeness of r. This time, we adapt the definition of recall from the information retrieval literature. In general, one could use any other measure to capture how much correct information was found by the record r.

We define the recall of r against e as follows.

$$Re(r, e) = \frac{\Sigma_{a \in r \cap e} w_{a.l}}{\Sigma_{a \in e} w_{a.l}}$$

If $\Sigma_{a \in e} w_{a.l} = 0$, we define Re to be 0. In our example, the recall of r against e is $\frac{2+1}{2+1+1+1} = \frac{3}{5}$.

The information retrieval literature suggests the harmonic mean as one way of combining correctness and completeness. Given the correctness Pr and completeness Re, the weighted harmonic mean is defined as $F_\beta = \frac{1}{\alpha/Pr + (1-\alpha)/Re} = \frac{(\beta^2+1) \times Pr \times Re}{\beta^2 \times Pr + Re}$ where $\beta^2 = \frac{1-\alpha}{\alpha}$.

The F_1 measure sets β to 1 and thus gives equal weight to precision and recall. In information retrieval, the F_1 measure captures how relevant a search result is against a given query. In comparison, the information leakage measure quantifies the relevance of a record r against the correct answer e. We can combine the precision and recall to produce a single record leakage measure L^0 where the "0" superscript indicates the leakage computation without confidences.

$$L^0(r, e) = F_1(Pr(r, e), Re(r, e)) = \frac{2 \times Pr(r, e) \times Re(r, e)}{Pr(r, e) + Re(r, e)}$$

In our example, the F_1 value is $\frac{2 \times 3/4 \times 3/5}{3/4 + 3/5} = \frac{2}{3}$.

2.3 Adversary Confidence

As mentioned earlier, the confidence that adversary Eve has on her data plays a role in computing leakage. For example, Eve may have gotten some information of r from an unreliable website. Or Eve may have heard rumors of the subject indirectly from someone else. If Eve is not so confident about r, then even if r has a high accuracy against e, the information leakage should be less than when Eve is more confident. Also, if Eve is highly confident about information that is not accurate, then the information leakage should be considered less than when Eve is not so confident about the inaccurate information.

To reflect the confidence of Eve, we extend our data model to have per-attribute confidence values. As a result, a record r consists of a set of attributes, and each attribute contains a label, a value, and a confidence (from 0 to 1) that captures the uncertainty of the attribute from Eve's point of view (the more Eve knows about Alice, the higher the confidence values). Any attribute that does not exist in r is assumed to have a confidence of 0. As an example, the following record may represent Alice:

$$r = \{\langle N, \text{Alice}, 1 \rangle, \langle A, 20, 0.5 \rangle, \langle A, 30, 0.4 \rangle, \langle Z, 94305, 0.3 \rangle\}$$

That is, Eve is certain about Alice's name, but is only 50% confident about Alice being 30 years old, 40% confident in Alice being 30 years old, and 30% confident about Alice's zip code 94305. For each attribute $a \in r$, we can access a's label $a.l$, a single value $a.v$, and confidence $a.c$. We assume that attributes in the reference e always have a confidence of 1 and omit the confidence values. No two attributes in the same record may have the same label and value pair.

The confidences within the same record are independent of each other and reflect "alternate worlds" for Eve's belief of the correct information of Alice. For example, if we have $r = \{\langle \text{name, Alice}, 1 \rangle, \langle \text{age}, 20, 0.4 \rangle, \langle \text{phone}, 123, 0.5 \rangle\}$, in Eve's view then there are four possible worlds: $\{\langle \text{name, Alice} \rangle, \langle \text{age}, 20 \rangle, \langle \text{phone}, 123 \rangle\}$ with probability $0.4 \times 0.5 = 0.2$, $\{\langle \text{name, Alice} \rangle, \langle \text{age}, 20 \rangle\}$ with probability $0.4 \times (1 - 0.5) = 0.2$, $\{\langle \text{name, Alice} \rangle, \langle \text{phone}, 123 \rangle\}$ with probability $(1 - 0.4) \times 0.5 = 0.3$, and $\{\langle \text{name, Alice} \rangle\}$ with probability $(1 - 0.4) \times (1 - 0.5) = 0.3$. We denote the possible worlds of a record r as the set of records without confidences

$$W(r) = \{\{\langle a.l, a.v \rangle | a \in r'\} | r' \in 2^r\}$$

where 2^r is the power set of r.

To help in our definition of leakage, we define the function $p(a, r)$ that simply gives the confidence of attribute a in record r:

$$p(a, r) = \begin{cases} b.c & \exists b \in r \text{ s.t. } a.l = b.l \wedge a.v = b.v \\ 0 & o.w. \end{cases}$$

We now extend our information leakage measure in the previous section to use confidences. Since, the confidence values of the attributes in r are independent, we can define the record leakage of r against the reference e as follows. (In Section 5, we show how to compute the record leakage efficiently.)

Definition 1. *Given confidence values, the record leakage of record r against the reference e is*

$$L(r, e) = E[L^0(\bar{r}, e)]$$
$$= \sum_{r' \in W(r)} (\prod_{a \in r'} p(a, r))(\prod_{a \notin r'} 1 - p(a, r))L^0(r', e)$$

where $\bar{r}$ is a random variable of r's possible worlds.

That is, we are computing the expected value of the F_1 value between a possible world and e. For example, suppose that $e = \{\langle\text{N, Alice}\rangle, \langle\text{A, 20}\rangle, \langle\text{P, 123}\rangle\}$ and $r = \{\langle\text{N, Alice, 0.5}\rangle, \langle\text{A, 20, 1}\rangle\}$. Also say that $w_N = 2$ while all the other weights have a value of 1. There are two possible values for $\bar{r}$: $r_1 = \{\langle\text{A, 20}\rangle\}$ and $r_2 = \{\langle\text{N, Alice}\rangle, \langle\text{A, 20}\rangle\}$. We then compute $L^0(r_1, e) = \frac{2\times1/1\times1/3}{1/1+1/3} = \frac{1}{2}$ and $L^0(r_2, e) = \frac{2\times2/2\times2/3}{2/2+2/3} = \frac{4}{5}$. Thus $L(r, e) = \frac{1}{2}\times L^0(r_1, e) + \frac{1}{2}\times L^0(r_2, e) = \frac{1}{2}\times\frac{1}{2} + \frac{1}{2}\times\frac{4}{5} = \frac{13}{20}$. Notice that L receives a record with confidences as its first input and a record without confidences as its second input. One can also define the precision and recall metrics using confidences by replacing $L^0(r', e)$ in Definition 1 with $Pr(r', e)$ and $Re(r', e)$, respectively.

$L(r, e)$ quantifies leakage when Eve has a single record r in her possession. What happens if Eve has a set of records R? There is no simple answer in this case, but we take a "conservative" approach and define leakage as the worst leakage that may occur when Eve looks at any one of her R records. That is, $L^0(R, e) = max_{r\in R}L(r, e)$. Note that we are overloading the symbol L: if the first parameter is a set, it refers to set leakage; if the first parameter is a single record, then it is record leakage. We use the "0" superscript to distinguish this basic set leakage from leakage after the adversary analyzes and possibly combines records (next subsection).

2.4 Adversary Effort on Data Analysis

In order to increase the information leakage, the adversary Eve may further improve the quality of the database by fixing errors, adding more information, or removing duplicates. We illustrate three possible data analysis operations below.

- *Error Correction*: The adversary Eve identifies and corrects erroneous data. For example, Eve may fix misspellings of words in the database.

- *Augment Information*: Eve fills in missing data either by inferring the data or copying the data from other sources. For example, if Eve knows the addresses of people, then she could fill in their zip codes automatically.

- *Entity Resolution* [17,4]: Eve can identify the records that refer to the same real-world entity and merge them into composite records. For example, if Eve has the three records r, s, and t in the database and know that r and s both refer to the same person, then she can merge r and s by combining the information of the two records into a single record $r+s$, resulting in a database with two records: $r + s$ and t. An ER operation can also use background information when resolving the records.

Among the operations, we will focus on the entity resolution (ER) operation. To illustrate how a data analysis operation can improve information leakage, say that we are running the ER function E on the database $R = \{r = \{\langle\text{N, Alice, 1}\rangle, \langle\text{P, 123, 1}\rangle\}, s = \{\langle\text{N, Alice, 1}\rangle, \langle\text{C, 999, 1}\rangle\}, t = \{\langle\text{N, Bob, 1}\rangle, \langle\text{P, 987, 1}\rangle\}\}$. (Notice that we have set all the confidence values to 1 for simplicity.) Also suppose we have the reference record $e = \{\langle\text{N, Alice}\rangle, \langle\text{P, 123}\rangle, \langle\text{C, 999}\rangle, \langle\text{Z, 111}\rangle\}$. Before running E, the information leakage is $L^0(R, e) = max_{r \in R} L(r, e) = max\{\frac{2 \times 2/2 \times 2/4}{2/2 + 2/4}, \frac{2 \times 2/2 \times 2/4}{2/2 + 2/4}, 0\}$ $= \frac{2}{3}$. While running E, suppose we conclude that r and s are the same person and produce the merged record $r + s = \{\langle N, \text{Alice}, 1 \rangle, \langle P, 123, 1 \rangle, \langle C, 999, 1 \rangle\}$. Then the new database $E(R) = \{r + s, t\}$ has the information leakage $L^0(E(R), e) = max_{r \in E(R)} L(r, e) = max\{\frac{2 \times 3/3 \times 3/4}{3/3 + 3/4}, 0\} = \frac{6}{7}$. Hence, by applying E, Eve has increased the information leakage of R from $\frac{2}{3}$ to $\frac{6}{7}$.

We can abstract any combination of data analysis operations as a function E, which receives the database R and returns another database $E(R)$ that may increase information leakage. For example, one can augment information to the database and then perform entity resolution.

While the above operations are powerful and may enhance information leakage, they require computation effort on Eve's side. For example, if a sophisticated ER algorithm takes quadratic time to run, then it may not be feasible to run the algorithm on all the hundreds of millions of people on the Web. If Eve uses a more relaxed and faster algorithm, then more records can be resolved.

To incorporate the adversary effort into our model, we define the cost function C that receives the adversary operation E and the database R, and returns the "cost" required to run E on R. The cost could be measured in computation steps, run time, or even in dollars. For instance, if has $O(n^2)$ complexity for resolving n records, then $C(E, R)$ could be $c \times |R|^2$ for some constant c.

Using the basic definition of information leakage and the data analysis operation E, we now define our information leakage measure as follows.

Definition 2. *Given an adversary operator E, the information leakage of R against p is $L(R, e, E) = L^0(E(R), e)$ with the cost $C(E, R)$.*

For example, say that there are 1000 records in the database R, and $L^0(R, e) = 0.3$. Also say that $C(E, R) = c \times |R|^2$ where $c = \frac{1}{1000}$. Now suppose that the operator E improves the information leakage where $L^0(E(R), e) = 0.9$. Hence, the data analysis using E has revealed an additional information of $0.9 - 0.3 = 0.6$ using a cost of $\frac{1}{1000} \times 1000^2 = 1000$. Notice that if E is an identity function where $E(R) = R$, then $L(R, e, E)$ reduces to the basic information leakage definition $L^0(R, e) = max_{r \in R} L(r, e)$.

We can extend our model to a scenario where Eve not just has a database of records R, but also has a "query" of interest. For example, Eve may be focusing on a person with name Alice who is 30 years old. In this case, Eve's query is $q = \{\langle \text{name}, \text{Alice}, 1 \rangle, \langle \text{age}, 30, 1 \rangle\}$. Eve can then look in R for records that are "related" to this Alice, thus expanding her information on this Alice. That is, starting with q, Eve may use ER to merge records in the database that refer to the same entity as q. Given an ER function E, we define the *dipping result* of q, $D(R, E, q)$, as the record $r \in E(R \cup \{q\})$ such that r is a merged result of q. For example, suppose we have the database $R = \{r = \{\langle N, \text{Alice}, 1 \rangle, \langle P, 123, 1 \rangle\}, s = \{\langle N, \text{Alice}, 1 \rangle, \langle C, 999, 1 \rangle\}, t = \{\langle N, \text{Bob}, 1 \rangle, \langle P, 987, 1 \rangle\}\}$. Also say that the ER function E merges all the records that have the same name. Given the query $q = \{\langle N, \text{Alice}, 1 \rangle\}$, we then obtain a dipping result $r + s + q = \{\langle N, \text{Alice}, 1 \rangle, \langle C, 999, 1 \rangle, \langle P, 123, 1 \rangle\}$ because both r and s have the same name as q. The information leakage of q can be defined as $L(D(R, E, q), e)$. (Reference [17] provides more details on ER and computing dipping results.)

3 Relationship to Other Measures

In this section, we compare our information leakage measure with two popular privacy models in data publishing. We first provide a detailed comparison of information leakage and the k-anonymity model [14]. Next, we briefly discuss how our measure relates to the l-diversity model [9]. Both models take an all-or-nothing approach where either all the records in a database are equally "safe" or none of the records are safe at all. In comparison, our information leakage model can be used to quantify various notions of privacy, e.g., the information leakage of an individual record within a database. Obviously, it is impossible to compare our model with every existing privacy model. For example, we do not directly compare our work with the t-closeness [8] or Differential Privacy [3] models. However, the same argument holds where information leakage can quantify various notions of privacy while the two existing models either deem the entire database safe or not safe.

3.1 k-Anonymity

In data publishing, the k-anonymity model [14] prevents the identity disclosure of individuals within a database. More formally, a database R satisfies k-anonymity if for every record $r \in R$, there exist $k - 1$ other records in R that have the same "quasi-identifiers." The quasi-identifers are attributes that can be linked with external data to uniquely identify individuals in the database. For example, suppose that all the records in R have three attributes: zip code, age, and disease. Given external information, if a person in R can be identified by looking at her zip code and age, then the quasi-identifiers are zip code and age. Also, a sensitive attribute is an attribute whose value for any particular individual must be kept secret from people who have no direct access to R. In our example, we consider the disease attribute as sensitive.

Table 1 illustrates a database R that contains the name, zip code, age, and disease information of patients. For example, patient 1 has the name Alice, zip code 111, an age of 30, and a heart disease. Table 2 shows the 3-anonymous version of R (called R_a) without the names. In order to anonymize a database, we "suppress" each quasi-identifier value by either replacing a number with a range of numbers or replacing one or more characters in a string with the same number of wild card characters. (A wild card character is denoted as '*' and represents any character.) For example, Dave's age 50 was suppressed to ≥ 50 while Alice's zip code 111 was suppressed to 1**. For any patient, there are two other patients that have the same zip code and age information. Each set of records that have the same quasi-identifiers form one equivalence class. We assume that the adversary Eve can view Table 2, but not Table 1.

Table 1. Database of Patients (R)

Name	Zip	Age	Disease
Alice	111	30	Heart
Bob	112	31	Breast
Carol	115	33	Cancer
Dave	222	50	Hair
Pat	299	70	Flu
Zoe	241	60	Flu

Table 2. 3-Anonymous Version of Table 1 (R_a)

Zip	Age	Disease
11*	3*	Heart
11*	3*	Breast
11*	3*	Cancer
2**	$\geq$50	Hair
2**	$\geq$50	Flu
2**	$\geq$50	Flu

Table 3. Background Information (R_b)

Name	Zip	Age
Alice	111	30

The k-anonymity model takes an all-or-nothing approach where either all the records satisfy k-anonymity or not. That is, if each record is indistinguishable from $k - 1$ other records in terms of quasi-identifiers, the released database is considered "safe." Otherwise, the database is not safe. In comparison, the information leakage model is more general and can quantify a wider range of privacy settings.

First, we can study the information leakage for individuals. For example, suppose that we compare the information leakage of Alice and Zoe. (For simplicity, we assume all attribute weights have the same value 1.) Say that we first run an ER algorithm E that merges all the records in Table 2 that have the same zip code and age. As a result, there are two merged records: r_1: $\{\langle$Zip, 11*, 1$\rangle$, $\langle$Age, 3*, 1$\rangle$, $\langle$Disease, Heart, 1$\rangle$, $\langle$Disease, Breast, 1$\rangle$, $\langle$Disease, Cancer, 1$\rangle\}$ and r_2: $\{\langle$Zip, 2**, 1$\rangle$, $\langle$Age, $\geq$50, 1$\rangle$, $\langle$Disease, Hair, 1$\rangle$, $\langle$Disease, Flu, 1$\rangle\}$. If the reference record of Alice is $e_a = \{\langle$Name, Alice$\rangle$, $\langle$Zip, 111$\rangle$, $\langle$Age, 30$\rangle$, $\langle$Disease, Heart$\rangle\}$, the information leakage of Alice is $max\{L(r_1, e_a), L(r_2, e_a)\} = max\{\frac{2\times3/5\times3/4}{3/5+3/4}, 0\} = \frac{2}{3}$. Here, we have made the simplification that a suppressed value (e.g., 1**) is equal to its non-suppressed version (e.g., 111). In practice, one could view a suppressed value as the original value with a reduced confidence value. If the reference record of Zoe is $e_b = \{\langle$Name, Zoe$\rangle$, $\langle$Zip, 241$\rangle$, $\langle$Age, 60$\rangle$, $\langle$Disease, Flu$\rangle\}$, then the information leakage of Zoe is $max\{L(r_1, e_b), L(r_2, e_b)\} = max\{0, \frac{2\times3/4\times3/4}{3/4+3/4}\} = \frac{3}{4}$. Again, we have simplified the comparison and considered a suppressed value (e.g, $\geq$50) to be equal to its unsuppressed version (e.g., 60). As a result, the information leakage of Zoe, $\frac{3}{4}$, is higher than that of Alice, $\frac{2}{3}$, although k-anonymity considers the records of both people to be equally safe.

Second, we can quantify the impact of background information on privacy. For example, say that the adversary knows additional information about Alice as shown in Table 2. The adversary can then combine the database R_b in Table 3 with Table 2 to measure Alice's information leakage. Using the same ER algorithm E as above, we now generate the two records r_1': $\{\langle$Name, Alice, 1$\rangle$, $\langle$Zip, 11*, 1$\rangle$, $\langle$Age, 3*, 1$\rangle$, $\langle$Disease, Heart, 1$\rangle$, $\langle$Disease, Breast, 1$\rangle$, $\langle$Disease, Cancer, 1$\rangle\}$ and r_2: $\{\langle$Zip, 2**, 1$\rangle$, $\langle$Age, $\geq$50, 1$\rangle$, $\langle$Disease, Hair, 1$\rangle$, $\langle$Disease, Flu, 1$\rangle\}$. The information leakage of Alice is thus $max\{L(r_1', e_a), L(r_2, e_a)\} = max\{\frac{2\times4/6\times4/4}{4/6+4/4}, 0\} = \frac{4}{5}$. Hence, in the presence of the background information R_b, Alice's information leakage has increased from $\frac{2}{3}$ to $\frac{4}{5}$.

3.2   l-Diversity

The l-diversity model [9] enhances the k-anonymity model by ensuring that the sensitive attributes of each equivalence class have at least l "well-represented" values. For example, in Table 2, the first equivalence class contains 3 distinct diseases while the second equivalence class has 2 distinct diseases. If $l = 3$, then we would like to enforce each equivalence class to have at least 3 distinct diseases. Suppose that we change Zoe's disease in Table 2 from Flu to Influenza. Then the modified database R'_a satisfies 3-diversity because each equivalence class has at least 3 different diseases.

Although R'_a is considered safe by l-diversity, the fact that Influenza is semantically similar to the Flu may result in less privacy for Zoe. We now illustrate how the information leakage model can quantify this change in privacy. First suppose that E considers the diseases Flu and Influenza to be different. Then using the ER algorithm E defined above, we generate the two records r_1: $\{\langle$Zip, 11*, 1$\rangle$, $\langle$Age, 3*, 1$\rangle$, $\langle$Disease, Heart, 1$\rangle$, $\langle$Disease, Breast, 1$\rangle$, $\langle$Disease, Cancer, 1$\rangle\}$ and r'_2: $\{\langle$Zip, 2**, 1$\rangle$, $\langle$Age, $\geq$50, 1$\rangle$, $\langle$Disease, Hair, 1$\rangle$, $\langle$Disease, Flu, 1$\rangle$, $\langle$Disease, Influenza, 1$\rangle\}$. Thus the information leakage of Zoe is $max\{L(r_1, e_b), L(r'_2, e_b)\}$ $= max\{0, \frac{2 \times 3/5 \times 3/4}{3/5 + 3/4}\} = \frac{2}{3}$. Now suppose that the operation E' is equivalent to E, but considers Influenza to be the same disease as the Flu and replaces all the occurrences of Influenza with Flu when merging records. In this case, the generated record r'_2 is now r''_2: $\{\langle$Zip, 2**, 1$\rangle$, $\langle$Age, $\geq$50, 1$\rangle$, $\langle$Disease, Hair, 1$\rangle$, $\langle$Disease, Flu, 1$\rangle\}$. As a result, the information leakage of Zoe becomes $max\{L(r_1, e_b), L(r''_2, e_b)\} = max\{0, \frac{2 \times 3/4 \times 3/4}{3/4 + 3/4}\} = \frac{3}{4}$. Hence, by exploiting the application semantics, the information leakage of Zoe has increased from $\frac{2}{3}$ to $\frac{3}{4}$. Notice that this measurement could not be done using the l-diversity model, which cannot capture the usage of application semantics.

4   Applications

Our information leakage framework can be used to answer a variety of questions as we show in the following sections. As we use our framework, it is important to keep in mind "who knows what". In particular, if Alice is studying leakage of her information, she needs to make assumptions as to what her adversary Eve knows (database R) and how she operates (the data analysis function E Eve uses). These types of assumptions are common in privacy work, where one must guess the sophistication and compute power of Eve. On the other hand, if Eve is studying leakage she will not have Alice's reference information e. However, she may use a "training data set" for known individuals in order to tune her data analysis operations, or say estimate how much she really knows about Alice. In the following sections, we formalize problems in information leakage both in Alice's point of view and in Eve's point of view.

4.1   Releasing Critical Information

In this section, we formalize problems for managing Alice's information leakage. Suppose that Alice tracks R, the information she has given out in the past. She now wants to release a new record r (e.g., her credit card information) which may fall in the hands of the adversary who might use the ER function E to resolve other records with r. Alice can compute the direct leakage involved in releasing the record r, i.e., $L(R \cup \{r\}, e, E)$. However, we may want to capture the information leaked by r only instead of computing the entire leakage of the database. We thus define the incremental leakage of r as follows.

$$I(R, e, E, r) = L(R \cup \{r\}, e, E) - L(R, e, E)$$

Since r may make it possible for Eve to piece together big chunks of information about Alice, the incremental leakage may be large, even if r contains relatively little data.

To illustrate incremental leakage for a critical piece of information, say that Alice wants to purchase a cellphone app from an online store and is wondering which credit card c_1 or c_2 she uses will lead to a smaller loss of her privacy. Each purchase requires Alice to submit her name, credit card number, and phone number. Due to Alice's previous purchases, the store already has some information about Alice.

In particular:

- Alice's reference information is $e = \{\langle N, n_1 \rangle, \langle C, c_1 \rangle, \langle C, c_2 \rangle, \langle P, p_1 \rangle, \langle A, a_1 \rangle\}$ where N stands for name, C for credit card number, P for phone, and A for address.

- The online store has two previous records $R = \{s = \{\langle N, n_1, 1 \rangle, \langle C, c_1, 1 \rangle, \langle P, p_1, 1 \rangle\}, t = \{\langle N, n_1, 1 \rangle, \langle C, c_2, 1 \rangle\}\}$. (We omit the app information in any record for brevity.)

- The store accepts one of the two records $u = \{\langle N, n_1, 1 \rangle, \langle C, c_1, 1 \rangle, \langle P, p_1, 1 \rangle\}$ or $v = \{\langle N, n_1, 1 \rangle, \langle C, c_2, 1 \rangle, \langle P, p_1, 1 \rangle\}$ for the cellphone app purchase. Since Alice is purchasing an app, again no shipping address is required.

Suppose that two records refer to the same entity (or match) if their names and credit card numbers are the same or their names and phone numbers are the same, and that merging records simply performs a union of attributes. Also say that all weights w have the same value 1.

Then the information leakage of Alice before her purchase is $L(R, e)$ $= max_{r \in E(R)} L(r, e) = max_{r \in \{s,t\}} L(r, e) = max\{\frac{2 \times 3/3 \times 3/5}{3/3 + 3/5}, \frac{2 \times 2/2 \times 2/5}{2/2 + 2/5}\} = max\{\frac{3}{4}, \frac{4}{7}\} = \frac{3}{4}$. If Alice uses c_1 and releases u to the store, then the information leakage is still $L(r, e) = \frac{2 \times 3/3 \times 3/5}{3/3 + 3/5} = \frac{3}{4}$ because u and s are identical and merge together, but not with t. If Alice uses c_2 and releases v instead, all three records merge together because v matches with both s and t. Hence the information leakage is $L(s + t + v, e) = \frac{2 \times 4/4 \times 4/5}{4/4 + 4/5} = \frac{8}{9}$. To compare Alice's two choices, we compute the incremental leakage values, i.e., the change in leakage values due to the app purchase. In our example, the incremental leakage of releasing u is $\frac{3}{4} - \frac{3}{4} = 0$ while the incremental leakage of releasing v is $\frac{8}{9} - \frac{3}{4} = \frac{5}{36}$. Thus, in this case Alice should use the credit card c_1 to buy her app because it preserves more of her privacy.

4.2 Releasing Disinformation

Releasing disinformation can be an effective way to reduce information leakage. Given previously released information R, Alice may want to release either a single record or multiple records that can decrease the information leakage. (The confidence values of the adversary remain the same.) We call records that are used to decrease the leakage *disinformation* records. Of course, Alice can reduce the information leakage by releasing arbitrarily large disinformation. However, disinformation itself has a cost. For instance, adding a new social network profile would require the cost for registering information. As another example, longer records could require more cost and effort to construct. We use $C(r)$ to denote the entire cost of creating r.

We define the problem of minimizing the information leakage using one or more disinformation records. Given one data analysis operator E, a set of disinformation records S and a maximum budget of C_{max}, the optimal disinformation problem can be stated as follows:

$$\text{minimize}\quad L(R \cup S, e, E)$$
$$\text{subject to } \Sigma_{r \in S} C(r) \leq C_{max}$$

The set of records S that minimizes the information leakage within our budget C_{max} is called an optimal disinformation.

We study the problem of releasing disinformation. Figure 2 shows a database $R = \{r, s, t, u, v\}$ where r and s refer to the entity e while t, u, and v refer to an entity other than e. The disinformation record can reduce the database leakage in two ways. First, a disinformation record can perform *self disinformation* by acting as disinformation itself and add its irrelevant information to a correct record. In our example, the disinformation record d_1 snaps with the correct record r and adds its own information to r. Second, a disinformation record can perform *linkage disinformation* by reducing the database leakage by linking irrelevant records in R to a correct record. For example, the disinformation record d_2 is linking the irrelevant record v to the correct record r and thus adding v's information to r. Using these two basic disinformation strategies, one can perform a combination of self and linkage disinformation as well.

When creating a record, we use a user-defined function called $Create(S, L)$ that creates a new minimal record that has a size less or equal to L and is guaranteed to match all the records in the set S. If there is no record r such that $|r| \leq L$ and all records in S match with r, the $Create$ function returns the empty record $\{\}$. A reasonable assumption is that the size of the record produced by $Create$ is proportional to $|S|$ when $L > |S|$. We also assume a function called $Add(r)$ that appends a new attribute to r. The new attribute should be "incorrect but believable" (i.e., bogus) information. We assume that if two records r and s

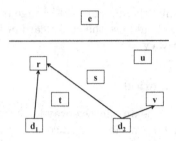

Fig. 2. Self and Linkage Disinformation

match, they will still match even if Add appends bogus attributes to either r or s. The $Create$ function is assumed to have a time complexity of $O(|S|)$ while the Add function $O(|r|)$. Reference [17] provides more detail how to use the $Create$ and Add functions to generate the optimal disinformation.

4.3   Enhancing a Composite Record

From the adversary Eve's point of view, there may also be interesting "opti-mization" questions to ask. Since Eve does not know Alice's full record e, the questions cannot be phrased in terms of e. Consider a composite record r_c that Eve has inferred from a set of facts in a set R. For whatever reason, Eve is very interested in r_c, but unfortunately there is some uncertainty in the attributes in r_c. We define r_e to be the same as r_c except that all confidences in r_c are set to 1 and omitted from the record. $L(r_c, r_e)$ is a measure of how certain r_c is: the closer $L(r_c, r_e)$ is to 1, the more certain Eve is of the information in r_c.

To improve $L(r_c, r_e)$ (i.e., make it closer to 1), Eve can try to increase her confidence in the attributes in R. For any given attribute $a = \langle l, v, c \rangle$ in some $r_i \in R$, Eve can improve the confidence of a by doing more research, bribing someone, issuing a subpoena, etc. The increase in the confidence of a will clearly have a cost associated with it. There are again many ways to model the cost, but for simplicity let us assume that the cost in changing the confidence from its current value of c to 1 is $C(a) = 1 - c$.

Now the question is, what is the most cost effective way to increase Eve's confidence in r_c. If Eve only wants to verify one attribute, then we want the one $a \in r_i$ that maximizes

$$\frac{L(r'_c, r_e) - L(r_c, r_e)}{C(a)}$$

where r'_c is the composite record Eve can infer when the confidence in a is increased to 1.

For example, suppose that we have the database $R = \{r_1 = \{\langle N, \text{Alice}, 1 \rangle, \langle A, 20, 1 \rangle\}, r_2 = \{\langle N, \text{Alice}, 0.9 \rangle, \langle P, 123, 0.5 \rangle, \langle C, 987, 1 \rangle\}\}$ where N stands for name, A stands for age, P stands for phone, and C stands for credit card number. We assume that all weights w have the value 1. Suppose that r_1 and r_2 merges into $r_c = \{\langle N, \text{Alice}, 1 \rangle, \langle A, 20, 1 \rangle, \langle P, 123, 0.5 \rangle, \langle C, 987, 1 \rangle\}$ where we take the maximum confidence value when merging two attributes with the same label and value pair. Then $r_e = \{\langle \text{N, Alice}\rangle, \langle \text{A, 20}\rangle, \langle \text{P, 123}\rangle, \langle \text{C, 987}\rangle\}$. If we enhance the name in r_2 to have a confidence of 1, then $r'_c = \{\langle \text{N, Alice}, 1\rangle, \langle \text{A, 20,} 1\rangle, \langle \text{P, 123, 0.5}\rangle, \langle \text{C, 987, 1}\rangle\}$ (which is identical to r_c), and $C(\langle \text{N, Alice}, 0.9\rangle) = 1 - 0.9 = 0.1$. Then $\frac{L(r'_c, r_e) - L(r_c, r_e)}{C(\langle \text{N,Alice},0.9\rangle)} = \frac{0}{0.1} = 0$. On the other hand, if we enhance the phone number of r_2, then $r'_c = \{\langle \text{N, Alice}, 1\rangle, \langle \text{A, 20, 1}\rangle, \langle \text{P, 123, 1}\rangle, \langle \text{C,} 987, 1\rangle\}$ with the cost $C(\langle \text{P, 123, 0.5}\rangle) = 1 - 0.5 = 0.5$. Then $\frac{L(r'_c, r_e) - L(r_c, r_e)}{C(\langle \text{P,123,0.5}\rangle)} = (\frac{2\times4/4\times4/4}{4/4+4/4} - (\frac{1}{2} \times \frac{2\times4/4\times4/4}{4/4+4/4} + \frac{1}{2} \times \frac{2\times4/4\times3/4}{4/4+3/4}))/0.5 = \frac{1-(1/2+3/7)}{0.5} = \frac{1}{28}$. Hence, verifying the phone number in r_2 results in a better enhancement of r_c than verifying the name of r_2.

5 Leakage Computation

Computing information leakage efficiently is important because the amount of information (i.e., the number of attributes) within a record can be large in practice. Given a database R and a data analysis operation E, the information leakage (see Definition 2) can be computed by running $E(R)$, and then computing the maximum record leakage by iterating each record r in $E(R)$ and computing $L(r, e)$. Given that computing the record leakage $L(r, e)$ takes $f(|r|, |e|)$ time and running E on R takes $g(|R|)$ time, the total complexity of computing the information leakage is $O(g(|R|) + \sum_{r \in E(R)} f(|r|, |e|))$.

A naïve approach for computing the leakage of each record r is to iterate through all possible worlds of r and add the record leakage values (without confidences) multiplied by their probabilities as shown in Definition 1. This solution has an exponential complexity of $O(2^{|r|} \times |r|)$.

We now propose efficient solutions for computing the record leakage $L(r, e)$. We first propose an exact algorithm that assumes equal attribute weights. We then propose an approximate algorithm that allows different attribute weights.

Algorithm 1 computes the exact value of information leakage in $O(|e| \times |r|^2)$ time assuming that all the weights have the same value. For example, suppose that $e = \{\langle \text{A, 1}\rangle, \langle \text{B, 2}\rangle\}$ and $r = \{\langle \text{A, 1, 0.1}\rangle, \langle \text{B, 3, 0.2}\rangle\}$. Also say that all the attribute weights have a value of 1. We first assign $b = \langle \text{A, 1}\rangle$ in Step 2 and set $Z = (0.2, (1 - 0.2)) = (0.2, 0.8)$ in Steps 8–11. We then set $Y = (0.2, 0.8)$ in Step 12 and continue to Steps 13–14 where we compute $L = 2 \times 0.1 \times \frac{0.2}{2+2-1+1} + 2 \times 0.1 \times \frac{0.8}{2+2-2+1} = \frac{19}{300}$. Next, we set $b = \langle \text{B, 2}\rangle$ in Step 2 and set $Z = (0.1\times0.2, 0.1\times(1-0.2)+(1-0.1)\times0.2, (1-0.1)\times(1-0.2)) = (0.02, 0.26, 0.72)$ in Steps 8–10. However, we add 0 to L in Steps 13–14 because $p(b, r) = 0$. Hence, we return $L = \frac{19}{300}$. Notice that we have the same result as computing $L(p, r)$ using the brute-force naïve approach: $0.1 \times 0.2 \times \frac{2\times1/2\times1/2}{1/2+1/2} + 0.1 \times 0.8 \times \frac{2\times1\times1/2}{1+1/2} + 0.9 \times 0.2 \times 0 + 0.9 \times 0.8 \times 0 = \frac{19}{300}$.

The proof of the correctness and complexity of Algorithm 1 in Proposition 1 can be found in our technical report [18].

Proposition 1. *Algorithm 1 computes $L(r, e)$ in $O(|e| \times |r|^2)$ time assuming equal weights.*

Algorithm 1. Record Leakage using Constant Weights

---

     input   : the records r, e
     output: the record leakage $L(r, e)$

1   $L \leftarrow 0$;
2   **for** $b \in e$ **do**
3        $Y \leftarrow (1.0)$;
4   **for** $a \in r$ **do**
5             $Z \leftarrow ()$;
6   **if** $a.l = b.l \wedge a.v = b.v$ **then**
7                 $\lfloor$ **continue to next loop**;
8             $Z.Add(Y.Get(0) \times p(a,r))$;
9   **for** $x = 0, \ldots, |Y| - 1$ **do**
10               $\lfloor$ $Z.Add(Y.Get(x) \times (1 - p(a,r)) + Y.Get(x + 1) \times p(a,r))$;
11             $Z.Add(Y.Get(|Y| - 1) \times (1 - p(a,r)))$;
12             $Y \leftarrow Z$;
13   **for** $x = 0, \ldots, |Y| - 1$ **do**
14           $\lfloor$ $L \leftarrow L + 2 \times p(b,r) \times \frac{Y.Get(x)}{|e| + |Y| - x}$;

15 **return** L;

We can also compute an approximation of $L(r, e)$ in $O(|e| \times |r|)$ time where the weights can be different. The idea is to compute the first few terms in the Taylor series of $L(r, e)$ (see our technical report [18] for details). While computing many terms leads to more accurate solutions, we show in Section 6.2 that an approximation based on the second order series is already quite accurate.

6   Experiments

We run experiments on synthetic data in order to observe trends and to study the scalability of our algorithms. Table 4 shows the configuration used. We first generate the reference record e by creating a set of n random attributes. We then generate a record $r \in R$ by iterating over each attribute in e and copying it with a probability p_c. However, each time there is a copy, we perturb the attribute with probability p_p into a new attribute. In addition, for each attribute in e we also add a new bogus attribute to r with probability p_b. The confidence value for each attribute generated was a random number between 0 and m, the maximum possible confidence. If $w = C$, then we set all the weights to 1, and if $w = R$, we randomly generated random real numbers between 0 and 1 for the weights. We repeated the generation of a record $|R|$ times. The last column of Table 4 shows the basic values of the parameters. Our base case does not represent any particular application or scenario; it is simply a convenient starting point from which to explore a wide range of parameter settings. Our algorithms were implemented in Java, and our experiments were run in memory on a 2.4GHz Intel(R) Core 2 processor with 4 GB of RAM.

Table 4. Parameters for Data Generation

Par.	Description	Basic
n	Size of the gold standard e	100
$\|R\|$	Number of records to generate	10,000
p_c	Probability of copying attribute from e to r	0.5
p_p	Probability of perturbing a copied attribute	0.5
p_b	Probability of adding bogus attribute to r	0.5
m	Maximum confidence value	0.5
w	Weights are constant (C) or random (R)	C

6.1   Trends

We plot the information leakage while varying the parameters p_c, p_p, and m. Any
parameter that was not varied was set to its basic value in Table 4. Figure 3(a)
shows the leakage when varying p_c from 0 to 1. As p_c increases, more of e's attributes are copied to r, increasing the recall and thus the information leakage as
well. Figure 3(b) shows the leakage when varying p_p from 0 to 1. This time, the
more frequent the perturbation of an attributed being copied, the lower the precision and thus the information leakage becomes as well. Finally, Figure 3(c) shows
the leakage when varying m from 0 to 1. As the average confidence increases, there
are two competing factors that determine the information leakage: the higher confidence of correct information increases the leakage while the higher confidence of
incorrect information decreases the leakage. In our setting, the correct information
dominates and leakage increases as confidence increases.

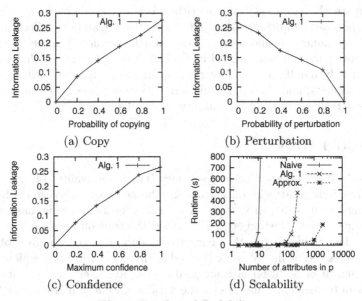

(a) Copy   (b) Perturbation

(c) Confidence   (d) Scalability

Fig. 3. Trends and Scalability

6.2   Accuracy of Approximate Algorithm

We now evaluate the accuracy of the approximate algorithm in Section 5. Table 5 shows the leakage values for Algorithm 1 and the approximation algorithm while varying the parameters n, p_c, p_p, b, m, and w. If $w = C$, we generated $|R| = 10,000$ records with constant weights and ran Algorithm 1 to compute the exact leakage. If $w = R$, we can only compute the exact leakage with the naïve algorithm (which is not scalable as shown in Section 6.3). Thus, we limited ourselves to records with only 10 attributes ($|e| = 10$), and gave each attribute a random weight ranging from 0 to 1. As we can see in Table 5, in all scenarios the exact and approximate leakage values are nearly identical, with a maximum error rate of 0.006%. We conclude that our approximate algorithm is highly accurate.

Table 5. Information Leakage Comparison

n	p_c	p_p	b	m	w	**Exact**	**Approx.**
100	0.5	0.5	0.5	0.5	C	0.1740179	0.1740178
200	0.5	0.5	0.5	0.5	C	0.1374662	0.1374661
100	1.0	0.5	0.5	0.5	C	0.2752435	0.2752431
100	0.5	1.0	0.5	0.5	C	0.0	0.0
100	0.5	0.5	1.0	0.5	C	0.1581138	0.1581135
100	0.5	0.5	0.5	1.0	C	0.2625473	0.2625469
100	0.5	0.5	0.5	0.5	R	0.4047125	0.4046881

6.3   Runtime Performance

We compare the scalability of Algorithm 1 and the approximate algorithm against the naïve implementation defined in the beginning of Section 6. We varied the parameter n and used constant weights while using the basic values for the other parameters as defined in Table 4. Figure 3(d) shows that the naïve algorithm only handle up to 12 attributes. In comparison, Algorithm 1 scales to 250 attributes, and the approximation algorithm scales to more than 2,000 attributes, demonstrating the scalability of our algorithms.

7   Related Work

Many works have proposed privacy schemes. The k-anonymity [14] model guarantees that linkage attacks on certain attributes cannot succeed. Subsequent works such as the l-diversity [9] and t-closeness [8] models have improved the k-anonymity model. Rastogi et al. [11] shows the tradeoff between privacy and utility in data publishing in the context of maintaining the accuracy of counting queries. A recent line of work [3] studies differential privacy, which ensures that a removal or addition of a single database item does not (substantially) affect the outcome of any analysis on the database. Finally, many works [2,7] use application-specific measures of privacy. In comparison, our information leakage measure is general and focuses on quantifying the privacy of an individual against a given database and has the following features. First, we assume that some of our data is already public (i.e., out of our control) and that there can be a wide range of scenarios where we need to measure privacy. Second, our information leakage reflects the four different factors of privacy: the correctness and completeness of the leaked database, the adversary's confidence on the database, and the adversary's analysis on the database.

A closely-related framework to ours is P4P [1], which seeks to contain illegitimate use of personal information that has already been released to an external (possibly adversarial) entity. For different types of information, general-purpose mechanisms are proposed to retain control of the data. More recently, a startup called Reputation.com [12] has started using disinformation techniques for managing the reputation of individuals focusing on improving search engine results. TrackMeNot [15] is a browser extension that helps protect web searchers from surveillance and data-profiling by search engines using noise and obfuscation. Finally, ICorrect [5] is a web site that allows one to clarify his/her misinformation on the Web. We believe that the works above show a clear need for using information leakage as a measure of privacy.

The information theoretic metric of entropy [13] is often used in the context of communication privacy and quantifies the amount of information an attacker is missing in verifying a hypothesis within a confidence interval. In comparison, the information leakage model focuses on capturing the intuitive notion of leakage: correctness, completeness, and the adversary confidence. In addition, our model incorporates the data analysis operations of the adversary and the costs for performing the operations.

Information retrieval [10] searches for relevant information within documents. Many different measures for evaluating the performance of information retrieval have been proposed. The notions of precision were first proposed by Kent et al.[6]. The F measure was introduced by van Rijsbergen [16]. Information leakage adopts these measures in a privacy setting. In addition, our measure reflects the adversary confidence and data analysis. Compared to probabilistic information retrieval [10] where documents are probabilistically ranked, our work probabilistically computes the information leakage itself using possible worlds semantics.

8   Conclusion

We have proposed a framework using information leakage as a measure for data privacy. In many applications, an important observation is that privacy is no longer an all-or-nothing concept because some of our data may inevitably become public through various interactions (e.g., buying a product from a vendor online). Our information leakage measure reflects four important factors of privacy: the correctness and completeness of the leaked data, the adversary's confidence on the data, and the adversary's data analysis. We have compared our information leakage model with the k-anonymity and l-diversity models.

We have described several challenges in managing information leakage that can be posed by our framework. We have proposed efficient algorithms for computing the exact and approximate values of information leakage. Finally, we have shown through extensive experiments on synthetic data that the information leakage measure indeed captures the important factors of privacy, and that our information leakage algorithms can scale to large data.

References

1. Aggarwal, G., Bawa, M., Ganesan, P., Garcia-Molina, H., Kenthapadi, K., Mishra, N., Motwani, R., Srivastava, U., Thomas, D., Widom, J., Xu, Y.: Vision paper: Enabling privacy for the paranoids. In: VLDB, pp. 708–719 (2004)
2. Becker, J., Chen, H.: Measuring privacy risk in online social networks. In: Workshop on Web 2.0 Security (2009)
3. Dwork, C.: Differential Privacy. In: Bugliesi, M., Preneel, B., Sassone, V., Wegener, I. (eds.) ICALP 2006, Part II. LNCS, vol. 4052, pp. 1–12. Springer, Heidelberg (2006)
4. Elmagarmid, A.K., Ipeirotis, P.G., Verykios, V.S.: Duplicate record detection: A survey. IEEE Trans. Knowl. Data Eng. 19(1), 1–16 (2007)
5. ICorrect, http://www.icorrect.com/
6. Kent, A., Berry, M.M., Luehrs Jr., F.U., Perry, J.W.: Machine literature searching VIII. Operational criteria for designing information retrieval systems. American Documentation 6(2), 93–101 (1955)
7. Krishnamurthy, B., Malandrino, D., Wills, C.E.: Measuring privacy loss and the impact of privacy protection in web browsing. In: SOUPS, pp. 52–63 (2007)
8. Li, N., Li, T., Venkatasubramanian, S.: t-closeness: Privacy beyond k-anonymity and l-diversity. In: ICDE, pp. 106–115 (2007)
9. Machanavajjhala, A., Gehrke, J., Kifer, D., Venkitasubramaniam, M.: l-diversity: Privacy beyond k-anonymity. In: ICDE, vol. 24 (2006)
10. Manning, C.D., Raghavan, P., Schtze, H.: Introduction to Information Retrieval. Cambridge University Press, New York (2008)
11. Rastogi, V., Hong, S., Suciu, D.: The boundary between privacy and utility in data publishing. In: VLDB, pp. 531–542 (2007)
12. Reputation.com, http://www.reputation.com
13. Reza, F.M.: An Introduction to Information Theory. Dover Publications (September 1994)
14. Sweeney, L.: k-anonymity: A model for protecting privacy. International Journal of Uncertainty, Fuzziness and Knowledge-Based Systems 10(5), 557–570 (2002)
15. TrackMeNot, http://cs.nyu.edu/trackmenot
16. van Rijsbergen, C.J.: Information Retrieval, 2nd edn. Butterworths, London (1979)
17. Whang, S.E., Garcia-Molina, H.: Managing information leakage. In: CIDR, pp. 79–84 (2011)
18. Whang, S.E., Garcia-Molina, H.: A model for quantifying information leakage. Technical report. Stanford University, http://ilpubs.stanford.edu:8090/1007/
19. Yao, D., Frikken, K.B., Atallah, M.J., Tamassia, R.: Private information: To reveal or not to reveal. ACM Trans. Inf. Syst. Secur. 12(1) (2008)

Privacy Protocol for Linking Distributed Medical Data

Daniel Janusz, Martin Kost, and Johann-Christoph Freytag

DBIS Group
Humboldt-Universität zu Berlin
Unter den Linden 6
10099 Berlin, Germany
{janusz,kost,freytag}@informatik.hu-berlin.de

Abstract. *Health care* providers need to exchange medical data to provide complex medical treatments. In general, regulations of *privacy protection* define strong constraints for exchanging such personal data within a distributed system. Privacy-preserving *query protocols* provide mechanisms for implementing and maintaining these privacy constraints. In this paper, we introduce a new two-phase protocol for protecting the privacy of patients. The first phase implements a private record linking. Thereby, the queried data provider links the received query with matching records in his data base. In the second phase, a requestor and a data provider perform an authorized exchange of matched patient data. Thus, our protocol provides a method for health care providers to exchange individual medical data in a privacy preserving manner. In contrast to other approaches, we actively involve patients in the exchange process. We apply the honest-but-curious adversary model to our protocol in order to evaluate our approach with respect to complexity and the degree of privacy protection.

1 Introduction

Health care providers use Hospital Information Systems (HIS) such as *Orbis* [1] or *i.s.h.med* [17] to manage patient data. In the course of a patient's treatment, lots of medical data is collected by various health care providers, e.g., hospitals or medical laboratories. In general, the HIS of these providers are not connected. Every provider manages a separate database to store the patient records.

Some medical treatments may involve the cooperation of several health care providers. Therefore, the involved health care providers exchange the required medical data, e.g., access blood analysis data from medical laboratories. Privacy concerns arise from communicating and processing such data. Moreover, exchanging medical records is often impossible due to legislative privacy reasons. For example, the privacy regulations of the European Union [8] restrict automatic exchange of personal data. A common way to overcome these restrictions is to hand over the records to the patient and he turns them over to the subsequent health care provider. Thus, patients implicitly authorize the receiving

W. Jonker and M. Petković (Eds.): SDM 2012, LNCS 7482, pp. 45–57, 2012.
© Springer-Verlag Berlin Heidelberg 2012

party to access this data. This procedure protects privacy, because the patient decides who should receive his/her data. However, the *data avoidance principle* is not addressed sufficiently. The approach described misses to check whether the receiver requires all record information for the intended treatment. Besides its benefits in terms of privacy, a manual data transfer of patient data may be too slow, e.g., in emergency scenarios.

In this paper, we present a protocol for exchanging medical data of one patient electronically while protecting the patient's privacy. Our approach protects patient's privacy with the same quality as the "manual approach". In addition, we address the data avoidance principle and provide an authorized remote data access mechanism. In our protocol, we use a two-phase approach. During the first phase, we identify patient records in the remote databases that may belong to the queried patient. Therefore, we utilize the observation that health care providers often collect the same medical attributes by means of family predispositions or baseline examinations. In the second phase, the required patient data is exchanged.

Our protocol protects privacy by guaranteeing the following two principles. First, the protocol enables health care provider to query remote data sources about a specific patient while not disclosing the identity of this patient. We call such queries *private fuzzy queries*. Second, the queried party requires that the query result can only be read if the patient is present and if the patient agrees to reveal the result data to the requestor. We call this principle an *authorized data exchange*.

In our approach, we guarantee that only those requesting parties get patient data that have the corresponding permission for receiving them. Moreover, we assume that health care providers do not trust each other; however we assume that they act honestly; i.e., all health care providers return accurate patient data. Such an approach resembles the *honest-but-curious adversary model* [11]. In a medical scenario, this adversary model is a proper assumption, as health care providers have no motivation for faking patient data. We will show that if only accurate patient data is submitted there is no attack on our protocol that may harm the privacy of patients.

As discussed before, our protocol aims at implementing and improving the manual approach of transfering patient data. Our approach includes that we do not implement more complex privacy principles such as limited data retention. There are still more open issues such as to update broken encryption keys at all data sources. Another challenge is to optimize our protocol in terms of communication overhead.

Outline. The remainder of this paper is organized as follows. Section 2 introduces preliminaries and basic definitions. In Section 3 we present our protocol, which we evaluate in terms of privacy and complexity in Section 4. Section 5 provides an overview of related work before Section 6 concludes the paper by outlining future work.

2   Background

In this section, we provide existing preliminaries and new definitions for introducing our approach.

2.1   Problem Definition

We implement a two-phase protocol that links distributed medical records. In the first phase, we identify health care providers that collect data of one specific patient. In the second phase, we exchange medical examination results of this patient that are relevant to the patient's intended medical treatment. Linking records stored on different databases has been widely discussed as the *record linkage problem* [9]. Record linkage is the process of identifying records belonging to the same entity, across two or more data sets. In contrast to general record linkage, our approach only localizes records belonging to one specific entity.

We call two records of different data sets *matching records* if these records belong to the same individual. In our scenario, we use *medical attributes* to find candidates for matching records. Medical attributes describe characteristics of a patient that belong to a patient's anamnesis, e.g., family predisposition, or biometric attributes, e.g., eye color.

Simple demographics like zip code and birth date are often sufficient to identify single individuals in a statistical database [18]. Medical attributes have similar characteristics [12]. Therefore, medical attributes are so-called *quasi-identifier*. To deal with measurement inaccuracies we can use ranges instead of exact values, e.g., if the height of a patient is 1,84m we search for a patient who's height is between 1,80m and 1,90m.

DEFINITION 1 (Table). *A table $\mathcal{T}$ is a set of tuples (records) with a schema $S = (A_1, ..., A_t), t \in \mathbb{N}$ and $\{A_1, ..., A_t\}$ is a set of attributes.*

DEFINITION 2 (Key). *Given a table $\mathcal{T}$ including a set of attributes $\mathcal{A}$. A key $\mathcal{K}$ of table $\mathcal{T}$ is a subset of the table attributes $\mathcal{K} \subseteq \mathcal{A}$ that uniquely identifies every record of the table $\mathcal{T}$.*

DEFINITION 3 (Quasi-Identifier). *Given a database table $\mathcal{T}$ including a set of personal attributes $\mathcal{A}$. A quasi-identifier in $\mathcal{T}$ is a subset of attributes $QID \subseteq \mathcal{A}$ that can be joined with external information to re-identify individual records with sufficiently high probability [19].*

We use quasi-identifying attributes to identify the searched patient. In order to hide the real identity of the searched patient from the queried party, we perform only fuzzy record matching. Fuzziness means not uniquely identify one person or in our context not less than k people. We call an identifier that performs a fuzzy record matching a *fuzzy matching pattern*. An example for these concepts is illustrated in Figure 1. In the table of hospital H, the attribute set {*sex, hair color, eye color*} forms a quasi-identifier. Consequential, *(sex, hair color)* forms a fuzzy matching pattern.

DEFINITION 4 (Fuzzy Matching Pattern). *Given a database table $\mathcal{T}$ including a set of personal attributes $\mathcal{A}_P$ and a quasi-identifier $QID \subseteq \mathcal{A}_P$ in $\mathcal{T}$. A fuzzy matching pattern $FMP = (A_y, ..., A_z)$ is an ordered list of attributes with: $\{A_y, ..., A_z\} \subset QID$.*

HOSPITAL *H*			Hair color	Eye color	Public biometric template	Radiograph
Patient ID	Name	Sex				
1	Allan	m	black	brown	x001	PIC1
2	Bob	m	black	green	x010	PIC2
3	Carl	m	blond	brown	x011	PIC3
4	Doris	f	black	brown	x100	PIC4

QUERY Q:
(MV₁,SHA1("m, black, brown"), Radiograph)

RESPONSE R:
encrypt("x001", PIC1)

EMERGENCY ROOM *E*		Hair color	Eye color	Private biometric template
Name	Sex			
Allan	m	black	brown	y001

Fig. 1. Hospital data and query example

2.2   Biometric Templates

Encryption methods [11] prevent unauthorized parties to access private data. Strong encryption keys are required to provide a secure encryption. By means of *biometric templates* such encryption keys can be generated. A biometric template is a digital description of distinct human characteristics that have been generated from biometric samples. After the generation of a biometric template the input samples must be deleted. Biometric templates are fault-tolerant against imprecise biometric input samples. In [3] the authors introduce a method to protect biometric templates based on *pseudonym identifier*. A pseudonym identifier is a diversifiable, protected binary strings, which does not reveal any information about the originally biometrics or the real identity of the related person.

Biometrics has been proofed to be valid for strong encryption [5]. We will utilize protected biometric templates to generate *public/private key-pairs* [11]. In the first version of our protocol, we will use a fixed set BIO of biometric sample attributes. In general, every party could use a different input for generating unique pseudonym identifier. In our approach, every patient holds a private and public encryption key. The private key is equal to the pseudonym identifier generated from BIO and will be called private biometric template BIO_{pr}. As public key and private key are interlinked, the public key must be generated using the private key, which we will call public biometric template BIO_{pu}.

2.3 Privacy Issues in Data Linking Scenarios

Usually, record linking is performed across data sets from different data sources. Privacy concerns arise whenever personal data is exchanged across companies. *Private record linkage* [10] addresses these concerns. However, the most private linking approaches do not consider one important privacy principle. That is, individuals have no control over the linkage process. In our approach, the individuals agree or disagree to the intended linkage process.

In the first phase of our protocol, we use special queries to identify matching records. We want even the query to be protected. Thus, the query must not leak any personal information. In order to realize such privacy-preserving queries, we define the notion of k-disguisebility. A *k-disguised* query performs fuzzy record matching. Let q be a query and ds a data source than we write $q(ds)$ to denote the result of the query q applied at the data source ds.

DEFINITION 5 (*k-disguisebility*). *Let $\mathcal{D}$ be a set of data sources in a distributed database setting, where every data source stores the same set of keys and (quasi-)identifying attributes. Let q be a query originated at one of the data sources $dr \in \mathcal{D}$ on keys or identifying attributes. The query q is said to satisfy k-disguisebility if and only if:*

$$|q(dr)| \geq k \qquad and \qquad \left| \bigcup_{d \in \mathcal{D} \setminus dr} q(d) \right| \geq k, \qquad (k \in \mathbb{N}).$$

The first property that must hold for k-disguisebility means that the result of query q at dr consists of at least k records. The second property states that the union of the results of query q at each of the remaining data source in $\mathcal{D} \setminus dr$ also consists of at least k records.

For an example consider the databases of hospital H (see Figure 1) and hospital G (see Figure 2). For these two databases a query on all tuples having "Hair Color = black" conforms to 2-disguisebility.

3 Privacy-Preserving Linking Protocol

In this section, we introduce our protocol. First, we exemplify the concepts of the approach before describing our protocol formally.

3.1 Example Scenario

We illustrate our approach using the following emergency scenario. After a serious car accident has occurred, a patient named Allan arrives at the emergency room E and needs a treatment. The physician wants to compare the current radiograph of his neck with an older image. Unfortunately, there is no prior record of Allan in the local HIS. The physician PE at E is allowed to access the remote database of hospital H (Figure 1) and starts a request for radiographs of Allan.

In order to protect the privacy of Allan the query Q conforms to k-disguise-bility. Therefore, the query Q is generated as follows: First, PE selects a fuzzy matching pattern FMP consisting of the attribute list $(sex, hair\ color, eye\ color)$. Next, the strings of Allan's values of the fuzzy matching pattern's attributes are concatenated. The result is hashed $h_{Allan} = SHA1("male, black, brown")$ using $SHA1$ [16]. Finally, the query $Q = (FMP, h_{Allan}, \{Radiograph\})$ is transmitted to hospital H. In section 4, we present an analysis verifying that Q now conforms to our notion of private fuzzy matching queries.

When hospital H receives the query Q from E, Q is processed as follows: For every record in H's database the $SHA1$ hash h_{temp} of the respective combined values of the attributes in FMP is generated. If h_{temp} equals h_{Allen}, the considered record matches. Thus, the image in the attribute $Radiograph$ is a candidate for being the searched prior radiograph. The algorithm adds all images of the matching records to the result set R. As seen in the table of Figure 1 h_{Allen} only matches the record with $PatientID = 1$. Therefore, $PIC1$ may be a radiograph of Allan.

The database of H contains the attribute $Public\ biometric\ template$. Public biometric templates BIO_{pu} are generated and stored at the first time a patient visits hospital H. The public biometric template is now used to encrypt the corresponding radiographs of the matching records in the response R. In case of Allan's record $PIC1$ is encrypted using his public biometric template $BIO_{pu}="x001"$ as encryption key.

After receiving the response R, E tries to decrypt all images in R using the private biometric template of Allan as decryption key. As Allan is physically present the emergency room gets Allan's permission to generate his private biometric template BIO_{pr} in order to access his previous medical data.

We now consider an example that includes an additional hospitals G (Figure 2). For G's database there will be two matching hashes for query Q. Therefore, the response of hospital G will contain the two encrypted radiographs $PIC11$ and $PIC12$. As Allan's private biometric template BIO_{pr} will only decrypt radiographs belonging to Allan, it is not possible to decrypt radiograph belonging to other patients such as John and Kevin.

HOSPITAL G			Hair	Eye	Public biometric	
Patient ID	Name	Sex	color	color	template	Radiograph
1	John	m	black	brown	x101	PIC11
2	Kevin	m	black	brown	x110	PIC22

Fig. 2. Data of the second hospital G

3.2   General Approach and Protocol

We now introduce our protocol formally. As mentioned before, our protocol protects privacy by implementing two selected privacy requirements (see Section 1). We introduce the following new type of private queries in order to realize our first privacy requirement, i.e., use private fuzzy matching queries. Let $\mathcal{D}$ be a set of independent medical data sources, e.g., hospitals or medical laboratories. Every data source in $\mathcal{D}$ stores or has access to the public biometric template BIO_{pu} of every individual in its database. Consider a patient $\mathcal{P}$ being at the health care provider $\mathcal{H}$. Let $\mathcal{A}$ be a set of all medical attributes of patient $\mathcal{P}$.

DEFINITION 6 (Privacy-Preserving Linking Query). *A privacy-preserving linking query $Q_{pr} = (\mathcal{FMP}, hash_{FMP}, X)$ on medical data of patient $\mathcal{P}$ is a triple with:*

1. *$\mathcal{FMP} \subset \mathcal{A}$ is a fuzzy matching pattern containing n attributes that are present in every schema of the databases in $\mathcal{D}$.*
2. *$hash_{FMP} = SHA1(val_1, ..., val_n)$ with val_i, $1 \le i \le n$, being the concrete value of the patient $\mathcal{P}$ for the i-th attribute in the fuzzy matching pattern $\mathcal{FMP}$.*
3. *$X \subset \mathcal{A}$ are the attributes of the patient $\mathcal{P}$, the health care provider $\mathcal{H}$ is interested in.*

If the fuzzy matching pattern $\mathcal{FMP}$ includes attributes that are not present in the schema of a queried databases, the query cannot be answered. However, in a medical scenario it is a realistic assumption that health care providers store a similar set of patient attributes. In our observations, we found that health care providers often collect the same attributes by means of family predispositions or baseline examinations. For example, every patient has to fill in an anamnesis questionnaire during the admission to a hospital. In many cases, such data may uniquely identify this patient.

In the first phase of our protocol the query Q_{pr} is sent to every data source in $\mathcal{D}$. Thereby, we assume that a global authentication method exists that identifies $\mathcal{H}$ as a valid health care provider, which is allowed to pose queries. Moreover, we assume communication is supposed to be end-to-end encrypted. A receiver $d \in \mathcal{D}$ of the query Q_{pr} processes a query as follows: For every record in d's database the $SHA1$ hash h_{temp} of the corresponding combined values of the attributes in the fuzzy matching pattern $\mathcal{FMP}$ is generated and compared to $hash_{FMP}$. If h_{temp} equals $hash_{FMP}$, then the record is marked as a matching record.

In order to realize our second privacy requirement, i.e., perform only authorized data exchange, every response R_{pr} of a data source $d \in \mathcal{D}$ to the query Q_{pr} is constructed as illustrated in Algorithm 1. It is important to highlight that for the encryption in line 5 the public biometric template BIO_{pu} of the corresponding individual must be used as encryption key. This guarantees that the encrypted items in the response R_{pr} can only be decrypted, if the corresponding indivial has agreed and provides his private biometric template BIO_{pu}. After constructing the response, R_{pr} must be returned to $\mathcal{H}$.

Algorithm 1. Generating the query response R_{pr}.

```
1:   r_k = ∅ ;
2:   for each record in d marked as a matching record , do :
3:       for each x in X , do :
4:           if x present in D , do :
5:               encrypt the concrete value/item of x
                 using the public biometric template BIO_pu
                 of the processed record as encryption key ;
6:               add the encrypted value/item to the set R_pr ;
7:           end if
8:       end for each
9:   end for each
```

During the last step, the health care provider $\mathcal{H}$ tries to decrypt the items in every response using $\mathcal{P}$'s private biometric template BIO_{pr}, which can only be gained directly from the patient $\mathcal{P}$. After all responses are evaluated the private biometric template BIO_{pr} of the patient $\mathcal{P}$ is deleted from $\mathcal{H}$'s databases.

4 Evaluation

To evaluate the proposed protocol, we analyze our protocol in terms of privacy and complexity. For the latter, we briefly compared our protocol with those of others.

4.1 Privacy Evaluation

As we stated in our introduction (Section 1), faking patient data is the only attack on our protocol that might harm the privacy of patients. In order to proof this statement, we apply the honest-but-curious adversary model to our protocol and look at attacks an initiator or a receiver of a query may execute.

An attacker may pose fake queries within our approach, i.e., a requester who is not authorized by the patient poses a query. A query may be generated, if the requester knows some medical attribute values of the patient. If the patient is not present the requester has no access to the private biometric template BIO_{pr}. Therefore, the requester will be unable to decrypt any response.

The worst case scenario for our protocol is, if the private biometric template BIO_{pr} of a patient gets leaked, i.e., someone gets access to the private biometric template BIO_{pr} who is not authorized by the patient. Such leakage of the private biometric template BIO_{pr} does not harm the privacy of the patient as biometric templates do not reveal any information about the originally biometrics or the real identity of the related person. In case of a leakage the public biometric template BIO_{pu} for this patient can no longer be used and must be changed. An infinite number of different protected biometric templates of a patient is available [3]. Thus, the challenge is to find out if a private biometric template got leaked and to update the public biometric template at all data sources. In the current state of our protocol, we do not handle such leakage.

A malicious receiver of a query $Q_{pr} = (\mathcal{FMP}, hash_{FMP}, X)$ may try to learn personal data from the query Q_{pr}. $\mathcal{FMP}$ and X include only sets of attribute types and include no personal information. Thus, the hash value $hash_{FMP}$ is the only part of the query that may be attacked. Brute-force is the only known attack on hash values created with $SHA1$. This attack may decrypt the original values of $hash_{FMP}$, if the attributes in $\mathcal{FMP}$ cover only small domains, e.g., the attributes in the fuzzy matching pattern $\mathcal{FMP} = (sex, hair\ color, eye\ color)$ in our example in section 3.1 cover small domains. In the worst case, an attacker gains the same knowledge that a query receiver having some matching records learns. As the query Q_{pr} must be k-disguised, the original values of $hash_{FMP}$ do only identify a group of at least k individuals. Moreover, a malicious receiver cannot learn from the query Q_{pr} whom of the individuals in the identified group the query poser was looking for. Finally, an attacker cannot even learn, if the queried patient is part of this group.

The challenge for a requester is to select an adequate fuzzy matching pattern for the query Q_{pr}. To generate a statistical large number of matching records, the requester may use local statistics about its database or global statistics of medical attributes.

Within the honest-but-curious attacker model our approach protects the privacy of patients. At last, we give an example of what may happen under a less restrictive attacker model where parties may deviate from the protocol. A malicious receiver of a query $Q_{pr} = (\mathcal{FMP}, hash_{FMP}, X)$ may harm the patient in two ways. First, matching records may be withheld. In this case, no private information is leaked. Second, if there are matching records, a malicious receiver may response false results. In both cases we end up having false or insufficient data of the patient, which may result in false-treatment. Faking query results can seriously harm the patient's health. Thus, our protocol may only be applied in scenarios where honest-but-curious behavior is a proper assumption.

4.2 Costs and Overhead

Most other approaches for privacy-preserving query protocols use secure multi party computations or homomorphic encryption (see Section 5 for related work). Current approaches use blocking strategies, which help to reduce costs. Nevertheless, the complete dataset of the queried party has to be encrypted to find the matching records. In our protocol, we use hashing to find matching records. Hash algorithms such as $SHA1$ are much less costly than secure multi party computations or homomorphic encryption. Moreover, once generated the hash values may be stored and reused for further query execution.

In our approach, responses can include false positive record matchings. This protects privacy but also increases communication complexity. In the worst case, the response includes the complete dataset of the queried party. To prevent such scenarios, the queried parties could demand a new query that uses a different fuzzy matching pattern. In general, we assume that a requester will try to reduce communication time and size. Therefore, requesters try to select adequate fuzzy matching patterns.

5   Related Work

Several approaches exist which provide methods for privacy-preserving query processing in distributed database settings. Exemplary, we compare our protocol with three recently proposed approaches. Subsequently, we discuss general concepts used in most of the existing approaches.

Chow et. al. [4] introduce a two-party computation model for privacy-preserving query execution. In their approach, they utilize the concept of two non-colluding parties. One party obfuscates the query and another party computes the query result (set intersection) on encrypted data. The advantage compared to our approach is that the query requester does not learn anything about the data sources. In our approach, we do not rely on non-colluding parties. Moreover, we do not require to hide the queried data sources as the patient explicitly permits the query requester for accessing his data from these remote data sources.

Allman et. al. [2] proposed an approach that resembles our query methodology to some extend. In this paper, the authors evaluate private queries for detecting attacks on network infrastructures. The queries include a hashed communication pattern. Every queried data source must try to rebuild the hash with its local data. Disregarding the different application domain of this approach, our approach is much more general and secure. Instead of a fixed fuzzy matching pattern we use a variable fuzzy matching pattern. Moreover, the proposed private matching approach is vulnerable as it suffers from a small domain of the fuzzy matching pattern (see section 4.2 for a privacy evaluation of our approach).

In [14] private record linkage is realized by combining secure blocking and secure matching. Before searching for matching records, all records are grouped into blocks. Blocking results in a huge decrease of record comparisons. Nevertheless, our matching method is more efficient as we do not use secure multi-party computation (see section 4.1 for efficiency and complexity of our approach). Furthermore, as in most other approaches individuals have no control over the linkage process.

Most of the existing privacy-preserving query approaches use some basic concepts. Thus, we evaluate the use of secure multi-party computation, third parties and privacy policies for our application scenario.

5.1   Secure Multi-party Computation

Methods for privacy-preserving query execution aim to prevent any revealing of personal information about the queried individual. Usually, existing implementations apply private record matching methods for finding query results. In order to protect privacy, existing approaches [13,14] combine record matching methods [6] with secure multi-party computations such as *secure set intersection* [10] or *private matching* [20].

Methods of secure set intersection as well as private matching methods focus on the problem of entities trying to find common data elements in their databases, without revealing the complete record pool to one another. In secure set intersection methods, the common elements are computed using *homomorphic encryption* [11]. On the other hand, private matching methods are based on commutative encryption. Both concepts suffer from high communication cost, because at least one party has to submit his complete encrypted dataset. Furthermore, computations on homomorphic encrypted data are very costly. In our approach, we only submit a very small subset of matching records and use hashing methods together with faster asymmetric encryption.

Disregarding the drawbacks, there are some benefits of using private record matching. Our matching algorithm is not capable of *approximate matching*. In order to handle typographical errors approximate matching algorithms use phonetic algorithms, string distance-based methods or bloom filters to find matching records [6].

5.2   Third Parties

The incorporation of *untrusted third parties* is another concept used for privacy-preserving queries [7]. An untrusted third party, e.g., cloud storage, may be used for storing encrypted records. The encrypted records are publicly available, but only authorized uses have access to the decryption keys. In contrast to our protocol, the integration of untrusted third parties involves more communication effort, as all parties have to upload their data. Another serious thread occurs if some encryption keys get leaked. Once encrypted records are released to an untrusted storage provider those record might stay online forever.

In complement to untrusted third parties, some approaches use *trusted third parties* to protect privacy. There are two functionalities which a trusted third party may provide. First, the trusted party may calculate the query results. In this case, all parties have to submit their data to the trusted party. Second, the trusted party may guarantee that all participating parties are honest and not curious. Many reasons exist why we should avoid using trusted third parties. For example, a trusted party may learn all input data for a query. Thus, there is a single point of failure which can be attacked. Furthermore, the approach requires to get control over the participating parties within a distributed database setting. Therefore, it is hard to guarantee an intended behavior for such distributed systems. In our approach, there does not exist a central point of failure and we require only minor behavioral guarantees of other parties.

5.3   Privacy Policies

In our protocol, the patient gives his consent for querying his data by providing his private biometric template. Using *privacy policies* is a common way to store and submit privacy preferences of individuals. Privacy policies such as *XACML* [21] or *P3P* [15] allow to define criteria such as the purpose of use, to restrict the set of external recipients, or retention constraints. Many applications running in distributed systems do not provide direct control for enforcing privacy policies. Thus, individuals have to trust in the self regulation of services providers. Moreover, often an expert is needed to write down or understand privacy policies. Our protocol establishes a simple mechanism which enables individuals for controlling the initialization of the query process. Moreover, we offer a method to securely enforce access control in a distributed database setting. However, we do not provide to define and enforce complex privacy preferences such as limited retention criteria.

6 Conclusions and Future Work

The current development of information systems in the healthcare domain raises new challenges for the integration of appropriate privacy-preserving query protocols. Often, existing implementations use a centralized trusted party or a complex multi party computation approach for protecting privacy while query processing. In this paper, we introduced a new two-phase protocol for privacy-preserving exchange of medical data. Within this protocol, we use private fuzzy queries to link distributed medical data of a patient. In addition, we provide a simple and effective access control mechanism. In contrast to other approaches, the patients directly authorize the intended query process. We analyzed and defined requirements for protecting the privacy of patients in a medical treatment scenario. Based on these requirements, we applied the honest-but-curious adversary model to our protocol in order to evaluate the introduced approach regarding complexity and privacy protection.

Currently, we are implementing a prototype of the proposed protocol. We are going to use this prototype for implementing a medical screening scenario. Next, we evaluate our implementation using real screening data.

In the future, we are going to provide a formal proof that our protocol implements our privacy requirements. Furthermore, we will include a mechanism for updating the public biometric templates in all data sources. Another challenge will be to extend the fixed schema of the fuzzy matching patterns by using individual fuzzy matching patterns for every data source. In order to improve record matching accuracy, we also want to include approximate matching capabilities in our protocol.

References

1. Agfa HealthCare, http://www.agfahealthcare.com
2. Allman, M., Blanton, E., Paxson, V., Shenker, S.: Fighting coordinated attackers with cross-organizational information sharing. In: Proceedings of 5th Workshop on Hot Topics in Networks, HotNets (2006)
3. Breebaart, J., Busch, C., Grave, J., Kindt, E.: A Reference Architecture for Biometric Template Protection based on Pseudo Identities. In: BIOSIG (2008)
4. Chow, S.S.M., Lee, J.-H., Subramanian, L.: Two-party computation model for privacy-preserving queries over distributed databases. In: NDSS 2009. The Internet Society, San Diego (2009)

5. Dodis, Y., Reyzin, L., Smith, A.: Fuzzy Extractors: How to Generate Strong Keys from Biometrics and Other Noisy Data. In: Cachin, C., Camenisch, J.L. (eds.) EUROCRYPT 2004. LNCS, vol. 3027, pp. 523–540. Springer, Heidelberg (2004)
6. Elmagarmid, A., Panagiotis, G., Verykios, S.: Duplicate record detection: A survey. IEEE Transaction on Knowledge and Data Engineering (2007)
7. Emekci, F., Agrawal, D., Abbadi, A.E., Gulbeden, A.: Privacy Preserving Query Processing Using Third Parties. In: ICDE (2006)
8. European Union. Directive 95/46/EC of the European parliament and of the council of 24 October 1995 on the protection of individuals with regard to the processing of personal data and on the free movement of such data (1995)
9. Felligi, I.P., Sunter, A.B.: A theory for record linkage. Journal of the American Statistical Society 64, 1183–1210 (1969)
10. Freedman, M.J., Nissim, K., Pinkas, B.: Efficient Private Matching and Set Intersection. In: Cachin, C., Camenisch, J.L. (eds.) EUROCRYPT 2004. LNCS, vol. 3027, pp. 1–19. Springer, Heidelberg (2004)
11. Goldreich, O.: General Cryptographic Protocols. In: The Foundations of Cryptography, vol. 2. Cambridge University Press (2004)
12. Gomatam, S., Carter, R., Ariet, M., Mitchell, G.: An empirical comparison of record linkage procedures. Statistics in Medicine, 1485–1496 (2002)
13. Inan, A., Kantarcioglu, M., Bertino, E., Scannapieco, M.: A hybrid approach to private record linkage. In: ICDE 2008, Cancun, Mexico. IEEE Computer Society (2008)
14. Karakasidis, A., Verykios, V.S.: Secure blocking + secure matching = secure record linkage. Journal of Computing Science and Engineering, 223–235 (2011)
15. P3P Preference Exchange Language v. 1.0 (APPEL1.0). W3C (2002), http://www.w3.org/TR/P3P-preferences
16. NIST. FIPS 180-3: Secure hash standard (SHS). Technical report, National Institute of Standards and Technology, NIST (2008), http://csrc.nist.gov/publications/fips/fips180-3/fips180-3_final.pdf
17. Siemens Healthcare, http://www.medical.siemens.com
18. Sweeney, L.: Simple demographics often identify people uniquely. Carnegie Mellon University, Data Privacy Working Paper 3 (2000)
19. Sweeney, L.: k-anonymity: a model for protecting privacy. International Journal on Uncertainty, Fuzziness and Knowledge-based Systems, 557–570 (2002)
20. Li, Y., Tygar, J., Hellerstein, J.: Private matching. In: Computer Security in the 21st Century, pp. 25–50 (2005)
21. eXtensible Access Control Markup Language (XACML) v. 2.0. OASIS Standard (February 2005), http://docs.oasis-open.org/xacml/2.0/accesscontrol-xacml-2.0-core-spec-os.pdf

Cloud and the City: Facilitating Flexible Access Control over Data-Streams*

Wen Qiang Wang, Dinh Tien Tuan Anh,
Hock Beng Lim, and Anwitaman Datta

Nanyang Technological University, Singapore

Abstract. The proliferation of sensing devices create plethora of data-streams, which in turn can be harnessed to carry out sophisticated analytics to support various real-time applications and services as well as long-term planning, e.g., in the context of intelligent cities or smart homes. A mature cloud infrastructure brings such a vision closer to reality than ever before, as more and more data owners are moving their data to the cloud. Hence, the ability to flexibly and easily control the granularity at which they share their data with other entities become more important. It makes data owners feel comfortable to share to start with, and also provide them a platform to realize different business models or logics. In this paper, we explore some basic operations to flexibly control the access on a data-stream and propose a framework *eXACML+* that extends the standard XACML model to achieve the same. We develop a prototype using the commercial StreamBase engine to demonstrate a seamless combination of stream data processing with (a small but important selected set of) fine-grained access control mechanisms, and to evaluate the framework's efficacy based on experiments in cloud like environments.

1   Introduction

Wide-scale deployments of sensors and smart mobile devices, and technologies for participatory sensing and Internet of Things (IoT) has given rise to numerous real-time data-stream driven applications. Those applications can be based either on the isolated data-streams generated by individual sources, or on mashing many streams together. Such services vary in scale and scope - from smart homes to intelligent cities [1], which may fuse together data owned by a single owner or from many parties. The pervasive cloud infrastructure is an important catalyst in enabling such visions, because (i) it is cost effective [1] for individual data owners since it provides the necessary computational and storage resources elastically, (ii) it allows fast prototyping, deployment and testing of new applications and analytics at large-scale, (iii) it naturally achieves collocation of data from different sources — the condition that is desirable to build many complex

---

* This work has been supported by A*Star TSRP grant no. 1021580038 for 'pCloud: Privacy in data value chains using peer-to-peer primitives' project. Contact author: Anwitaman Datta (`anwitaman@ntu.edu.sg`)

[1] `http://en.wikipedia.org/wiki/Intelligent_cities`

W. Jonker and M. Petković (Eds.): SDM 2012, LNCS 7482, pp. 58–74, 2012.

applications. For example, a flu outbreak in one or several cities can be tracked, studied (and necessary intervention measures taken) using real-time data from various sources such as hospitals, transport departments, weather stations, as well as telecom companies. In the pre-cloud era, finding and sharing such data would need to overcome several layers of barriers.

However, in order to facilitate meaningful sharing of data, it is crucial that the data-owners have adequate controls on what they wish to share and with whom. Such controls are desirable for several reasons, including maintaining ownership of data, content privacy, and monetization of the data by differentiated pricing by exposing data in different details to different users. In absence of fine-grained control, or if the control comes only at prohibitive costs (either in negotiating, interpreting or implementing), it will more likely dissuade data-owners from sharing. In our previous work [2], we have proposed some simple extensions to XACML [3] that can represent and enforce fine-grained access controls (such as time-window based aggregation, trigger/threshold based access, etc.) on archived data, i.e., data stored in a relational database (RDBMS). In this paper, we look at how to achieve similar fine-grained access control on data-streams. In particular, while the sharing predicates we explore remain the same as in our previous work, the main challenges and contributions of this work is precisely to deal with data-streams, which rely on fundamentally different set of technologies than data stored in a RDBMS. Developing access control model and mechanism on data-streams is more challenging due to the characteristics of stream data and Data-stream Management System (DSMS). Specifically:

- DSMS deals with unbounded and fast changing time-series tuples in data-streams. Access control enforcement, particularly when it is based on the content (such as, say a value based trigger or range predicate) is not a one-time operation, but a continuous procedure applied on the data-streams. Whenever a new data tuple arrives, corresponding access control actions must be taken on it. Therefore, models and technologies developed for access control enforcement on RDBMS such as those in [4] cannot be readily adapted for DSMS.

- Temporal constraints, i.e., sliding windows, plays a crucial role in DSMS. In addition to normal constraints such as selection and projection, window-based aggregation is a popular operation..

In this work we propose the *eXACML+* framework, by extending our previous work on fine-grained access control in RDBMS, namely eXACML [2], which in itself extends the popular XACML [3] standard. The *eXACML+* framework adds fine-grained access control mechanism to a popular data-stream management model, namely the Aurora model [5]. We assume a trusted cloud service provider, which itself has access to all the stored data, and furthermore honestly enforces the sharing constraints specified by the data-owners. Content confidentiality from the cloud service provider itself, and the service provider's accountability are also important and much researched topics, which are necessary extensions for the presented work, but are out of the scope of this paper. The main contributions of this paper are:

1. We extend XACML to enable fine-grained access control for *continuous queries* [6]. We express the policies within *obligations* blocks of XACML policies and utilize the Policy Enforcement Point (PEP) to generate corresponding continuous queries from the obligations, provided that the Policy Decision Point (PDP) grants necessary access[2]. These continuous queries are in the form of query graphs and are sent to the back-end DSMS for processing. We refer to this approach as *XACML+*.

2. We design various components to realize the *eXACML+* framework. They include a data server, *XACML+* instances, a proxy server and a client interface. Users send requests for data-streams together with customized continuous queries to the server, from which they get back stream handles which point to the unique resource identifiers (URIs) of the processed data-streams.

3. We show that customized queries that are issued by users, if not taken care of carefully, can give rise to information leak in case of sliding window policies (which our framework can detect and prevent). We also discuss possible improvements to the system efficiency by informing users of empty/partial results due to policy and query mismatches.

4. We instantiate the eXACML+ framework using Aurora's commercialized software StreamBase [7] as the back-end DSMS. We evaluate the performance of our prototype in a cloud-like environment. The results suggest that the framework incurs relatively constant overhead and is scalable.

The rest of the paper is organized as follows. Section 2 describes details of XACML+ — out extension to XACML to support stream data. Section 3 discusses the design of the *eXACML+* framework. The prototype and evaluation of the framework are presented in Section 4. Section 5 discusses related work, and finally we conclude our work and propose future work in Section 6.

2   XACML Policies for Stream Data

2.1   Overview of XACML and Aurora Model

The *eXtensible Access Control Markup Language* [3] is a OASIS framework for specifying and enforcing access control. Policies are written in XML and contain elements including *subjects, resources , actions, obligations, etc.*. The framework consists of two main components: a Policy Decision Point (PDP) and a Policy Enforcement Point (PEP). The former manages policies and evaluates user requests against the stored policies, the result of which are *permit* or *deny* decisions. PEP's main role is to marshal user requests and the PDP results. In addition to permit/deny decision, the PDP also returns a set of *obligations* to the PEP. We extend this process for fine-grained access control by embedding parts of the policies in obligations which are then processed by the PEP.

Aurora[5] is a popular model for stream data, which has matured into a commercial product, i.e. the StreamBase engine[7]. In Aurora, a data-stream consists

---

[2] PEP and PDP are standard terms associated with XACML technology stack, and will be described in detail in next Section.

of an append-only sequence of tuples with the same schema. A query on a data-stream is modeled as a directed acyclic graph (or *query graph*), of operators (or boxes). The query graph is applied to each tuple from the input stream, hence every tuple in the output data-stream satisfies the predicate defined by the query graph. StreamBase also comes with support for StreamSQL,which is SQL-like representation of query graphs.

The Aurora model supports a number of operators, in this work we focus on three common ones: *filter* (selection), *map* (projection) and *window based aggregation* (aggregate functions applied on sliding windows). A filter operator has a condition C — a boolean expression composed of logic operators (*AND, OR, NOT*), equality and inequality operators ($<, >, \leq, \geq, =, \neq$). A map operator contains a set of projected attributes S. A *window-based aggregation* operator consists of the sliding window (specified by the window type, size, advance step), the set of attributes and the aggregate functions to be computed over each window.

2.2   Fine-Grained Access Control Policies

To better illustrate our access control model for stream data, we use the following example throughout the paper.

Example 1. The National Environmental Agency (NEA) wishes to provide real-time weather data service through the cloud platform. The data has the schema (*samplingtime, temperature, humidity, solar radiation, rain rate, wind speed, wind direction, barometer*) and is generated every thirty seconds by a weather station. Instead of creating one customized data-stream for each individual customer, NEA decides to use the cloud's access control mechanism. Benefits of this approach has been discussed in [2]. The Land Transport Authority (LTA) is developing an automatic warning system that alerts drivers of possible traffic congestion due to heavy rain. The warning system requires real-time weather data from NEA which specifies the following policy: 1) only samplingtime, rain rate, and wind speed data are visible 2) data should come in windows of size 5 and advance step of size 2, and the functions applied on samplingtime, rain rate and wind speed are *lastValue*, *average* and *maximum*, respectively 3) data is visible only when the rain rate is greater than 5mm/hour.

Table 1. Obligation types

Description	Obligation Id
Filter	*exacml:obligation:stream-filtering*
Map	*exacml:obligation:stream-mapping*
Window-Based Aggregation	*exacml:obligation:stream-window-aggregation*

Figure 1 shows the Aurora query graph that transforms the original weather data-stream so that it satisfy the above access control scenario. Using the obligation-based approach described in [2], we create new obligation elements, each for every operator (listed in Table 1). The content of each element is as follows:

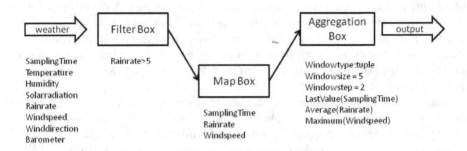

Fig. 1. Aurora query graph for the example in section 2.2

1. Filter: consists of a string attribute with attribute ID: *exacml:obligation: stream-filter-condition-id*. The value is a string representing a boolean expression used as the filter condition C.

2. Map: consists of a set of string attributes with ID: *exacml:obligation:stream-map-attribute-id*. The values are attribute names, used used to restrict access to only authorized attributes, such as rain rate and wind speed in the example.

3. Window-Based Aggregation: consists of a number of attributes:

- Window type: string attribute with attribute id: *exacml:obligation:stream-window-type-id*. It specifies if the window size is based on number of tuples or number of time unit.

- Window size: integer attribute with attribute id: *exacml:obligation:stream-window-size-id*. It specifies the size of the window in the number of tuples or time units.

- Window advance step: integer attribute with attribute id: *exacml:obligation: stream-window-step-id*. It specifies how fast the window advances on the stream.

- Aggregation attribute: string attribute with attribute id: *exacml:obligation: stream-window-attr-id*. It specifies the attribute in the data-stream schema that is to be aggregated, and what the aggregate function is. Its value is of the form *attribute-id:aggregate-function*, where *attribute-id* is the name of the attribute and *aggregate-function* is an element from the set of aggregate functions {*Avg, Max, Min, Count, LastValue, FirstValue,...*}.

Having defined these elements, we can now combine them to form the Obligations element of the XACML policy, as shown in Figure 2.

3   The eXACML+ Framework

We describe in this section the design of the *eXACML+* framework which is a natural extension of the *eXACML* [2] with additional functionality to manage Aurora query graphs and customized user queries. The architecture of *eXACML+* resembles that of *eXACML* except that: 1) *XACML+* instances are

```
<Obligations>
  <Obligation ObligationId="exacml:obligation:stream-filter" FulfillOn="Permit">
    <AttributeAssignment AttributeId="pCloud:obligation:stream-filter-condition-id"
    DataType="http://www.w3.org/2001/XMLSchema#string">rainrate > 5 </AttributeAssignment>
  </Obligation>
  <Obligation ObligationId="exacml:obligation:stream-map" FulfillOn="Permit">
      <AttributeAssignment AttributeId="pCloud:obligation:stream-map-attribute-id"
      DataType="http://www.w3.org/2001/XMLSchema#string">samplingtime</AttributeAssignment>
      <AttributeAssignment AttributeId="pCloud:obligation:stream-map-attribute-id"
      DataType="http://www.w3.org/2001/XMLSchema#string">rainrate</AttributeAssignment>
      <AttributeAssignment AttributeId="pCloud:obligation:stream-map-attribute-id"
       DataType="http://www.w3.org/2001/XMLSchema#string">windspeed</AttributeAssignment>
  </Obligation>
  <Obligation ObligationId="exacml:obligation:stream-window" FulfillOn="Permit">
    <AttributeAssignment AttributeId="pCloud:obligation:stream-window-step-id"
    DataType="http://www.w3.org/2001/XMLSchema#integer">2</AttributeAssignment>
    <AttributeAssignment AttributeId="pCloud:obligation:stream-window-size-id"
    DataType="http://www.w3.org/2001/XMLSchema#integer">5</AttributeAssignment>
    <AttributeAssignment AttributeId="pCloud:obligation:stream-window-type-id"
    DataType="http://www.w3.org/2001/XMLSchema#string">tuple</AttributeAssignment>
    <AttributeAssignment AttributeId="pCloud:obligation:stream-window-attr-id"
    DataType="http://www.w3.org/2001/XMLSchema#string">samplingtime:lastval</AttributeAssignment>
    <AttributeAssignment AttributeId="pCloud:obligation:stream-window-attr-id"
    DataType="http://www.w3.org/2001/XMLSchema#string">rainrate:avg</AttributeAssignment>
    <AttributeAssignment AttributeId="pCloud:obligation:stream-window-attr-id"
    DataType="http://www.w3.org/2001/XMLSchema#string">windspeed:max</AttributeAssignment>
  </Obligation>
</Obligations>
```

Fig. 2. Obligation portion of the XACML policy for the example in section 2.2

used to handle access control needs on data-streams and 2) the policy management module is updated to accommodate changes in the data model. Figure 3(a) illustrates the architecture of eXACML+. It includes a *cloud server*, *XACML+* and *XACML** instances, a *proxy* with cache feature and a *client* interface. We also discuss two issues which have not been addressed in the original eXACML framework: 1) allowing multiple windows on the same data-stream can lead to violation of data privacy and 2) how to alert users if their queries contradict with the access control policies enforced on the data-streams, resulting in empty/partial result sets.

3.1   Handling User Query

In many cases, the data-stream accessible by the user may not directly fit the actual requirements. In our example, suppose that the LTA finds out that only rain rate over 50mm/hr has influence on traffic condition, and the warning system only needs the data from sliding windows of size 10 (instead of the original 5) tuples. The LTA could process the incoming data steam locally. However, having such additional filtering done by a server (the cloud) is more preferable. In our framework, the user sends a customized query to the PEP, which acts as a request to apply additional operation on the authorized stream. We implement the query in XML form, as shown in Figure 4(a). The PEP transforms this into

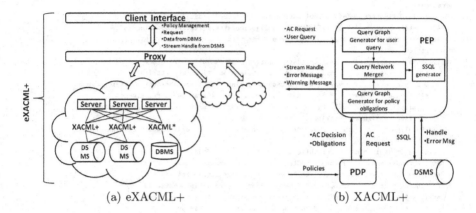

Fig. 3. Architecture of XACML+ and eXACML+ framework

an Aurora query graph similar to that in Figure 1, and then combines it with the query graph derived from the policy obligations. One could simply concatenate the two graphs, but properly merging them together gains advantages such as reducing the number of operators in query graph and therefore improving efficiency. It also allows for detection of empty/partial result (which we refer to as *NR* and *PR*).

Merging two query graphs is equivalent to merging each type of operators in the graphs. We explain how *NR* and *PR* can be detected during the merging process later in Section 3.5. The rules for merging individual types of operators are:

- Two filter operators F_1 and F_2 with condition C_1 and C_2 are merged into a filter F_3 with the condition $C_3 = (C_1 \text{ AND } C_2)$. There are cases that C_3 can be further simplified. For example, if $C_1 = x > v_1$ and $C_2 = x > v_2$, C_3 can be written as $x > v_2$ iff $v_2 \geq v_1$.

- Two map operator M_1 and M_2 with attribute sets S_1 and S_2 are merged into new operator M_3 with the attribute set $S_3 = S_1 \cup S_2$.

- Two window-based aggregation operator A_1 and A_2 are merged only if the following conditions are met: 1) window types are the same 2) suppose A_1 is derived the policy obligations and A_2 from user query, A_1's window size and advance step are must be less than or equal to those of A_2. The second condition is to ensure that user are not given more fine-grained data than permitted by the policy. The new operator A_3 will have the same window type as A_1 and A_2, and the window size and advance step are the same as those of A_2. The aggregation function and attribute sets are the intersection of those from A_1 and A_2.

Figure 4(b) shows the StreamSQL statements after merging the query graph in Figure 1 with user query in Figure 4(a).

```
<UserQuery>
   <Stream name="weather" />
   <Filter>
      <FilterCondition>
      RainRate > 50
      </FilterCondition>
   </Filter>
   <Map>
      <Attribute>RainRate</Attribute>
   </Map>
   <Aggregation>
      <WindowType>tuple</WindowType>
      <WindowSize>10<WindowSize>
      <WindowStep>2<WindowStep>
      <Attribute>avg(RainRate)</Attribute>
   </Aggregation>
</UserQuery>
```

```
CREATE INPUT STREAM weather (
samplingtime timestamp , temperature double ,
 humidity double , rainrate double ,
 windspeed double,winddirection int,
 barometer double );

CREATE STREAM internal_0;
SELECT * FROM weather WHERE rainrate > 50 INTO internal_0;

CREATE OUTPUT STREAM internal_1;
SELECT internal_0.samplingtime,internal_0.rainrate,
FROM internal_0 INTO internal_1;

CREATE OUTPUT STREAM output;
CREATE WINDOW _10tuple( SIZE 10 ADVANCE 2 TUPLES);
SELECT lastval(samplingtime) AS lastvalsamplingtime,
avg(rainrate) AS avgrainrate
FROM internal_1[_10tuple] INTO output;
```

(a) User Query in XML   (b) StreamSQL statements

Fig. 4. User Query and StreamSQL

3.2   Design of XACML+

Figure 3(b) shows the design of XACML+, which is an extension of the original oasis XACML model [3]. The work-flow is as follows:

1. PEP receives a user's request for accessing a stream, together with a customized query, which are then forwarded to the PDP. The customized query is also converted into a Aurora query graph.

2. PDP evaluates the request against the stream's policies and returns the decision and obligations (if any) to the PEP. If the decision is permit, PEP will generate a query graph from the obligations.

3. PEP checks that for the credentials included the request, no query is currently being applied to the same data-stream. The reason for this is given in Section 3.4.

4. PEP merges the two query graphs derived from obligations and user query, during which PR or NR are checked.

5. If there is no PR or NR warning detected, the merged query graph is converted into a StreamSQL script and sent to the data-stream engine. A handle, in the URI form, is returned to the user.

3.3   Query Graph Management

In the original eXACML framework, PDP is called whenever a data request is received and only when the decision is permit, SQL queries are generated from obligations and sent to database to retrieve data. This work flow guarantees that removing or updating a policy does not affect the privacy of the data owner. However, this is not the case when dealing with unbounded stream data. Instead of actual data, only a handle used to retrieve the actual data-stream from data-stream engine is returned as the response to user's request. The user then uses this handle to connect to the back-end data-stream engine for data-streams. If the data-stream owner for some reason has removed or modified the policy that grants the user for a particular data-stream, the user may still connected to the data-stream though he is not supposed to be able to access the data-stream any longer.

To solve this issue, we in-cooperate query graph management into the framework. In additional to keeping track of policies loaded, data server also keeps track of query graphs that are generated by PEP and have already been sent to back-end data-stream engines. In eXACML+, whenever a policy has been removed or modified by user, all query graphs that are spawned by the policy are immediately withdrawn from back-end data-stream engines. This may not be a flexible solution, but it ensures data privacy.

3.4   Multiple Aggregation Windows

As described in Section 3.2, only a single access is permitted on a particular data-stream for one user at any time. We justify this constraint by showing a example in which one can reconstruct the raw data steam by combining outputs from multiple aggregation windows of different window sizes or advance steps.

Example 2. Suppose we have a single-attribute stream $S = a_0,a_1,a_2,a_3,a_4,a_5,..,a_n$. The access control policy for S allows for aggregation window w, where $w.size = 3$, $w.advancestep = 2$, $w.type = tuple$, $w.attribute=a$ and $w.function =sum$. An user can request an aggregation window v using a customized query, provided that $v.size>=w.size, v.advancestep >= w.advancestep$, $v.type = w.type$, $v.attribute = w.attribute$ and $v.function = w.function$. If multiple accesses are allowed, the user can obtain multiple result stream using different v simultaneously. Let $v_1.size = 3$, $v_2.size = 4$, $v_3.size = 5$ and all other window specifications be identical to w, the framework will return the user three aggregated data-streams S_1, S_2 and S_3, such that:

$S_1 = (a_0+a_1+a_2), (a_2+a_3+a_4),(a_4+a_5+a_6), ...$
$S_2 = (a_0+a_1+a_2+a_3),(a_2+a_3+a_4+a_5),(a_4+a_5+a_6+a_7),...$
$S_3 = (a_0+a_1+a_2+a_3+a_4),(a_2+a_3+a_4+a_5+a_6), ...$

By computing $S_2 - S_1$ and $S_3 - S_2$, we obtain two new streams $S' = a_3,a_5,a_7,...$ and $S'' = a_4,a_6,a_8,...$ Merging S' and S'', we can reconstruct all of the original stream except for first three tuples.

In general, given a set of output streams derived from different aggregation windows with fixed advance step M and different window size N, $N+1$, $N+2$,.., $N+M$, we can reconstruct the original stream from the Nth tuple. The inductive proof is as follows. Suppose we have three sum aggregation windows with sizes N, $N + Q_1$, $N + Q_2$, where $Q_1 < Q_2$, and a fixed step size M, the first k tuples of the three streams are: $S_0 =(a_0 + ... + a_{N-1}),(a_M + ... +a_{N+M-1}),...,(a_{kM} + ... +a_{N+kM-1})$; $S_1 =(a_0 + ... + a_{N+Q_1-1}),(a_M + ... +a_{N+M+Q_1-1}),...,(a_{kM} + ... +a_{N+kM+Q_1-1})$; $S_2 =(a_0 + ... + a_{N+Q_2-1}),(a_M + $

... $+a_{N+M+Q_2-1}),...,(a_{kM} + ... +a_{N+kM+Q_2-1})$. Let $T_1 = S_1 - S_0$ and $T_2 = S_2 - S_1$, we can have $T_1=(a_N +...+a_{N+Q_1-1}),..., (a_{N+kM}+...+a_{N+kM+Q_1-1})$ and $T_2=(a_{N+Q_1} +...+a_{N+Q_2-1}),..., (a_{N+kM+Q_1}+...+a_{N+kM+Q_2-1})$.

In a similar fashion, we can construct subsequence streams until T_i such that $T_i=(a_{N+Q_{i-1}}+...+a_{N+Q_j-1}), ...,(a_{N+kM+Q_{i-1}} + ... + a_{N+kM+Q_j-1})$. Let $Q_1=1$,$Q_j=Q_i+1$, i.e., each window contains one more element than previous windows, and $Q_j < M$, we can simplify T_1 to T_i as: $T_1=a_N,a_{N+M},...,a_{N+kM}$, $T_2=a_{N+1},a_{N+M+1},...,a_{N+kM+1},...,T_M=a_{N+M-1},a_{N+2M-1},...,a_{N+(k+1)M-1}$. Combine T_1 to T_M in an interleave manner, we can obtain stream $a_N,a_{N+1},...,$ $a_{N+(k+1)M-1}$, which is the original stream except for first (N-1) tuples.   ∎

3.5   Checking for Empty or Partial Result Set (NR/PR)

As mentioned earlier, NR and PR warnings occur while the framework merges two query graphs. Since the query graphs are built with filter, map and window based aggregation operators, we simplify this problem by checking how merging each type of operators causes NR/PR cases. Let us first define NR and PR and present examples of NR/PR cases.

Partial Result Warning (PR): some tuples in the requested stream may not be returned to the user due to conflict between the user query and some policies enforced on the streams.

Empty Result Warning (NR): none of the tuples in the request stream will be returned to the user due to conflict between the user query and some policies enforced on the streams. This is different to the case where the user does not have access to the stream.

Example 3. Suppose we have a stream S with single attribute a and filter condition F_1: $a > 8$ from policy obligation, filter condition F_2: $a > 5$ is from user query. Let a part of S be (..., 9,10,11,3,2,6,9,8,7,2,13,...), the user query expects output to be like, (...,9,10,11,6,9,8,7,13,...). However, due to $F1$, tuples like 6,8,7 are filtered out and the actual stream the user will get is (... 9,10,11,9,13,...). In this case, a PR warning will be issued to the user stating that there are possibilities that some tuples that fit his requirement are not returned to him due to certain access control policies enforced on the data-stream. If we change F_1 to be $a < 4$, the predicate "$a < 4$ AND $a > 5$" will always be false no matter what value a may take. Therefore, none of the tuples will be returned to the user and a NR warning will be issued.

The method to generate NR/PR warnings for each operator is as follows:

Map Operator: Suppose we have two map operators: M_1 from policy and M_2 from user query with attribute sets S_1 and S_2. If $S_1 \cap S_2 = \emptyset$, alert NR. Otherwise, alert PR if $S_1 \neq S_2$.

Aggregate Operator: Suppose we have two aggregation operators A_1 and A_2, where A_1 comes from the policy and A_2 comes from user query. We apply following rules: (1) If $A_1.size > A_2.size$, alert NR (2) If $A_1.advancestep >$

$A_2.advancestep$, alert NR (3) If $A_1.type \neq A_2.type$, alert NR (4) If different aggregation functions are applied for the same attribute in A_1 and A_2, alert NR (5) For every attribute a in A_2, if a is an attribute in A_1 and the aggregation functions applied to a in both A_1 and A_2 are the same, do not alert (6) In all other cases, alert PR.

Filter Operator: Checking if merging two filter operators gives rise to NR or PR warnings is more complicated. A *simple expression* S is an expression of the form "$x \ op \ v$", where x is a variable (in our case, an attribute name of a stream schema), $op \in \{<,>,\geq,\leq,=,\neq\}$, and v is a number, or a string (only when op is = or $\neq$). A *complex expression* C is an logical predicate that is formed by connecting *simple expressions* with NOT, OR or AND. In our case, C is the filter condition of a filter operator that belongs to a policy or a user query.

Suppose we have two filter operators F_1 and F_2 with condition C_1 and C_2 respectively. The checking procedure follows the steps below:

Step 1: Let $P = C_1$ AND C_2. Eliminate NOT operator in P. Let the result expression be P_1.

Step 2: Convert P_1 into its disjunctive normal form (DNF) P_2 [8]. Note each variable S in P_2 is a *simple expression*.

Step 3: Check for NR and PR in P_2, by pair-wisely calling function *checkT-woSimpleExpression* on every two simple expression S within the same conjunctive expression. If any function call returns with NR or PR, mark the whole conjunctive expression with NR or PR. If all conjunctive expressions are marked with PR or NR, alert PR or NR, respectively. The cost of the whole procedure is bound by $O(kn^2)$, where k is the number of conjunctive expressions in P_2 and n is the maximum number of S in a single conjunctive expression.

The function *checkTwoSimpleExpression* takes as inputs two simple expressions S_1 and S_2 and returns either NR or PR. Note that checking is only necessary when $S_1.x = S_2.x$. Since there are six possible values of $op \in \{<,>,\leq,\geq,=,\neq\}$, we need to do 36 comparisons to include all cases that op may take in S_1 and S_2. For each comparison, there are three cases, i.e., $S_1.v > S_2.v$, $S_1.v < S_2.v$ and $S_1.v = S_2.v$. We show here an example of how to generate NR and PR alerts for one comparison. Let $S_1 = x \geq v_1$ and $S_2 = x \leq v_2$, Figure 5 shows how the warnings are produced given different values of v_1 and v_2 and Example 4 better illustrates how the whole procedure works.

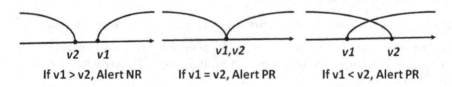

v2 v1	v1,v2	v1 v2
If v1 > v2, Alert NR	If v1 = v2, Alert PR	If v1 < v2, Alert PR

Fig. 5. Checking PR/NR for $S_1 = x \geq v_1$ and $S_1 = x \leq v_2$

Example 4. Suppose we have C_1 =(a>20 AND a<30) OR NOT(a$\neq$40), C_2 = NOT(a$\geq$10) AND b=20. After the first step, we have P_1 = (a>20 AND a<30) OR a=40 AND a<10 AND b=20. Denote A as $a > 20$, B as $a < 30$, C as $a = 40$, D as $a < 10$, E as $b = 20$, & as AND, $\|$ as OR. P_1 is then expressed as ((A&B)$\|$C)&(D&E). Next, P_2= E & D & C $\|$ E & D & B & A. Finally, we apply function *checkTwoSimpleExpression* on simple expressions of the two conjunctive expressions in P_2, which are e_1 = E & D & C and e_2 = E & D & B & A. For e_1, 3 calls are made on simple expression pairs (E,D), (E,C) and (D,C). For e_2, 6 calls are made on (E,D),(E,B),(E,A),(D,B),(D,A) and (B,A). Among all these function calls, (D,C) returns NR as $a < 10$ and $a = 40$ cannot be true for any given a value. Similarly, function call on (D,A) also returns NR as $a < 10$ and $a > 20$ contradicts. Both e_1 and e_2 cannot be true for any a value, means that $e_1\|e_2$ cannot be true for any a value. In this case, a NR warning will be returned to the user.

4   Prototype and Evaluation

4.1   Prototype Implementation

We have implemented a prototype of *eXACML+* in Java. We use APIs provided by StreamBase to manage and query data-streams. Communications between clients, proxies and servers are based on sockets. For XACML+, we extended Sun's XACML implementation [9] , which is also based on Java.

4.2   System Evaluation

The performance of the system is measured by the time taken to fulfill user's requests on data-streams.We compare the results with that of a system that query directly to StreamBase DSMS, which is refer to as *direct-query* system.

Hardware Setup: The prototype system is deployed in a cloud-like environment. We make use of four machines in the experiments, which run data server, StreamBase, proxy and client interface accordingly. Machines running the server and the StreamBase are both IBM x3650 servers located in a server room and each has two Quad-Core Intel Xeon E5450 processors and 32GB memory. The machine running the proxy is a mini work station and the client machine is a personal laptop. All machines are connected via University's 100Mbps Intranet. The StreamBase DSMS maintains a number of real-time data-streams from various projects, including weather data feeds from a number of weather stations producing weather data at one minute interval, as well as GPS information from personal mobile devices.

Workloads: The workloads consist of sequences of continuous queries. Each query corresponds to three files in the experiment: (1) a StreamSQL script as the input to direct-query system, (2) a XACML policy file whose obligations forms the query graph exactly as that in the above StreamSQL script, (3) a XACML request file for requesting data-streams from eXACML+, which may also have user query embedded inside. The request file contains credentials such that the PDP will always return a permit decision. Query graphs are generated randomly. In the experiment, we create query graphs with a pre-defined set of combinations for Filter(FB), Map(MB) and Aggregation (AB) operators. The sequence of continuous queries can have one of the two settings: (1) each continuous query and corresponding request appears only once (i.e. is unique) in the sequence (2) the sequence follows Zipf distribution, which models the scenario where a small number of popular streams are requested frequently. Such request pattern is popular in P2P file-sharing and web caching [10,11] and we use it to verify the performance improvement brought by cache mechanism on query graphs in the proxy. The parameters used to generate the workloads are illustrated in Table 2

Table 2. Summary of parameters used experiments

Variable	Value	Description
$nDirectQueries$	1500	number of direct queries
$directQueryDist$	160:170:130:124:254:290:372	query graph composition (Single FB : Single MB : Single AB : FB+MB : FB+AB : MB+AB : FB+MB+AB)
$nPolicies$	1000	number of unique policies
$nRequests$	1500	number of matching requests
α	0.223	skew parameter for Zipf distribution
$maxRank$	300	maximum rank of unique requests from which Zipf distribution is generated

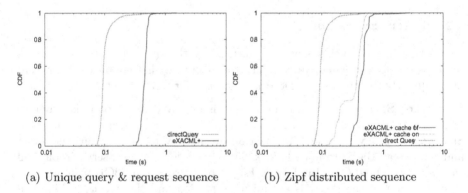

(a) Unique query & request sequence   (b) Zipf distributed sequence

Fig. 6. Overall Performance

Experiments: We measure system performance in terms of time taken to fulfill authorized data-stream requests. The access control mechanism accounts for the overhead incurred when handling request from users. Before any user request is made, we load policies onto the data servers so that PDP can make decisions based on them. This process takes a small amount of time with respect to the number of policies already loaded. The average loading time is 0.25 second with standard deviation of 0.06 second.

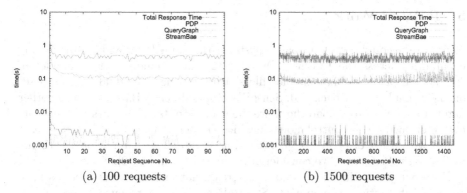

(a) 100 requests   (b) 1500 requests

Fig. 7. Detailed Processing Time of AC Requests

Figure 6(a) presents the result obtained by running the unique query/request sequence. Since there is no actual data transferred in the system, most direct queries and most requests to *eXACML+* are responded quickly, i.e. in less than one second. The response time for direct queries are consistent, which is as expected because only the query graphs and data-stream handles are exchanged between the direct query system and DSMS. Given a stable environment, the response time should not vary much. *eXACML+* incurs overheads and the curve is less smooth compared to that of direct query system, which is mainly caused by additional network traffic among clients, proxies and servers, which occupies about two-third of the total response time. The cost for communication between multiple entities is also subject to change. Figure 7(a) and Figure 7(b) represent the detailed elapsed time for processing 100 and 1500 AC requests with *eXACML+*, respectively. We can see that time taken to make access control decisions and to manipulate query graphs take less than 0.01 second in all requests and are rather consistent despite the increment number of requests and loaded policies, which are 50 for 7(a) and 1000 for 7(b). Elapsed time for sending query graphs to DSMS occupies one third of the total response time on average and has much larger variance. We notice that there are a few cases where sending query graphs to DSMS take much longer time than average and these cases take place only in the beginning of the request sequences. We believe this is due to the behavior of StreamBase API, which needs longer time to establish initial connections to StreamBase than to send subsequence queries. In general, the response time for *eXACML+* to process AC requests is consistent for over 99% of the requests, which verifies that the whole system is scalable with respect to the number of requests and polices.

Figure 6(b) shows how the overhead changes when the proxy enables caching. Although *eXACML+* does not outperform direct query systems, the performance improvement brought by caching is substantial. Unlike *eXACML*, what cached in the proxy is not actual data, but data-stream handles, whose sizes are significantly smaller. The performance indicates over 100% improvement over non-cached requests for nearly 40% of the number of quests and at least 10% improvement for the rest requests.

5   Related Work

There are a couple of cloud-based systems that aim to provide data sharing capabilities across the Internet. Dropbox[12] and iCloud[13] are examples of commercial products that enables file sharing among individual devices bases on their cloud storage back-end. SenseWeb[14] and SensorBase[15], on the other hand, allows users to upload the share their sensor data. Theses systems support coarse-grained access control model in which an user either makes his data public, shares with a list of people or just keeps it private. They cannot deal with the access control scenarios we considered in this paper and in [2].

In recent years, time-series data, or stream data management systems have enjoyed substantial development. StreamBase [7] — a renowned commercial DSMS — has evolved from the Aurora system [5] and its distributed version Borealis [16]. Enforcing access control on data-streams is still a fresh topic. Perhaps closest to our work are those by Carminati et al. [17], [18] which proposed model and framework for enforcing access control over stream data, but our work has integrated the access control model with XACML and presented an implementation and evaluation based on StreamBase engine. Rimma, et al. [19], [20] proposed to make use of embedded punctuation in the data-stream to enforce access control, while Lindner. et al. [21], [22] proposed to build an additional static layer on top of query engines.

Using of XACML in Cloud systems is yet to receive further development. [23] uses XACML in grid environment where its role is to unify database access control mechanisms from multiple parties. We foresee that XACML will be more widely used in the industry as the standard and is constantly evolving in response to new access control requirements. To the best of our knowledge, our work in this paper is the first to use XACML model to enforce fine-grained access control policies over stream data.

6   Conclusion and Future Work

In this paper, we have proposed *eXACML+* framework that allows data-stream owners to share their data-streams with other users in a secure and flexible manner over a trusted cloud infrastructure. The main challenges are due to the differences between bounded data (as in RDBMS) and unbounded stream data (as in DSMS). We have explored the problem of possible privacy leak caused by a single user having access to multiple aggregated streams of one master data-stream. We have demonstrate a possible performance improvement by detecting if a user query will return empty or only partial result due to mismatches with access control policies. We have implemented a prototype of our framework using StreamBase data-stream management system. Preliminary experiments show the framework's efficacy. It incurs constant and consistent overhead compared with direct queries (without access control) on the data-stream engine. The source-code for the implementation will be made available at http://code.google.com/p/e-xacml/.

Our immediate plans are to migrate the framework to commercial cloud environments such as Amazon EC2 [24] and Microsoft's Azure [25] for more comprehensive evaluations with practical workloads instead of synthetic ones. Moreover, we intend to use other stream base engines like APE [26] and DB2 DSE [27] to broaden the range of applications that our framework supports. On the conceptual front, relaxing the trusted cloud model to incorporate more accountability mechanisms, or by employing cryptographic approaches is our next challenge.

References

1. Geambasu, R., Gribble, S.D., Levy, H.M.: CloudViews: Communal Data Sharing in Public Clouds. In: HotCloud (2009)
2. Dinh, T.T.A., Wenqiang, W., Datta, A.: City on the sky: Extending xacml for flexible, secure data sharing on the cloud. Journal of Grid Computing (2012)
3. OASIS: OASIS eXtensible Access Control Markup Language (XACML) TC (2011), http://www.oasis-open.org/committees/xacml/
4. Ferrari, E., Thuraisingham, B.: Secure database systems. Advanced Databases: Technology and Design (2000)
5. Abadi, D.J., Carney, D., Cetintemel, U., Cherniack, M., Convey, C., Lee, S., Stonebraker, M., Tatbul, N., Zdonik, S.: Aurora: a new model and architecture for data stream management. In: VLDB (2003)
6. Babu, S., Widom, J.: Continuous queries over data streams. ACM SIGMOD Record (2001)
7. StreamBase: Streambase systems inc., http://www.streambase.com/
8. IBM: Evaluate mathematical expressions quickly and accurately, http://www.ibm.com/developerworks/library/j-w3eval/index.html
9. Sun Microsystem, Inc.: Sun's xacml implementation (2004), http://sunxacml.sourceforge.net
10. Adamic, L.A., Huberman, B.A.: Zipf's law and the internet. Glottometrics (2002)
11. Klemm, A., Lindemann, C., Vernon, M.K., Waldhorst, O.P.: Characterizing the query behavior in peer-to-peer file sharing systems. In: SIGCOMM (2004)
12. Dropbox Inc.: Dropbox, http://www.dropbox.com
13. Apple Inc.: icloud, http://www.icloud.com
14. Microsoft Research: Senseweb, http://research.microsoft.com/en-us/projects/senseweb/
15. Center for Embedded networked sensing (UCLA): Sensorbase, http://sensorbase.org
16. Ahmad, Y., et al.: Borealis distributed stream processing engine, http://www.cs.brown.edu/research/borealis/public/
17. Carminati, B., Ferrari, E., Tan, K.L.: Specifying Access Control Policies on Data Streams. In: Kotagiri, R., Radha Krishna, P., Mohania, M., Nantajeewarawat, E. (eds.) DASFAA 2007. LNCS, vol. 4443, pp. 410–421. Springer, Heidelberg (2007)
18. Carminati, B., Ferrari, E., Tan, K.L.: Enforcing access control over data streams. In: SACMAT (2007)
19. Nehme, R.V., Rundenseinerr, E.A., Bertino, E.: A security punctuation framework for enforcing access control on streaming data. In: ICDE (2008)
20. Nehme, R.V., Lim, H.-S., Bertino, E., Rundenseinerr, E.A.: Cstreamshield: a stream-centric approach towards security and privacy in data stream environments. In: SIGMOD (2009)

21. Lindner, W., Meier, J.: Towards a Secure Data Stream Management System. In: Draheim, D., Weber, G. (eds.) TEAA 2005. LNCS, vol. 3888, pp. 114–128. Springer, Heidelberg (2006)
22. Lindner, W., et al.: Securing the borealis data stream engine. In: IDEAS (2006)
23. Power, D., Slaymaker, M., Politou, E., Simpson, A.C.: A Secure Wrapper for OGSA-DAI. In: Sloot, P.M.A., Hoekstra, A.G., Priol, T., Reinefeld, A., Bubak, M. (eds.) EGC 2005. LNCS, vol. 3470, pp. 485–494. Springer, Heidelberg (2005)
24. Amazon: Amazon elastic compute cloud, http://aws.amazon.com/ec2/
25. Microsoft: Windows azure platform, http://www.microsoft.com/windowsazure/
26. APE: Ape project organization, http://www.ape-project.org/
27. IBM: Ibm corporate,
    http://www-01.ibm.com/support/docview.wss?uid=swg27009727

Policies for Composed Emergencies in Support of Disaster Management

Barbara Carminati, Elena Ferrari, and Michele Guglielmi

Department of Theoretical and Applied Science
University of Insubria, Varese, Italy
{barbara.carminati,elena.ferrari,michele.guglielmi}@uninsubria.it

Abstract. Recently, some proposals have appeared to achieve timely
and flexible information sharing in support of emergency management.
This is obtained by means of an emergency description language able
to specify both emergency situations and temporary access control poli-
cies/obligations that have to be activated during emergencies. In this
paper, we show that these languages have some limitations in capturing more critical emergency situations, which might arise when atomic
emergency events are combined. Moreover, we show that such critical
situations might require a new response plan (i.e., new temporary access
control policies and obligations), with respect to those already in place
for atomic emergencies. Therefore, we introduce the concept of *composed
emergency* and related *emergency policies*. We also propose some overriding strategies to determine how temporary access control policies and
obligations associated with a composed emergency have to be combined
with those associated with atomic emergencies. Finally, we propose a
tree-data structure in support of efficient emergency policy enforcement.

1 Introduction

Disaster management is the organization and management of resources and responsibilities to address all the aspects of an emergency. One of the most important aspects of disaster management is information sharing among involved
parties. For example, it has been demonstrated that during emergency situations,
like the attacks of 9/11 and hurricane Katrina [1,3], the lack of information sharing among federal, state, local, agencies and government cost a lot in terms of
human lives. To cope with this issue in [10] we have proposed an emergency
description language to specify *emergency situations* as well as *temporary access
control policies (tacps)* and *obligations* that have to be activated during such situations. More precisely, each emergency has associated one or more tacps, stating
the new access rights the entities involved in the emergency management might
need to carry on their activities. Moreover, since the triggering of an emergency
could require the immediate execution of some activities, an emergency may also
be associated with one or more obligations. The binding of an emergency with
the corresponding tacps and obligations is modeled by the so-called *emergency
policies*. In this paper, we show that even though the model proposed in [10]

W. Jonker and M. Petković (Eds.): SDM 2012, LNCS 7482, pp. 75–92, 2012.

allows the Emergency Manager to capture complex event patterns, there exist critical scenarios that cannot be handled. These are the cases of a combination of different emergency situations that may give rise to a new and more critical situation, requiring a new response plan, different from those plans already in place for the management of atomic emergencies. Therefore, in this paper we introduce the concept of *composed emergencies*, to describe how and which sub-emergencies have to be combined together to form a composed one. Moreover, as described by the examples provided in this paper, in some cases a composed emergency may require overriding the tacps/obligations that have been activated as response plans of sub-emergencies, whereas in other cases tacps/obligations of composed emergencies should coexist with those of sub-emergencies. Therefore, we associate with each policy for composed emergencies an *overriding strategy* according to which we can specify if tacps/obligations of sub-emergencies have to be maintained, deleted or temporarily blocked until the end of the composed emergency. Overriding also supports *exceptions*, which are defined at two distinct granularity levels: emergencies and single tacp/obligation. A further contribution of the paper is related to policy enforcement that requires determining, as soon as an emergency is detected, the new tacps/obligations to be inserted in the system. Moreover, it requires also determining those tacps/obligations to be deleted/blocked due to the selected overriding strategy. It is important to note that in an emergency situation it is mandatory to make immediately available the needed information to the right person, as well as to immediately trigger the required obligations. Therefore, to speed up policy enforcement, we make use of a tree-data structure (called Emergency Composition Tree - ECT), which helps us in pre-computing, for each emergency, the lists of tacps/obligations to be maintained, deleted or blocked.

Some models in support of controlled information sharing for disaster management have been already proposed, in addition to [10]. Relevant examples are those based on the concept of Break-the-Glass (BtG) policies [2,6,8,4,11,12,17]. However, none of these models support the concept of composed emergency and related policies, which is the focus of the current paper. Since our proposal deals with policy overriding, it may be considered in some relationship with work for policy composition [5,7,16,19,13,9,18]. However, it is important to note that the focus of our work is different from that of the proposals for policy composition, since we deal with composition of emergencies, to which we associate new emergency policies, rather than composition of polices. As such, while policy combination strategies focus on operators to combine policies and resolution strategies for conflicts among positive and negative policies, in our proposal we are interested in composition of emergencies and solutions for the overriding or coexistence of their corresponding temporary access control policies. Finally, our approach is related to the problem of information sharing in *dynamic coalitions*. Dynamic coalitions are formed during international crisis, i.e., emergency situations, therefore there are similarities between our model and dynamic coalitions models [21,20,15]. However none of those proposals address the dynamic reconfiguration of access control rights upon the triggering of an emergency.

Rather, they address the possibility of enforcing information sharing among heterogeneous entities and related security issues.

The remainder of the paper is organized as follows. Section 2 presents some motivating scenarios. The formal definition of composed emergencies and related policies is given in Section 3, whereas Section 4 presents the data structure used for the enforcement. Policy enforcement is addressed in Section 5. Section 6 presents the complexity analysis of policy enforcement, whereas, Section 7 concludes the paper.

2 Motivating Scenario

There exist critical scenarios characterized by combination of different emergencies, leading to a new more critical situation that requires a new response plan.

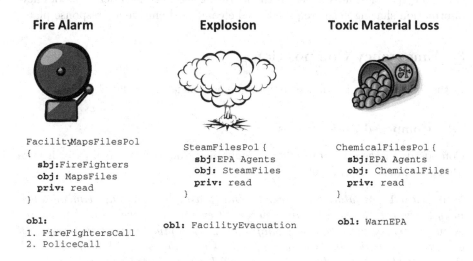

Fire Alarm	Explosion	Toxic Material Loss

```
FacilityMapsFilesPol
{
  sbj:FireFighters
  obj: MapsFiles
  priv: read
}

obl:
1. FireFightersCall
2. PoliceCall
```

```
SteamFilesPol {
  sbj:EPA Agents
  obj: SteamFiles
  priv: read
}


obl: FacilityEvacuation
```

```
ChemicalFilesPol {
  sbj:EPA Agents
  obj: ChemicalFiles
  priv: read
}

obl: WarnEPA
```

Fig. 1. Industrial Facility Scenario: emergencies and related tacps/obligations

Example 1. Consider the scenario of an industrial company facility which produces plastic material. Suppose that the facility is equipped with sensor networks detecting fire alarms, explosions and presence of toxic substances in air/water. Suppose that the system enforces the emergency policies represented in Figure 1: (1) when a fire alarm is detected, the firefighters and police agents are automatically called (i.e., *FireFightersCall* and *PoliceCall* obligations) and they are allowed to access the facility map files (i.e., *FacilityMapsFilesPol* temporary access control policy); (2) when an explosion emergency is detected, facility evacuation is enforced (i.e., *FacilityEvacuation*) and the Environmental Protection Agency (EPA) personnel is allowed to read the files with information about steams processed in the facility (i.e., *SteamFilesPol*); (3) when a high level of toxic substances is detected, the EPA should be warned about the emergency (i.e., *WarnEPA*) and information on the chemical substances used in the facility should be immediately available to EPA staff (i.e., *ChemicalFilesPol*). The situation might get much more critical if two or more of the above described emergencies are detected at the same time or in a sequence. Indeed, if the fire alarm is followed by an explosion, and the explosion is in turn followed by a toxic material loss emergency, it means that the fire and explosion caused damage with toxic material release. As such, the emergency situation requires the modification of the ongoing response activities. Since the risk of ecological disaster is high a higher level authority, such as the Department of Homeland Security (DHS), should be warned and any information about the processes executed in the facility should be immediately available to DHS staff.

Situations like the one presented in Example 1 cannot be handled by the model in [10], since they require the new concepts of composed emergencies and related emergency policies, introduced in the following sections, in order to model new information sharing needs required by the composed emergency response plan.

3   Emergency Composition

In the following, we introduce composed emergencies and related polices.

3.1   Composed Emergencies

Composed emergencies are built by combining atomic emergencies which were originally introduced in [10].

Definition 1. *An atomic emergency emg is a tuple (init, end, timeout, priority), where init and end are emergency events, such that init denotes the event triggering the emergency emg, end is the optional event that turns off emg, timeout is the time within emg expires even though end has not occurred. Priority ∈ {high, low} denotes the priority level associated with emg.*

Events describing the beginning/ending of an emergency are defined according to a language, called Core Event Specification Language (CESL) [10], by using: (i) query stream operators such as *selection, projection, aggregation*, and *join*; (ii) basic event operators, like *event type, event instance* and *array of event instances*; and (iii) complex event pattern operators, such as *sequence, negation* and *iteration* of events.

Example 2. Consider the scenario of an industrial company facility presented in Example 1. Suppose the steam pressure in the pipes is controlled through sensors. When a pressure higher than 100 Pa (Pascal) is detected, then an explosion is forthcoming, therefore an explosion emergency is raised. According to Definition 1, this emergency can be modeled as follows:

```
Explosion {
    init: PS1 p₁
    PS1 = σ(pressure > 100)(PipeSensors);
    end: PS2 p₂
    PS2 = σ(pressure ≤ 100)(PipeSensors);
    timeout: ∞;
    priority: high;
}
```

The emergency starts when an event p_1 coming from output stream $PS1$ is received. Output stream $PS1$ receives events from input stream $PipeSensors$ selecting those events whose *pressure* attribute is higher than 100, i.e., the emergency starts when the pressure of a pipe is higher than 100 Pa. The emergency ends when an event p_2 coming from output stream $PS2$ is received. Output stream $PS2$ receives events from input stream $PipeSensors$ selecting those events whose *pressure* is lower than or equal to 100, i.e., the emergency ends when the pressure returns lower than or equal to 100 Pa.

We support two ways to specify how emergencies have to be combined together to form a composed emergency. The first represents the composed emergency as a list of multiple occurrences of the same emergency type. The second represents the composed emergency as a pattern of different emergencies. Formally, composed emergencies are defined as follows.

Definition 2. *A composed emergency ce is a pair (*combination, priority*), where* priority $\in \{high, low\}$ *indicates the priority of the composed emergency, whereas* combination *indicates the sub-emergencies and how they are combined together to form ce. More precisely, the combination component can be of one of the following forms:*

- $\{oc_1, ..., oc_n\}$, *such that* $oc_j = (emg_j, n_j)$, *where* emg_j *is an emergency identifier, whereas* $n_j \in \mathbb{N}$ *is the minimum number of* emg_j *instances necessary to trigger ce.*
- *pattern, which can be: (1) a sequence* emg_1, $emg_2[emg_1, s_2]$, $...$, emg_n $[emg_{n-1}, s_n]$, *where* emg_i *is an atomic or composed emergency, whereas* $emg_i[emg_{i-1}, s_i]$ *indicates that* emg_i *should happen between* emg_{i-1} *and a time interval of size* s_i, *defining in this way the sequence of emergencies* $emg_1, emg_2, ..., emg_n$; *(2) a negation* $\neg$ $emg[w]$, *which specifies the non-occurrence of emergency emg in a given time window w.*

Example 3. Consider the situation presented in Example 1, where three atomic emergencies generate a critical situation, which can be modeled by the following composed emergency:

$$EcologicalDisaster = (Pattern, high)$$

$$Pattern = \begin{cases} FireAlarm, \\ Explosion[FireAlarm, 1h], \\ ToxicMaterialLoss[Explosion, 1h] \end{cases}$$

If an explosion emergency is detected within one hour after the fire alarm emergency and a toxic material loss emergency is detected within one hour after the explosion, then the composed emergency *EcologicalDisaster* is raised.

3.2   Emergency Policies

The binding of an atomic or composed emergency with the corresponding tacps and obligations is modeled through emergency policies. In order to manage critical situations represented by composed emergencies, it is often necessary that the tacps and obligations that have been activated as response plan to sub-emergencies are overridden by tacps/obligations associated with composed emergencies.

For instance, consider again the scenario presented in Example 1, and suppose that the obligations associated with the sub-emergency fire alarm are: call firefighters and call police. When the composed emergency *EcologicalDisaster* is detected, while the police call should be deleted in order to not endanger the lives of police men with the released toxic material, the firefighters call should be maintained, since the fire must be extinguished regardless the release of toxic substances.

To handle situations like these, we enable the Emergency Manager to specify the overriding strategy determining how to behave with respect to the tacps/obligations associated with sub-emergencies involved in the composition. More precisely, we support three overriding strategies, that is, *maintain, delete,* and *block* that imply, respectively, that tacps/obligations associated with sub-emergencies are maintained, deleted or blocked until the end of the corresponding composed emergency.

The *block* overriding strategy is extremely important, since it allows to temporary block tacps/obligations for the duration of the composed emergency. For instance, consider an emergency of power loss in a generator of a power plant and the consequent obligation *CallMaintenance*. If the emergency gets more critical, e.g., the generator is burning, a new obligation *FireFightersCall* should be enforced. In this case the *CallMaintenance* obligation should be blocked to not endanger maintenance staff lives, but it should be restated as soon as the fire is extinguished.

We are aware that there could be emergencies whose relevance requires not stopping any of the associated tacps/obligations, even in case these are involved in a composition. As an example, consider once again the scenario in Example 1, when the ecological disaster emergency is detected, although this composed emergency is more serious than its sub-emergency fire alarm, the related firefighter call should not be deleted/blocked until the fire is extinguished.

To prevent overriding of critical tacps/obligations, we introduce an *exception mechanism* at the emergency level. This is done by exploiting the priority level associated with each emergency (cfr. Definitions 1 and 2). More precisely, the tacps/obligations associated with any high priority emergency can be never deleted/blocked even though this emergency is involved in a composed emergency, and even though this latter requests for tacps/obligations overriding.[1] Moreover, considering that, given an emergency, not all of its response procedures have the same importance, we introduce a more fine-grained exception level, that is, the tacp/obligation level. More precisely, we enable the Emergency Manager to specify, for each emergency with low priority, those tacps/obligations that do not have to be deleted/blocked even in case the emergency is involved in a composed emergency which requests for tacps/obligations overriding. The formal definition of emergency policy is therefore the following.

Definition 3. *An* Emergency Policy *is a tuple (*emg, tacps, obligations, overriding*), where* emg *is the identifier of an atomic or composed emergency;* tacps *is a set of pairs (*tacp,[2] exception*), where* tacp *is a temporary access control policy, whereas* exception ∈ *{*true, false*}*; obligations *is a set of pairs (*obl, exception*), where* obl *is an obligation, whereas* exception ∈ *{*true, false*}*. *An* exception *will be used to denote whether a tacp or obligation enforces a policy/action that cannot be deleted or blocked (* exception = true*) by the overriding strategies. The* overriding *component consists of (*tacpOver, oblOver*), whose values in {*maintain, delete, block*} denote the overriding strategy for tacps/obligations, respectively.*

It is worth noting that in case *emg* is an atomic emergency, the *overriding* field is empty.

Example 4. Consider the scenario in Example 1. The requirement to automatically warn the DHS, allowing its personnel to access information about any process in the facility (i.e., all files), when the *EcologicalDisaster* emergency (cfr. Example 1) is raised, can be modeled by associating the following policy to the *EcologicalDisaster* emergency, as shown in Figure 2.

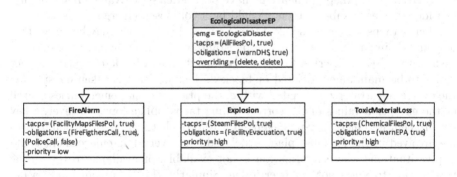

Fig. 2. EcologicalDisaster Emergency Policy

---

[1] In this paper, we just consider two priority levels (i.e., high, low). We postpone as future work the definition of a more sophisticated exception mechanism.

[2] Tacps are expressed in terms of subject, object, privilege and context information. See [10] for more details.

In Figure 2, the *EcologicalDisasterEP* emergency policy is represented, where *AllFilesPolicy* is a tacp granting DHS access to any file containing information about processes in the facility and *WarnDHS* obligation warns EPA about the ecological disaster emergency. Suppose now that the *FireAlarm* emergency has a low priority, whereas we assume that its tacp *FacilityMapsFilesPol*, allowing firefighters and police agents to access the facility maps files, has a true exception value. Moreover, two obligations are associated with *FireAlarm*, requiring to call firefighters and police agents, which we assume having a true and false exception value, respectively. Additionally, the *Explosion* emergency has a high priority and its tacp (called *SteamFilesPol*) and obligation (called *FacilityEvacuation*) have both true as exception value. Finally the *ToxicMaterialLoss* emergency has a high priority and its tacp (called *ChemicalFilesPol*) and obligation (called *WarnEPA*) have both true as exception value. Let us now explain the overriding strategies. Since *tacpOver* is set to delete, the tacp related to the low priority sub-emergencies (i.e., *FireAlarm*) with exception field set to false (none in case of *FireAlarm*) are deleted, whereas those with a true exception value (i.e., *FacilityMapsFilesPol*) are maintained. Similarly, since the flag *oblOver* is set to delete, obligations related to low priority sub-emergencies (i.e., *FireAlarm*) with exception field set true (i.e., the obligation requiring to call firefighters) are maintained, whereas those with false exception value (i.e., the call police obligation) are deleted.

4   Emergency Composition Tree

The introduction of composed emergencies brings new issues mainly related to overriding enforcement. Indeed, when a composed emergency ce is triggered, its sub-emergencies, say $e_1, \ldots, e_n$ have been already instantiated. This implies that the corresponding tacps/obligations have been already activated. If we further consider that each sub-emergency could be a composed emergency as well, the number of tacps/obligations linked to a composed emergency may be large. This may greatly impact the time needed to instantiate the new emergency e, since for each of the already inserted tacps/obligations it should be determined whether it has to be maintained, deleted or blocked. This decision is taken considering the overriding strategy associated with e, the priority of sub-emergencies as well as the exception values of the corresponding tacps/obligations. However, a key requirement for emergency management is to provide timely information to people involved in the response plan. A delay due to overriding enforcement could imply situations where information is not available, or available to the wrong people, due to tacps not yet overridden. Similarly, this delay can imply a delayed stop of risky activities imposed by obligations. To avoid these situations, we propose a solution where, for each composed emergency e for which a policy has been specified, the corresponding lists of tacps/obligations to be deleted, maintained or blocked are statically *pre-computed*. More precisely, we organize the tacps/obligations that have to be instantiated due to the triggering of an atomic/composed emergency as well as the lists of tacps/obligations to be overridden, into a set of tree data structures, called *Emergency Composition Tree*. In the following, we introduce the tree data structure and the algorithm for its generation.

4.1   Tree Data Structure

An Emergency Composition Tree (*ECT*) is defined such that each emergency is represented as a node, whereas all information related to the corresponding policies are modeled as its attributes. The formal definition of an ECT is given in what follows.

Definition 4. *Given a composed emergency ce consisting of n sub-emergencies $e_1, ..., e_n$ and its corresponding emergency policy* cep=(ce, tacps, obligations, overriding),[3] *the corresponding ECT is defined as a pair $\langle N, E \rangle$ where:*

- $N = \{n_{ce}, n_{e_1}, ..., n_{e_n}\}$ *is the set of nodes. Node n_{ce} represents the composed emergency ce and has the following attributes:* tacps, obligations, priority, tacpOver, oblOver, tacpToDelete, tacpToBlock, oblToDelete, *and* oblToBlock. *In particular,* tacps *and* obligations *contain the list of tacps/obligations specified in* cep.tacps[4] *and* cep.obligations, priority *is the priority of emergency ce,* tacpOver *and* oblOver *represent the overriding strategies specified in* cep.overriding, tacpToDelete, tacpToBlock, oblToDelete *and* oblToBlock *contain, respectively, the tacps and obligations that have to be deleted or blocked in case of the triggering of ce. Each node $n_{e_i} \in N$, $i \in [1, n]$ represents a sub-emergency e_i. It has the same attributes as node n_{ce}, where* tacps *and* obligations *contain the list of tacps/obligations specified in the emergency policy related to e_i,* priority *is the priority of emergency e_i,* tacpOver *and* oblOver *represent the overriding strategies specified in the emergency policy associated with e_i, whereas the overriding lists (i.e.,* tacpToDelete, tacpToBlock, oblToDelete *and* oblToBlock*) contain tacps/obligations that have to be deleted or blocked in case of the triggering of e_i.*
- $E = \{(n_{ce}, n_{e_1}), ..., (n_{ce}, n_{e_n})\}$ *is the set of edges.*

Attributes related to overriding (i.e., *tacpOver, oblOver, tacpToDelete, tacpToBlock, oblToDelete* and *oblToBlock*) are optional. For instance, in case of a node denoting an atomic emergency they are unnecessary, as the following example clarifies.

---

[3] For simplicity, in Definition 4, we assume that each emergency is associated with a single policy. If an emergency is bound to multiple policies, Definition 4 can be easily extended.

[4] Here and in the following we use dot-notation to indicate fields of emergencies or polices (e.g., tacps, obligations).

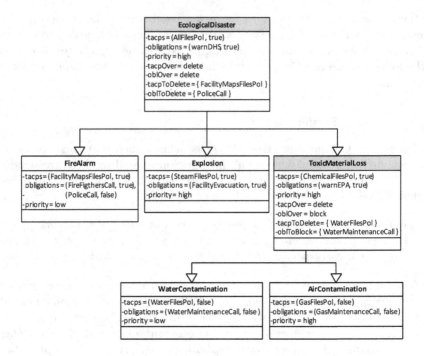

Fig. 3. Emergency Composition Tree

Example 5. Consider the policy presented in Example 4 referring to the composed emergency *EcologicalDisaster* in Example 3. Suppose that *ToxicMaterialLoss* is defined as the composition of two atomic emergencies: *WaterContamination* and *AirContamination*. Suppose moreover that *WaterContamination* is a low priority emergency associated with the tacp *WaterFilesPol*, which allows water maintenance personnel to access files containing information about water usage in the facility. In contrast, *AirContamination* is a high priority emergency associated with the tacp *GasFilesPol* allowing the gas maintenance personnel to access files containing information about gas processed in the facility. The ECT corresponding to the *EcologicalDisaster* emergency is represented in Figure 3. The node associated with the composed emergency *ToxicMaterialLoss* has a *tacps* attribute which contains a tacp, called *ChemicalFilesPol*, with true exception value. *ChemicalFilesPol* allows EPA personnel to access files with information about chemical substances processed in the facility. The *obligations* attribute of *ToxicMaterialLoss* contains an obligation, called *warn EPA*, that warns EPA about the toxic material loss emergency. The *tacpOver* attribute is set to delete meaning that *ChemicalFilesPol* overrides the sub-emergency tacp *WaterFilesPol*, but not *GasFilesPol*. This is because *GasFilesPol* is associated with *AirContamination* which is a high priority emergency, whereas *WaterFilesPol* is associated with the low priority emergency *WaterContamination*.

The *oblOver* attribute of *ToxicMaterialLoss* is set to block. However, *GasMaintenanceCall* has to still be enforced, since it is associated with the high priority emergency *AirContamination*, whereas the obligation *WaterMaintenanceCall* is temporary blocked until the end of *ToxicMaterialLoss*, since it is associated with the low priority emergency *WaterContamination*. Therefore, the overriding lists of *ToxicMaterialLoss* are the following: *tacpToDelete* = { *WaterFilesPol* }, *tacpToBlock* = ∅, *oblToDelete* = ∅, *oblToBlock* = { *WaterMaintenanceCall* }. The overriding lists of *EcologicalDisaster* are computed in a similar way.

4.2   ECT Generation

In this section, we show how we create the set of ECTs for composed emergencies. Note that the same emergency could be part of one or more composed emergencies. To avoid storage of redundant information, we make use of an indexing data structure (i.e., a hash table), which maps each emergency with information about the position of the corresponding subtree in existing ECTs. The position is encoded as index[emg] = (t_j, l_m, c_n), where t_j denotes an ECT, whereas l_m and c_n denote the position of the node related to emg in t_j (i.e., its level l_m and relative position c_n in the level, from left to right). Algorithm 1 receives as input the policy base *CEP* containing policies for composed emergencies and returns the set of created *ECTrees* and the associated indexing structure. For each policy $cep_j \in CEP$, it calls the *createECT()* function, which returns an ECT called *tree* and the modified *index* (line 3). *Tree* is then inserted into the *ECTrees* (line 4). Atomic emergencies that are not part of a composed emergency are not considered by Algorithm 1, therefore they are not indexed and during enforcement, they are activated/deactivated as explained in [10].

Algorithm 1. Emergency Composition Trees generation

Input   : *CEP* the composed emergency policy base
Output: *ECTrees*, the set of ECTs, and the *index* hash table
1 Let *index* be an empty hash table, *root* be an empty variable;
2 **foreach** $cep_j \in CEP$ **do**
3   <tree, index> = createECT (cep_j, root, 0, 0, index);
4   Insert tree Into ECTrees;
5 **end**
6 **return**   <*ECTrees,index*>

The *createECT()* function receives as input: an emergency policy *cep* for a composed emergency; the *root* node of the ECT under construction (needed for the indexing); *depth* and *chNum*, denoting the level and number of children, where nodes created by the function will be inserted; the indexing hash table *index*. The *createECT()* function returns a pair <*parent, index*> where *parent* is the node created for the input *cep* and *index* is the modified hash table. To better explain the meaning of *root*, *depth* and *chNum*, suppose to have a composed emergency ce_1 consisting in turn of two composed sub-emergencies

ce_2 and ce_3. When the createECT function is called for ce_1 by Algorithm 1, *root* is an empty variable, *depth = 0* and *chNum = 0* (see line 3 in Algorithm 1), therefore *root* will be assigned to the node related to ce_1, say n_1 and $index[ce_1]$ = $(n_1, 0, 0)$. When createECT is recursively called for ce_2, *root = n_1*, *depth = 1* and *chNum = 0*, therefore $index[ce_2] = (n_1, 1, 0)$. Finally, when createECT is recursively called for ce_3, *root = n_1*, *depth = 1* and *chNum = 1*, therefore $index[ce_2] = (n_1, 1, 1)$.

Function createECT(cep, root, depth, chNum, index)

1 <parent, index, root> = createNode (cep, root, depth, chNum, index);
2 depth++;
3 Let *SubEmg* be the set of sub-emergencies in cep.emg;
4 **foreach** $sub_j \in SubEmg$ **do**
5   Let ep_j be the emergency policy associated with sub_j;
6   **if** sub_j *is an atomic emergency* **then**
7   <child, index, root> = createNode (ep_j, root, depth, chNum, index);
8   **else**
9   <child, index> = createECT (ep_j, root, depth, chNum, index);
10   **end**
11   Create an edge between node *parent* and node *child*;
12   chNum++;
13   parent = createOverLists (parent, child);
14 **end**
15 **return** <parent, index>

Function createECT calls function *createNode()*, by passing it *cep, root, depth, chNum* and *index* (line 1). This function returns a node, called *parent*, defined according to Definition 4, the modified *index* table and *root*. Then, function createECT analyzes each of the sub-emergencies sub_j involved in the input composed emergency (lines 4-14). If sub_j is an atomic emergency (line 6), then the function calls *createNode()*, which returns the *child* node (line 7), the modified *index* table and *root*. If sub_j is a composed emergency, then the *child* node is created calling recursively function *createECT()* (line 9). In both the cases, the *child* node is added as direct child of *parent* node (line 11). Finally, function createECT calls the *createOverLists()* function which inserts the proper tacps/obligations related to the *child* node into the overriding lists of the *parent* node (line 13). When all sub-emergencies have been analyzed, then the createECT function returns *parent* node, i.e., the root of the created ECT and the modified *index* table (line 15).

The createNode function takes as input an emergency policy *ep*, the *root* of the ECT under construction, *depth* and *chNum*, denoting the level and number of children where the new node will be inserted. If a node associated with the emergency *ep.emg* already exists, then the createNode function gets that node through the *getNode* function (line 1), otherwise, a new node is created (line 3).

Function createNode(ep, root, depth, chNum, index)

---

1   if $index[ep.emg] \neq \emptyset$ then   n = getNode(index[ep.emg]);
2   else
3   n = **new** node;
4   n.tacps = ep.tacps;
5   n.obligations = ep.obligations;
6   n.priority = ep.emg.priority;
7   if *ep.emg is composed* then
8   n.tacpOver = ep.tacpOver;
9   n.tacpOver = ep.oblOver;
10   n.tacpToDelete = n.tacpToBlock = n.oblToDelete = n.oblToBlock = $\emptyset$;
11   end
12 end
13 if *depth = 0* then   root = n;
14 Insert (root, depth, chNum) Into index[ep.emg];
15 **return** $<n, index, root>$;

The *tacps, obligations* and *priority* attributes are initialized for the new node (lines 4, 5, 6). If *ep.emg* is a composed emergency (line 7), then also the overriding strategies attributes are initialized (lines 8, 9) and the overriding lists are created (line 10). Finally, the createNode function creates the index (*root*,[5] *depth, chNum*) for node n (line 14) and returns the node itself, the modified *index* table and the *root* node (line 15).

Function createOverLists(parent, child)

---

1   if $child.priority \neq high \wedge parent.tacpOver \neq maintain$ then
2   **foreach** $tacp_j \in child.tacps$ **do**
3   if $tacp_j.exception \neq true$ then
4   if $parent.tacpOver = delete$ then
5   Insert $tacp_j$ Into parent.tacpToDelete;
6   else
7   Insert $tacp_j$ Into parent.tacpToBlock;
8   end
9   if $child.priority \neq high \wedge parent.oblOver \neq maintain$ then
10   **foreach** $obl_j \in child.obligations$ **do**
11   if $obl_j.exception \neq true$ then
12   if $parent.oblOver = delete$ then
13   Insert obl_j Into parent.oblToDelete;
14   else
15   Insert obl_j Into parent.oblToBlock;
16   end
17 **return** *parent;*

---

[5] The *root* variable is already set if *depth* is greater than zero, but in case *depth* is equal to zero it means that node n is the root of its ECT, thus variable *root* is set to n (line 13).

The createOverLists function takes as input a *parent* and a *child* node, inserts the proper tacps/obligations related to *child* into the overriding lists of *parent* and returns the modified *parent* node. If the *child* node is not linked with a high priority emergency and *parent* requests to override/block tacps (line 1), then the tacps related to *child* should be deleted or blocked. Therefore, each $tacp_j \in child.tacps$ is analyzed (lines 2-8) and if *exception* is not set to true (line 3) then: (i) if $parent.tacpOver = delete$ (line 4), $tacp_j$ is inserted into *parent.tacpToDelete* (line 5), (ii) if $parent.tacpOver = block$ (line 6), $tacp_j$ is inserted into *parent.tacpToBlock* (line 7). In lines 9-16, a similar overriding strategy is enforced for obligations.

5 Policy Enforcement

Emergency policy enforcement is done by making use of ECTs. More precisely, when an emergency e is detected, then: if e is an atomic emergency, its tacps and obligations are inserted into the system as explained in [10], whereas if it is composed, tacps and obligations contained into *tacps* and *obligations* attributes of the corresponding ECT node are inserted into the system and those contained in *tacpToDelete/ oblToDelete, tacpToBlock/oblToBlock* are deleted and/or blocked, respectively.

Example 6. Consider the ECT in Figure 3. When the composed emergency *EcologicalDisaster* is detected, active tacps are: *FacilityMapsFilesPol* (linked to *FireAlarm*), *SteamFilesPol* (linked to *Explosion*), *GasFilesPol* (linked to *AirContamination*) and *ChemicalFilesPol* (linked to the *ToxicMaterialLoss*). In contrast, the *WaterFilesPol* tacp was already overridden by the *ChemicalFilesPol* tacp. The node related to *EcologicalDisaster* is retrieved using the indexing data structure. Then, the system enforces tacps and obligations related to *EcologicalDisaster*. The system also retrieves the tacps contained in the overriding lists. Since *tacpToDelete* = { *FacilityMapsFilesPol* }, *FacilityMapsFilesPol* is deleted. The obligations in place in the system are: *FireFightersCall* and *PoliceCall* (linked to *FireAlarm* emergency), *FacilityEvacuation* (linked to *Explosion*), *GasMaintenanceCall* (linked to *AirContamination*), and *warn EPA* (linked to the *ToxicMaterialLoss*), whereas the *WaterMaintenanceCall* obligation was already blocked until the end of the *ToxicMaterialLoss* emergency. The system checks the obligations contained in the list associated with the *EcologicalDisaster* node. Since *oblToDelete* = { *PoliceCall* }, *PoliceCall* is deleted.

6 Complexity Analysis

In this section, we estimate the time needed to create the set of ECTs, which are generated at policy specification time, as well as the time needed for composed emergency policy enforcement using the generated ECTs.

6.1   ECTs Generation

To estimate the time required to create the set of ECTs, we analyze Algorithm 1. We first analyze createECT function, then we draw conclusions about complexity of Algorithm 1.

Function createECT: As a first step, createECT calls createNode by passing as input cep, a policy for composed emergencies (line 1). The time required by all operations in the createNode function is a constant time c except the time to copy the list of tacps and obligations (lines 4, 5) which is linear in the number of tacps n_t and the number of obligations n_o. Therefore the total time required by the function is $n_t + n_o + c$, i.e., $O(n_t + n_o)$. Then, the createECT function considers each sub-emergency sub_j contained into cep (lines 4-14). When sub_j is an atomic emergency, the function creates the corresponding node, by calling function createNode (line 7), whereas if sub_j is a composed emergency, it recursively calls itself (line 9). For each sub-emergency the createECT function calls also the $createOverLists$ function (line 13) which implements the overriding strategy. The time required by this function depends again on the number of tacps and obligations in $child$ node, i.e., $O(n_t + n_o)$. To give an estimation of the total time required by createECT function, we assume that the number of sub-emergencies that are involved at any level in cep is n and all sub-emergencies are composed,[6] which means that createECT is recursively called n times. The overall time is, in the worst case, $O(n \times (max(n_t) + max(n_o)))$ where $max(n_t)$ and $max(n_o)$ denote the maximum number of tacps/obligations associated with policies of all sub-emergencies. Therefore, the overall time is linear in the number of sub-emergencies.

Main Algorithm: Algorithm 1 calls function createECT for each policy associated with a composed emergency (lines 2-5). Let m be the number of emergency policies associated with composed emergencies. Then, the overall time required for Algorithm 1 is: $O(m \times n \times (max(n_t) + max(n_o)))$. Thus, Algorithm 1 is linear in the number of emergency policies for composed emergency and, since the creation of each ECT takes a linear time in the number of sub-emergency, Algorithm 1 is efficient and scalable.

6.2   Emergency Policy Enforcement Analysis

Thanks to the proposed tree and indexing data structures, composed emergency enforcement is efficient in terms of time needed to decide which tacps/obligations have to be inserted, deleted or blocked. We recall that, for a policy associated with a composed emergency ce, the enforcement consists of the following steps: (i) retrieval of the ECT node related to the emergency, (ii) reading of the tacps and obligations attributes and (iii) insertion in the policy bases of the retrieved

---

[6] Actually, at least one emergency among those involved in the composition has to be atomic, but to estimate the worst case, we are assuming that they are all composed as this requires more time.

tacps/obligations, (iv) reading of the overriding lists, and (v) execution of the overriding operations (i.e., delete/block the overridden tacps/obligations). By using the defined data structures, the time needed to perform step (i) is expected to be short. Indeed, given a composed emergency ce, retrieving the root node of the corresponding subtree in an ECT requires just to access the first entry in the hash table associated with ce, which requires a constant small time. Once index (t, l, c) has been retrieved from the hash table, the time needed to access the indexed node is again very small, as it requires to access node at level l and internal position c, i.e., the complexity is $O(l*c)$. Steps (ii) and (iii) require reading two node attributes (i.e., *tacps* and *obligations*) and inserting their content into the proper repository. Assuming that read and write operations require a constant time, then these steps have a time complexity of $O(n_t + n_o)$, where n_t is the number of tacps and n_o is the number of obligations. The time required by both steps (iv) and (v) is linear in the lists size (i.e., the number of items to be read and written). As such, let $max(n_l)$ be the maximum size of the overriding lists, the overall complexity is $O(max(n_l))$. Therefore, the overall cost of policy enforcement is $O(l * c + n_t + n_o + max(n_l))$.

7   Conclusions

In this paper, we have proposed an extension of the emergency access control model presented in [10] with the possibility of defining composed emergencies and related emergency polices. We have presented a suitable data structure to represent policies for composed emergencies in support of an efficient enforcement. A key concept, in our model, is the combination of atomic emergencies, therefore, besides combination techniques presented in these paper, we plan, as future work, to investigate more complex combination patterns. We also plan to extend the prototype implemented in [10] with the support for composed emergencies. Moreover, we plan to extend the model with administration policies in order to specify who are the subjects authorized to create/modify emergency policies. Additionally, we aim to implement incremental maintenance strategies of the ECT data structure to efficiently manage policy updates. Regarding access control, we plan to investigate efficient buffering or caching techniques to avoid the loss of information due to emergency policies enforcement (see for instance [14] or [22]). Finally, we plan to complement our system with new cloud computing techniques in order to enable information sharing under emergencies among heterogeneous entities. In particular, we aim using public cloud for information sharing protecting data with cryptographic policy enforcement schemes allowing queries on encrypted data.

Acknowledgment. Research presented in this paper was partially funded by the European Office of Aerospace Research and Development (EOARD).

References

1. The 9/11 commission report. Technical report, National Commission on Terrorist Attacks Upon the United States (July 2004)
2. Break-glass: An approach to granting emergency access to healthcare systems. White paper, Joint NEMA/COCIR/JIRA Security and Privacy Committee, SPC (2004)
3. Federal response to hurricane Katrina: Lessons learned. Technical report, Assistant to the President for Homeland Security and Counter Terrorism (February 2006)
4. Brucker, A.D., Petritsch, H., Weber, S.G.: Attribute-Based Encryption with Break-Glass. In: Samarati, P., Tunstall, M., Posegga, J., Markantonakis, K., Sauveron, D. (eds.) WISTP 2010. LNCS, vol. 6033, pp. 237–244. Springer, Heidelberg (2010)
5. Alghathbar, K., Wijesekera, D.: Consistent and Complete Access Control Policies in Use Cases. In: Stevens, P., Whittle, J., Booch, G. (eds.) UML 2003. LNCS, vol. 2863, pp. 373–387. Springer, Heidelberg (2003)
6. Ardagna, C.A., De Capitani di Vimercati, S., Foresti, S., Grandison, T., Jajodia, S., Samarati, P.: Access control for smarter healthcare using policy spaces. Computers and Security 29(8), 848–858 (2010)
7. Bertolissi, C., Fernández, M.: A rewriting framework for the composition of access control policies. In: Proceedings of the 10th International ACM SIGPLAN Conference on Principles and Practice of Declarative Programming, PPDP 2008, pp. 217–225. ACM, New York (2008)
8. Brucker, A.D., Petritsch, H.: Extending access control models with break-glass. In: Proceedings of the 14th ACM Symposium on Access Control Models and Technologies, SACMAT 2009, pp. 197–206. ACM, New York (2009)
9. Bruns, G., Huth, M.: Access control via belnap logic: Intuitive, expressive, and analyzable policy composition. ACM Trans. Inf. Syst. Secur. 14(1), 9:1–9:27 (2011)
10. Carminati, B., Ferrari, E., Guglielmi, M.: Secure information sharing on support of emergency management. In: Proceeding of the Third IEEE International Conference on Information Privacy, Security, Risk and Trust (PASSAT), pp. 988–995 (October 2011)
11. Ferreira, A., Chadwick, D., Farinha, P., Correia, R., Zao, G., Chilro, R., Antunes, L.: How to securely break into RBAC: The BTG-RBAC model. In: Proceedings of the 2009 Annual Computer Security Applications Conference, ACSAC 2009, pp. 23–31. IEEE Computer Society, Washington, DC (2009)
12. Ferreira, A., Cruz-Correia, R., Antunes, L., Farinha, P., Oliveira-Palhares, E., Chadwick, D.W., Costa-Pereira, A.: How to break access control in a controlled manner. In: Proceedings of the 19th IEEE Symposium on Computer-Based Medical Systems, pp. 847–854. IEEE Computer Society, Washington, DC (2006)
13. Dantas, D., Bruns, G., Huth, M.: A simple and expressive semantic framework for policy composition in access control. In: Proceedings of the 2007 ACM Workshop on Formal Methods in Security Engineering, FMSE 2007, pp. 12–21. ACM, New York (2007)
14. Kohler, M., Brucker, A.D.: Access control caching strategies: an empirical evaluation. In: Proceedings of the 6th International Workshop on Security Measurements and Metrics, MetriSec 2010, pp. 8:1–8:8. ACM, New York (2010)
15. Krishnan, R., Niu, J., Sandhu, R., Winsborough, W.H.: Group-centric secure information-sharing models for isolated groups. ACM Trans. Inf. Syst. Secur. 14(3), 23:1–23:29 (2011)

16. Lockhart, H., Marinovic, P.B.: Extensible access control markup language (XACML) specification 3.0 (August 2010)
17. Marinovic, S., Craven, R., Ma, J., Dulay, N.: Rumpole: a flexible break-glass access control model. In: Proceedings of the 16th ACM Symposium on Access Control Models and Technologies, SACMAT 2011, pp. 73–82. ACM, New York (2011)
18. Ni, Q., Bertino, E., Lobo, J.: D-algebra for composing access control policy decisions. In: Proceedings of the 4th International Symposium on Information, Computer, and Communications Security, ASIACCS 2009, pp. 298–309. ACM, New York (2009)
19. De Capitani di Vimercati, S., Bonatti, P., Samarati, P.: An algebra for composing access control policies. ACM Trans. Inf. Syst. Secur. 5(1), 1–35 (2002)
20. Phillips Jr., C.E., Ting, T.C., Demurjian, S.A.: Information sharing and security in dynamic coalitions. In: Proceedings of the Seventh ACM Symposium on Access Control Models and Technologies, SACMAT 2002, pp. 87–96. ACM, New York (2002)
21. Warner, J., Atluri, V.I., Mukkamala, R., Vaidya, J.: Using semantics for automatic enforcement of access control policies among dynamic coalitions. In: Proceedings of the 12th ACM Symposium on Access Control Models and Technologies, SACMAT 2007, pp. 235–244. ACM, New York (2007)
22. Wei, Q., Crampton, J., Beznosov, K., Ripeanu, M.: Authorization recycling in hierarchical rbac systems. ACM Trans. Inf. Syst. Secur. 14(1), 3:1–3:29 (2011)

Indexing Encrypted Documents
for Supporting Efficient Keyword Search

Bijit Hore[1], Ee-Chien Chang[2], Mamadou H. Diallo[1], and Sharad Mehrotra[1]

[1] Donald Bren School of Information and Computer Sciences, University of California, Irvine
[2] School of Computing, National University of Singapore
{bhore,mamadoud,sharad}@ics.uci.edu, changec@comp.nus.edu.sg

Abstract. We propose a scheme to index encrypted documents on an untrusted server and evaluate keyword search queries against them. The proposed scheme provides better security than deterministic encryption schemes and is far more efficient than existing searchable encryption schemes in literature. Furthermore, it provides the user with a set of control parameters to adjust the level of exposure against the efficiency of the indexing scheme. It also allows easy updates and deletions unlike most existing encrypted searching schemes. We carry out preliminary experiments to test the effectiveness of the proposed scheme and give an intuition for the security properties along with a fairly detailed outline of the security formalism that we are currently developing to analyze the security of our scheme.

1 Introduction

Enabling efficient search over encrypted data has been a deeply investigated problem in computer science [15,7,2,5,6,3,14,16,12]. Specifically, the problem of keyword based retrieval over an encrypted document collection has received a lot of attention, especially from the cryptographic research community [15,7,2,5,12,6]. In a typical setup, *Alice* the data owner, wants to store her document collection in an encrypted format with *Bob*, a remote (untrusted) server and be able to access them over the network. She wants to be able to retrieve documents by conducting keyword searches on the collection - given a search keyword w, Bob should be able to return all the documents containing the word w to Alice. However, the problem remains inherently challenging and solutions to date are not scalable to large databases. The barrier to scalability has been primarily one - secure encryption techniques (such as probabilistic encryption schemes that ensure semantic security) do not allow the data to be indexed on the server. The only alternative out there is to employ the much less desirable deterministic encryption that allows the ciphertexts to be indexed and therefore enable keyword matching in logarithmic time[1]. However, deterministic encryption reveals statistical information, such as frequency of keywords which Bob can then use to infer the actual keyword and/or identify a document. Moreover, in all these techniques the association of a keyword to a document is completely revealed to Bob once that particular keyword has been issued as a query by Alice. Therefore, none of the existing techniques are asymptotically secure.

---

[1] The time taken being logarithmic in the number of documents plus the number of actual documents that contain the keyword.

W. Jonker and M. Petković (Eds.): SDM 2012, LNCS 7482, pp. 93–110, 2012.

The above mentioned shortcomings of existing techniques lead us to explore a new approach in this paper. In our approach Alice can control how much information gets revealed about the underlying document-keyword relationship to Bob, and also allow him to evaluate the search queries efficiently. Specifically, we develop a novel technique to encode keyword-document relationship that can be indexed on the server for fast retrieval. As in *bucketization* based approaches proposed previously for range queries [10,9], Alice has to carry out some post-processing to weed out the false positive matches returned by Bob. The average number of false positives depend upon the encoding parameters, which also determines the degree of information loss. In this work, we specifically look at two important kinds of information: keyword-to-document relationship and document-to-document relationship. Our security analysis estimates the confidence with which Bob can establish whether a given keyword is present in a document and if two documents have one or more words in common. Before we go into the description of our technique, we will briefly review the existing techniques for this problem and their performance and security characteristics.

Related Work: Amongst the first papers to address this problem in a non-trivial manner were Song et al. [15]. They proposed an interesting cryptographic technique that prevented the server from learning any information about the contents of the documents, and yet conduct a keyword search and retrieve the matching documents once the "search capability" was given by the owner. However, their mechanism incurs a computational overhead of $O(Nd)$ for each search, where N is the number of documents in the repository and d is the average number of keywords in a document. This is inherently non-scalable for large repositories. Goh et al. in [7] overcome this limitation by exploiting *Bloom filters* for indexing documents. They reduce the search complexity to $O(N)$ from $O(Nd)$ since now the presence or absence of a word in a document can be detected in $O(1)$ time as opposed to $O(d)$ time as in [15]. One of the few sublinear time algorithm till date is one due to Curtmola et al. [6]. They propose an oblivious inverted-list traversal based technique to retrieve all documents containing the search keyword. The idea is to build a standard inverted keyword list as typically done in information retrieval applications, and then permute the rows corresponding to the keywords (i.e., the headers of each list) as well as the order of the entries in the postings list. The structure of the linked list is protected using cryptographic means: if node u points to node v, the node v is encrypted using a key stored in node u. Given the header node of a linked list, one can iteratively decrypt and obtain the whole list. On the other hand, without the knowledge of the header node, it is computationally difficult to derive useful information. Hence, this provides security in the sense that the server is unable to derive useful information from the encrypted linked lists.

Shortcomings of Existing Techniques: Most previous works focus on adversary who has access to the data-structure but does not have access to the historical queries issued by the user. For instance, in [6], since the query on a word reveals the corresponding header node, a linked list will be revealed after a legitimate query is issued. Likewise, under the method proposed by Goh [7], the hashed value of word is rehashed using the document identity. Although, it is computationally difficult for the server to determine the hashed value associated with the document, once a query on a particular value is issued, the server is able to find the associated documents. Similar problem exists in the technique of [15]. Furthermore, once a trapdoor for a keyword w has been revealed to the server (say, while issuing a search query in the schemes of [15,7]), it has the capability to determine whether w is present in all new documents that are created from that point onwards. As will become clear, our technique is more robust than most of the existing ones in preventing such attacks/inferences by the server. Also, many of these techniques rely too heavily on the client machine for the index creation part, which is traditionally the task of the server. For instance, in [6] the inverted list needs to be built on the client-side, therefore, requiring substantial processing effort on part of the client. Furthermore, this technique cannot support updates and deletions of nodes in an efficient manner. It requires the encrypted data structure to be brought onto the client machine, to be decrypted and then traversed to facilitate the operations. This is clearly infeasible in cases where a substantial fraction of operations consists of updates. Last, but not the least, none of the existing approaches offer any means to trade-off performance for security. Each scheme has a fixed notion of security and corresponding fixed cost-overheads for insertion, updates and deletions operations that are imposed.

Our goal in this paper is to develop a practical technique for keyword retrieval that is tunable - wherein different parameter combinations can be used to tune the tradeoff. Our experimental results illustrate that one is often able to find the parameters that result in a pretty good efficiency as well as high levels of security.

The remainder of the paper is as follows. In the next section, we present some preliminaries detailing our approach and the security analysis. In Section 3 we first present the two randomized techniques followed by detailed security analysis. In the subsequent section we present some preliminary experimental results that show the overheads associated with the color-based indexing mechanism and the relation between performance to security. In section 5 we present an optimal indexing algorithm that can potentially decrease the overheads while providing sufficient security. Finally, we conclude and discuss ongoing and future directions for this work.

2   Preliminaries

Indexing and Search Mechanism: The keyword search algorithm has two basic phases - *setup* and *query evaluation*.

Setup Phase: Given a set of documents $\mathbf{D} = \{d_1, \ldots, d_n\}$, the dataset is pre-processed with the Alice's secret key k, giving an index structure $\mathbf{I}$ and a sequence of encrypted documents, $\widetilde{\mathbf{D}} = \langle \tilde{d}_1 = E_k(d_1), \ldots, \tilde{d}_n = E_k(d_n) \rangle$.

Traditionally, where no encryption is involved, Alice would simply upload her documents, which would then get parsed and indexed by Bob (server). The unique searchable keywords are extracted from the document. The server stores an inverted keyword list data structure where a list is maintained for every word in the dictionary. The list corresponding to a keyword consists of all the documents containing the keyword. For text data stored in relational tables, the inverted list contains row ids (rids) of the records that contain the specified keyword in the text field specified in the query. This is called a *postings list*. An inverted list facilitates efficient retrieval of documents containing a specified keyword(s). For instance, given a multi-keyword query where all keywords need to be present (AND queries), the server computes the intersection of the respective lists of rids (postings lists) and the resulting set of documents are retrieved. Similarly, for OR queries the union of the respective rid lists needs to be computed. Fast algorithms have been developed for such merging of large rid lists [13,11].

However, when a document is encrypted the server is unable to extract the keywords in the usual manner, and therefore the user needs to provide auxiliary information to facilitate indexing of some sort. (Note, in many of the cryptographic approaches like those proposed in [15,7], there is no concept of server-side indexing. Instead, Alice generates the trapdoor (using her secret key and the plaintext of the keyword) which is revealed to Bob when a query consisting of the keyword is issued. Bob then scans the entries to detect the correct matches. Only Curtmola's technique [6] is different, but it needs to be built on the client!). In the approach presented in this paper, we will see how some simple hashing like techniques (we call it *coloring*) can allow the user to play a nice tradeoff between information revealed and search overhead.

Query Evaluation Phase: Given a word w and the secret key k, the user generates and sends a query q to the server. The server, from q and the index structure $\mathbf{I}$, obtain a set of indices $i_1, \ldots, i_q$. The documents in $\tilde{\mathbf{D}}$ with the indices, i.e. $\{\tilde{d}_{i_1}, \ldots, \tilde{d}_{i_q}\}$ are then sent to the user.

In this paper, we focus on creation of the index $\mathbf{I}$ to enable the server to efficiently retrieve documents against a query that is issued by the user. The index of an encrypted document is a set of colors which encode the presence of the keywords while not giving out their exact identities. The server can use any suitable data structure to index the encrypted documents by their color codes. The main operations it has to carry out is "retrieval of all documents indexed by a color and being able to efficiently compute the union of multiple such color lists". It will become clear soon as to why these two operations are required. In its simplest form, given a query keyword, Alice computes its color code and sends it to the server. The server then determines all documents whose index entries have at least one of the specified colors and returns these to Alice. This method will retrieve some false positives which Alice would subsequently need to weed out. Note, however, this does not leave out any true positives.

Overview of Security Analysis: The server keeps the dataset $\tilde{\mathbf{D}}$, the index structure $\mathbf{I}$ and a sequence of queries $\mathbf{Q}$ issued by the user. The adversary's goal is to derive "useful" information. We consider two forms of information desired by the adversary: *document to document* relationship and *word to document* relationship.

Document to Document: Given two indices i_1 and i_2, the adversary wants to infer the relationship between d_{i_1} and d_{i_2}. One particular relationship we study in this paper is whether $d_{i_1} \cap d_{i_2} \neq \emptyset$, that is, both contain at least one common word. Note that under method by Goh et al [7] and Curtmola et al [6], if the observed queries contain a common word, then the adversary know for sure that there are common words. When there is noise in the query-result as in our scheme, even if a query on the common word has been issued, there is uncertainty in their relationship. An interesting question is, whether randomization helps in hiding the relationships?

Word to Document: Given the color code $code(w)$ of a word w (this is typically, a set of s colors where s is fixed for all words) and a color index i_d of a document d, the adversary wants to infer whether the word w is present in d or not. We will show that larger s implies more uncertainty has to be overcome in determining the word-document relationship.

Next, we describe our basic coloring based indexing approach and carry out a deeper security analysis of these schemes.

3   Basic Coloring Algorithm and Security Analysis

Let us begin with some of the notations we will be using in this section. We then describe a baseline randomized algorithm, a simple enhancement of the baseline algorithm and finally, a detailed security analysis of these schemes.

Notations:

w, w_i: A word.

$\mathcal{W}$:   Dictionary, which is a collection of words.

N: Total number of words, i.e. $|\mathcal{W}|$.

d: A document, which is a collection of words.

D: Set of documents.

M: Number of documents, i.e. $|\mathbf{D}|$.

t: Number of words in a document.

A: The incidence matrix of words and documents.

C: Total number of colors.

$code(w)$: The set of colors assigned to a word.

s: Number of colors assigned to a word,
        i.e. $|code(w)| = s$ for all w's.

c, c_d: Number of colors assigned to a document (d).

$\mathcal{S}$:   A selection algorithm that, on input a
        collection of words, outputs a set of colors.

C_d: Expected number of colors per document,
        i.e. $\mathcal{E}[|\mathcal{S}(d)|]$.

Bold font letters refer to the random variable, for example $\mathbf{W}$ is the random variable on a word w.

3.1   Simple Randomized Approach

Index Building: Given the dictionary $\mathcal{W}$, Alice assigns a color code $code(w)$ (i.e., a set of s distinct colors) to each word $w \in \mathcal{W}$ which is chosen at random from the set of C colors. Given a document d, Alice extracts all the indexable keywords from d and adds the corresponding color to the document's color-index c_d. The actual document is then encrypted and appended to its color-index and shipped off to Bob for indexing and storage.

Search: For a query keyword w, Alice determines its color-code and sends it to Bob. Bob, then retrieves all documents whose index contains the specified color and returns them to Alice. The returned set is bound to contain all the documents that truly contain the search keyword. Alice, then decrypts the documents and checks for the presence of the search term and discards the false positives.

Note, Alice could easily eliminate all false positive retrievals (with probability very close to 1) by composing the above color-based technique with a cryptographic scheme such as Goh's [7]. For instance, she could simply retrieve to the client, the encrypted Bloom filters corresponding to the color-matched documents. Then, decrypt these Bloom filters, determine the exact set of documents containing the search keyword and fetch exactly those from the server. Bloom filters being much smaller in size than the corresponding documents, the color-based index would then act as a pure indexing mechanism, used simply to speed up the $O(N)$ complexity of the cryptographic protocol. However, this would also deny the user the additional benefit of "hiding the access patterns", which is naturally provided by the color-based retrieval mechanism.

The cost of our indexing scheme is proportional to the number of false positive documents that are retrieved. Like hashing, the number of collisions will be determined by the total number of colors C used. We will present a more detailed performance analysis later in the section.

3.2 Enhanced Randomized Algorithm

Now consider a slightly more complex technique, one where Alice chooses s $(s > 1)$ distinct colors at random as the color code of each word in the dictionary. To encode the presence of a word in a document d, she picks $s' \leq s$ random color from this set of s colors and adds it to the color-index of d. To search on a keyword w, Alice specifies all the s colors in its code and Bob returns all documents whose color-index has at least s' colors from this set. As before, Alice would need to sift through the returned set of documents and discard the false positives.

Note that the proposed technique can be seen as a general form of a Bloom filter based representation of a set. If we set $s' = s$, then this color-index of a document is exactly that of a Bloom filter with C bits[2]. The main benefit of the enhanced approach is that it affords more control of the security to the owner. Consider the case when $s' = 1$. Here, given a document d, for every word w we choose one color from $code(w)$ to include in color-index of d ($index(d)$). Depending upon the value of s and C, the proposed scheme can obfuscate the color-word relation in d. For instance, given n words in a document, there is a certain (non-zero) probability of multiple words mapping to the same color in d's index. The probability of such collisions can be controlled more effectively using the parameters s, C and s'.

3.3 Security Model

Adversarial Model and Security Analysis: The optimal adversary is a *maximum likelihood decoder*, who makes his choice based on the conditional probabilities given the index structure and the queries. However, it is difficult to derive such conditional probabilities, especially in practice where the underlying distribution on the database is not known. Hence, in this paper, we consider specific attacks and empirically determine the

---

[2] It is easy to see that the random choice of s colors for code can be simulated by using s different hash functions with range $[0, s - 1]$ and the keyword as the key.

right values of parameters that will leak the minimum amount of information to such attackers.

Full versus Partial View: As mentioned in the introduction, the algorithms we studied essentially maintain a sequence of linked lists, and it is possible to protect the structure using method described by Curtmola et al. [6]. The nodes along a particular linked list would be revealed to the server once a query containing information of the header-node is issued. We can have two settings, *protected* and *unprotected*. When the index structure is not protected, the server has the full view of the index structure even without knowing any queries. When the index structure is protected, the server only see the linked list revealed by the queries, that is, the server only has a *partial view*. In this paper, for security analysis, we simply consider servers as having full view of the index, which is the worst case assumption.

Distribution of Dataset: In our analysis, we consider a simplified distribution of the dataset and conduct empirical studies on a dataset where the documents are modeled as follows: Let $\mathcal{D}$ be the distribution on the dataset $\mathbf{D}$, and $\mathcal{Q}$ be the distribution on the set of queries. Under the simplified model, the dataset consists of M documents, where each document contain, possibly with repetition, t words. The words are uniformly and randomly chosen from a dictionary $\mathcal{W}$ of N words. Let us denote this distribution as $\mathcal{D}_{M,t,N}$.

Next, we present the security analysis for one of the attack models, "word-document relationship".

3.4   Word-Document Relationship

Now, we look at what the adversary can learn about the relationship between a document and a word, given the color-index of the document and color code of the word. In our model, the adversary is an entity who has access to the server. Therefore, his knowledge is exactly the same as what the server sees. For instance, when the search query $q = code(w)$ is issued by the user, the server (adversary) only gets to see the s colors in $code(w)$. Now, he knows that some $s' \leq s$ of these colors have been used to encode the presence of w in each document that contains w. However, since color codes of words may overlap, the adversary cannot be certain about the presence of the word (w in this case) in a document even if he sees that some s' colors ($\subseteq q$) are present in its color-index. In the following analysis, we try to determine the average probability (*confidence*) with which a particular kind of adverary (i.e., a maximum-likelihood decoder) would make the correct guess. Such an adversary guesses the answer (presence or absence of the word in a document) by estimating the likelihood of the observed number of common colors between q and $index(d)$.

We analyze only the enhanced randomized algorithm for the case where $s' = 1$, i.e., when exactly one color from the code of each word in d is added to $index(d)$. (Note, the simple randomized algorithm described in Section 3.1 is a special case). Given a positive integer t denoting the number of distinct words in a document, a dictionary of keywords $\mathcal{W}$, $code(\cdot)$, γ ($0 \leq \gamma \leq 1$) and an algorithm $\mathcal{S}$ (denoting the enhanced randomized algorithm), consider the following game between an adversary and a user.

GAME(W-D): *Let w_0 be a randomly chosen word from $\mathcal{W}$. The user chooses a bit b where $b = 0$ with probability γ. The user next chooses a document d with t words. When $b = 0$, d is a collections of t randomly chosen words from $\mathcal{W}$. Otherwise, when $b = 1$, user constructs d as a collections of $t - 1$ randomly chosen words together with w_0. The adversary, when given $\mathcal{S}(d)$ and $code(w_0)$, outputs either 0 or 1.*

We say that the color assignment gives at most δ advantage[3] if, for any adversary, the probability of the adversary's output equal to b is at most $\max\{\gamma, 1 - \gamma\} + \delta$.

Note, there is no constraint on the adversary's running time. Hence, this is an information theoretic notion. When $b = 0$, there is a chance that the t randomly chosen words contain w_0. While one could modify the formulation so that the document will not contain w_0, we decide on the stated formulation for ease of analysis.

Analysis of Enhanced Randomized Algorithm w.r.t. GAME(W-D): Let us consider the randomized scheme with $|code(w)| = s$ for all w's, and the total number of colors is C. We consider any $code(\cdot)$ that chooses s distinct colors from C for each word in the dictionary (however, two different words may share colors in their code). Hence, the process of randomly choosing a word w and then computing $code(w)$, is equivalent to randomly choosing a set of s colors from C. In the analysis, we consider a modified randomized strategy that leaks slightly more information - if the same color is selected for h different words in the document, the color appears h times in the color-index of the document. Thus $\mathcal{S}(d)$ is a multi-set.

Given $f = \mathcal{S}(d)$, the color-index of document d, the optimal adversary amounts to a maximum likelihood decoder, who chooses the output bit corresponding to the larger of the following two probabilities:

$$p_0 = Prob(\mathbf{B} = 0 \mid \mathcal{S}(\mathbf{D}) = f), \text{ and} \tag{1}$$
$$p_1 = Prob(\mathbf{B} = 1 \mid \mathcal{S}(\mathbf{D}) = f). \tag{2}$$

Given f, the probability that the adversary succeeds is the maximum among p_0 and p_1. We want to find the expected probability taken over all possible f's.

Let k be the number of common colors in f and $code(w_0)$. Note, due to symmetry, the probability (1) is the same for two different f's when they have the same number of common colors with $code(w_0)$. Hence, we can rewrite (1) & (2) as:

$$p_0 = Prob(\mathbf{B} = 0 \mid |f \cap code(w_0)| = k), \text{ and}$$
$$p_1 = Prob(\mathbf{B} = 1 \mid |f \cap code(w_0)| = k).$$

Given that $\mathbf{B} = 0$, the number of common colors k follows a binomial distribution with t trials and probability $\frac{s}{C}$ where C is the total number of colors in the universe. To see that, let $\mathbf{X}_i = 1$ if the color selected by $\mathcal{S}$ for the i-th word is also in $code(w_0)$, and 0 otherwise. As the algorithm randomly chooses a color from a word and assigns it to the document, $Prob(\mathbf{X}_i = 1) = \frac{s}{C}$. Since $\mathbf{K}|(\mathbf{B} = 0)$ is $\sum_{i=1}^{t} \mathbf{X}_i$, and $\mathbf{X}_i$ are i.i.d, the distribution $\mathbf{K}|(\mathbf{B} = 0)$ follows $B(t, \frac{s}{C})$. By similar argument, $\mathbf{K}|(\mathbf{B} = 1)$ follows the distribution $1 + B(t - 1, \frac{s}{C})$.

---

[3] As δ is typically small, we sometime use $-\log_2(\delta)$ for comparisons, and seek for a scheme with large $-\log_2(\delta)$.

Hence the task of the adversary is same as distinguishing the two distributions $B(t, \frac{s}{C})$ and $1 + B(t - 1, \frac{s}{C})$. Let us write $P_0(x) = Prob(\mathbf{K} = x | \mathbf{B} = 0)$ and $P_1(x) = Prob(\mathbf{K} = x | \mathbf{B} = 1)$. Let us consider the case where $\gamma \leq \frac{1}{2}$. Note, while the total number of common words between $code(w_0)$ and $\mathcal{S}(D)$ cannot be greater than s, for ease of analysis, we count the common colors as many times as they occur in f. Therefore, the summation below goes from 0 to t instead of 0 to s. Now, the probability that the maximum likelihood decoder gives the correct answer is:

$$\mathcal{E}_{k \leftarrow \mathbf{K}}[\max\{Prob(\mathbf{B} = 0 \mid \mathbf{K} = k), Prob(\mathbf{B} = 1 \mid \mathbf{K} = k)\}]$$

$$= \sum_{k=0}^{t} Prob(\mathbf{K} = k) \cdot$$

$$\max\{Prob(\mathbf{B} = 0 \mid \mathbf{K} = k), Prob(\mathbf{B} = 1 \mid \mathbf{K} = k)\}$$

$$= \sum_{k=0}^{t} \max\{P_0(k)Prob(\mathbf{B} = 0), P_1(k)Prob(\mathbf{B} = 1)\}$$

$$= \sum_{k=0}^{t} \max\{\gamma P_0(k), (1 - \gamma)P_1(k)\} \tag{3}$$

Let x_0 be the smallest integer where $(1 - \gamma)P_1(x) > \gamma P_0(x)$ for all $x \geq x_0$. Then we can rewrite (3) as

$$\left(\gamma \sum_{k=0}^{x_0-1} P_0(k) + (1 - \gamma) \sum_{k=x_0}^{t} P_1(k) \right)$$

$$= (1 - \gamma) + \gamma F\left(x_0 - 1; t, \frac{s}{C}\right) - (1 - \gamma)F\left(x_0 - 2; t - 1, \frac{s}{C}\right) \tag{4}$$

Where $F()$ is the cumulative density function for binomial distribution. The factor $F\left(x_0 - 2; t - 1, \frac{s}{C}\right)$ in the last term comes from the fact that the case $\mathbf{B} = 1$ results in a distribution of the form "$1 + Binomial(t - 1, s/C)$". Therefore, subtracting 1 gives us a cumulative distribution with the upper-bound of the summation reduced by 1.

Analysis of SingleColor Scheme: Consider the scheme where $|code(w)| = 1$, i.e. $s = 1$. It can be shown that the probability of success is:

$$\frac{1}{2} + \frac{1}{2}\left(\frac{C - 1}{C}\right)^t$$

$$\approx \frac{1}{2} + \frac{1}{2}\left(1 - \frac{t}{C}\right)$$

Discussion: The model assumes that the dictionary give all possible set of colors, each with equal probability. In cases where the dictionary is small, the bounds hold when the adversary only knows the color of the given word and document. In the above analysis, the term for $k = 0$ signifies the case when there are no colors in common between the code of a word and the document's color index. This would be the case for a large number of cases where it is trivial for the adversary to guess that the particular word is not present in the document. Leaving out this term from expression 4 would only decrease the advantage of an adversary of making the correct guess in the really interesting cases, i.e., when there is at least one color in common.

In the appendix section, we present some analysis of the other attack model mentioned earlier, i.e., "document-to-document relationship".

4 Experimental Evaluation

We provide some preliminary experimental results that illustrate the cost-overheads associated with the color-based indexing scheme, specifically, as a function of security. However, we are only considering security in the word-document sense. Recall, higher the ratio s/C implies greater security, where s is the size of the color-code of a word and C is the total number of colors in the universe. Assuming $s/C < 0.5$, it is easy to see that the advantage of the adversary decreases with increasing value of s. In short, higher the number of colors used in the code of a word, higher is the security on an average. (This holds true assuming all documents are sampled from the same distribution).

We use the following parameters for all our experiments:
Number of Documents = 10,000
Total Keywords in Documents = 1,070,450
Average Keywords/Document = 107.045
Keywords in Dictionary = 27,830
Number of Queries = 1,000
We also used all possible combinations of 5 different sets of colors (having 2000, 4000, 6000, 8000, and 10000 different colors respectively) and 6 different sizes of code-sets for words (1, 5, 10, 15, 20, 25).

Results for *Randomized Coloring* Algorithm

Precision versus Security: We measure precision (accuracy) as *Number of correct docs / Number of docs retrieved*. We executed 1000 queries on the data set, and counted the number of documents retrieved and the total number of correct documents. Then, we measured the ratio of the number of correct documents and the total number of documents retrieved. We plotted this against the size of the code-set (s) for different values of C. Recall, our measure of security is s/C. The plot is shown in Figure 1.

Savings versus Security: We measure the savings as the # Total docs - # docs retrieved. We computed the average saving by taking the difference between the number of documents retrieved by the algorithm for each of the 1,000 queries and the total number documents in the repository (10,000). The plot is shown in Figure 2. In particular, it gives us an idea of how much savings one can expect over typical $O(N)$ schemes such as Goh's [7] by using the color-based index.

Size: This plot shows the # Documents per color for the various runs (i.e., different code-set sizes). This is shown in Figure 3.

Cover: This plot (Figure 4) Number of Colors Per Document on an average as a funtion of the code-set size.

The last two plots show (as expected), the size of the inverted lists and the document indices do not vary with the size of the code-sets.

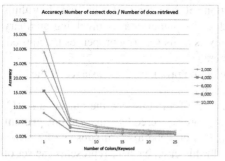

Fig. 1. Randomized Coloring: Accuracy as a function of code-set size

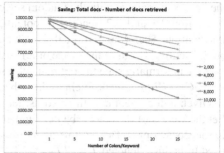

Fig. 2. Randomized Coloring: Savings (# of documents eliminated) as a function of code-set size

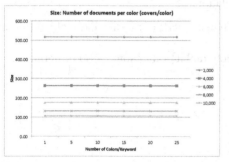

Fig. 3. Randomized Coloring: Size of inverted color-lists

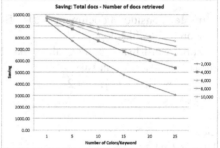

Fig. 4. Randomized Coloring: Average size of color-index of documents

5   Optimal Coloring Algorithm

One can see that the number of queries on which a document is retrieved is proportional to the number of colors in its index (c). Therefore, making the index smaller is beneficial both for Alice and Bob. For Alice, smaller number of false positives mean lesser post-processing. For Bob, a smaller index means maintaining smaller lists/sets of colors per document. Given that more than one word in a document may have the same set of colors in its code-set, if we select smartly, the number of total colors needed to cover each word in the document can be significantly reduced. However, the question one has to ask is whether such an attempt at "folding" (reducing) the set of colors reduces security?

Recall, greater the value of s/C (while it remains substantially smaller than 0.5), smaller is the advantage of the adversary. Therefore, the folding mechanism can in fact, be seen as a mechanism to simultaneously increase efficiency as well as security of the color-based indexing scheme. In any case, the proposed optimal algorithm is certainly a better choice in trying to reduce the cost overheads than naively reducing the value s or increasing value of C. Nonetheless, the optimal selection of colors tends to reduce the benefit associated with the random selections of the naive and enhanced algorithms of Section 3.1 and 3.2, leading to potential side channel attacks involving auxiliary information. Therefore, a more thorough analysis of its security properties is required, but it is currently out of the scope of this paper.

We can formally state the optimal color selection problem as an instance of the *Minimum Cost Hitting Set* problem as described below.

Given a document d with n words, let the set of all colors be the universal set C. Let the weight of the color c be the number of words covered by c that are **not present** in the document d. Denote this as $weight(c)$[4]. Let T be a set of subsets of C (that need to be hit), denoted $T = \{T_1, \ldots, T_n\}$. In this case, each T_i represents the set of colors in the code for word w_i in d. Then, it is easy to see that solving the *minimum weighted hitting set* problem for the above instance will ensure that the colors selected will cover all the words in the document at least once and minimizing the weight will result in minimizing the number of words covered that are not present in the document. The following example illustrates the formulation.

Example: Consider 3 documents - d1: {Bob likes cats}; d2: {Alice likes rabbits}; d3: {Bob and Alice like dogs}.

Global word-list: {cat, dog, alice, like, bob, rabbit} (after some form of normalization and stop-word removal)
$C = \{c_1, c_2, c_3, c_4, c_5\}$, $s = 2$,
$D_w = $ cat, $< c1, c2 >$
dog, $< c3, c4 >$
Alice, $< c1, c5 >$
like, $< c2, c4 >$
Bob, $< c3, c5 >$
rabbit, $< c1, c3 >$

For d_1 we will have the following matrix shown in figure 5. The marked rows are shown with an arrow.

There are many candidate selections that cover each one of "Bob", "like" and "cat" at least once (in general, we can require at least k colors to be chosen out of the s in $code(w)$), for example, (c_1, c_2), (c_2, c_3), (c_1, c_4, c_5), (c_2, c_5) etc., all are feasible covers. We need to select one that minimizes coverage of non-marked rows. Therefore (c_2, c_5) is an optimal color-code for document d_1 as it leads to only one extra word's coverage (of "Alice" which is not in the document). The selected colors are the highlighted columns and the circles in each column show the words in document d_1 that are covered by that color. The un-circled "X" in each highlighted column contributes to the cost of the chosen scheme. Similarly, select the color-code for the remaining 2

---

[4] The weight of a color for a document is supposed to reflect the likelihood of the document being a false-positive match for any keyword (query) associated with that color. As a concrete example, let the color c be associated with the keywords "cat", "bat" and "mat". If the document d contains only the word "cat" in it and color c is chosen to be in its cover (C_d), then assuming that all keywords are equally likely to be issued as a search term, $weight(c)$ in this case = 2. This captures the fact that whenever keywords "bat" and "mat" are issued as the query term, this document will also be retrieved falsely.

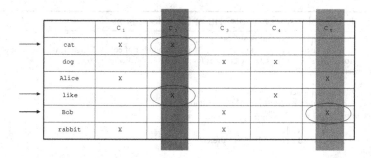

Fig. 5. Example of color based coverage of words

documents independently and annotate the document entry on the server with its corresponding color-code. The search is carried out as described in the algorithm above.◇

We now present the main algorithm for creation of the color index.

Minimum-Weight Color Indexing of Document: 1. Choose parameters: C (set of colors,) $|C| = t$ (# colors); m (size of the Bloom filter for each document), s (the # colors to be chosen for each word).

2. Create the word dictionary $D_w = \{(w, C_w)\}$ where C_w is the set of s colors assigned to the word w (use some random assignment technique for creating the C_w's). We refer to C_w as $code(w)$. Let there be N words in the dictionary.

3. For each document d, extract the list of keywords, call it L_d. Let $|L_d| = r_d$.

(We now select the unique color for each word under which it will be encoded)

4. For coloring a document d, create a $(N \times t)$ matrix where each row corresponds to a unique word in the dictionary and each column corresponds to a unique color from C. For each row insert a "X" in the column corresponding to every color in its code-set.

5. Mark the r_d rows corresponding to the words in the document (these are the rows that need to be covered).

6. (Optimization problem) Select a set of columns (colors) such that each marked row in matrix has at least k intersections with the chosen columns and the number of intersections with the unmarked rows are minimized. A row "i" is said to intersect with column "j" if there is a "X" in the cell (i, j) of the matrix. Output the set of colors corresponding to the chosen columns.

7. Now, take the union of all colors chosen in step 6 and set it as the color-code of the document d (denote it as C_d).

The optimal color selection step (step 6) is done according to the algorithm below.

The color selection algorithm is similar to the greedy algorithm for set cover problems where in each iteration we choose the next best available candidate, i.e., one that hits (covers) the maximum number of keywords that are not already covered. When a cost is associated with a color as in our case, the best candidate (in each iteration) is the color that maximizes the ratio of the number of new words covered to the cost associated with the color. We will refer to this ratio as the *benefit* of the candidate. The minimum-cost hitting set problem being equivalent to the minimum-cost set cover problem, we know that Algorithm 1 gives a solution that is within $1 + lnN_D$ times the optimal. Here N_D denotes the number of words in document D.

Algorithm 1. 1st color selection algorithm for a document

1: **Input**:W_D,M,Weight$[1, \ldots, M]$,$ColorCodes_{dict}$;
2: /* W_D is the list of distinct words in document D, M is total number of colors, Weight[i] is the weight of color 'i'
    w.r.t D, $ColorCodes_{dict}$ is the set of color-codes for all words in the dictionary */;
3: **Output**: cover;
4: Initialize $cover \leftarrow \phi$;
5: **while** $\exists \, w \in W_D$ that is not covered **do**
6:      find color $c^* \notin cover$ s.t. $benefit(c^*)$ is maximized;
7:      where $benefit(c) = \frac{\#\text{NEW WORDS COVERED BY c}}{Weight[c]}$;
8:      $cover \leftarrow cover \cup \{c^*\}$;
9:      Mark all newly covered words in W_D as 'covered';
10: **end while**
11: Return $cover$;

Search: When searching for a keyword, look up its code-set and ask the server to retrieve all documents whose index contains one or more of these colors.

6 Conclusions and Future Work

In this paper we proposed a new "bucketization" (hashing) based technique for indexing of encrypted documents on an untrusted server. The goal is to facilitate more efficient retrieval of documents than is currently possible for encrypted document, i.e., when the document contents cannot be revealed to the server. Existing techniques are either inefficient in terms of search (requiring time linear in the number of documents) or need the client to do a lot of pre-processing and indexing work before writing the encrypted document to the server. Our scheme is more secure than any deterministic keyword-encryption based schemes in literature. It is also more efficient and far more practical than pure cryptographic approaches that strive to achieve "semantic security" of representation. In fact, our scheme is more secure than most others in hiding of access pattern corresponding to queries. It is able to obfuscate access patterns better since it retrieves excess records from the server. Additonally, our mechanism provides a parametic way to trade off degree of security with efficiency by proper adjustment of a few design parameters. And, last but not the least, our technique is completely composable with other, more secure encryption schemes – our scheme can be used to pre-process metadata corresponding to a larger fraction of documents that satisfy the query, and then retrieve a smaller, more accurate subset to the client, which can then be decrypted and matched against the queries.

However, at present, our security analysis is far from complete. In this paper, we have included only a snippet of the approach we are currently developing for security analysis. Since, there is not much prior work on formally analyzing the security guarantees of hashing-based techniques, this is a significant component of our ongoing research. Specifically, the security properties of the optimal indexing algorithm discussed in Section 5 has not been analyzed. While optimization does bring down the "randomness" of the scheme, the inherent entropy of large document repositories would likely make such optimizations harmless from security point of view. However, a more rigorous security analysis is certainly desirable for all indexing algorithms and therefore, it remains an important direction for our future work. Also, we plan to carry out more extensive experimentations with larger document repositories and more complicated queries, like conjunctive and disjunctive queries. The efficient indexing of color codes and computation of union and intersection of postings list is also an important component of our experimental framewok which is currently under development.

References

1. Ballard, L., Kamara, S., Monrose, F.: Achieving Efficient Conjunctive Keyword Searches over Encrypted Data. In: Qing, S., Mao, W., López, J., Wang, G. (eds.) ICICS 2005. LNCS, vol. 3783, pp. 414–426. Springer, Heidelberg (2005)
2. Boneh, D., Di Crescenzo, G., Ostrovsky, R., Persiano, G.: Public Key Encryption with Keyword Search. In: Cachin, C., Camenisch, J.L. (eds.) EUROCRYPT 2004. LNCS, vol. 3027, pp. 506–522. Springer, Heidelberg (2004)
3. Boneh, D., Waters, B.: Conjunctive, Subset, and Range Queries on Encrypted Data. In: Vadhan, S.P. (ed.) TCC 2007. LNCS, vol. 4392, pp. 535–554. Springer, Heidelberg (2007)
4. Briney, A.: Information Security Industry Survey (2001), http://www.infosecuritymag.com/archives2001.shtml (cited in October 2002)
5. Chang, Y.-C., Mitzenmacher, M.: Privacy Preserving Keyword Searches on Remote Encrypted Data. In: Ioannidis, J., Keromytis, A.D., Yung, M. (eds.) ACNS 2005. LNCS, vol. 3531, pp. 442–455. Springer, Heidelberg (2005)
6. Curtmola, R., Garay, J., Kamara, S., Ostrovsky, R.: Searchable symmetric encryption: improved definitions and efficient constructions. In: CCS (2006)
7. Goh, E.: Secure Indexes (2003) (unpubished manuscript)
8. Golle, P., Staddon, J., Waters, B.: Secure Conjunctive Keyword Search over Encrypted Data. In: Jakobsson, M., Yung, M., Zhou, J. (eds.) ACNS 2004. LNCS, vol. 3089, pp. 31–45. Springer, Heidelberg (2004)
9. Hore, B., Mehrotra, S., Canim, M., Kantarcioglu, M.: Secure Multidimensional Range Queries over Outsourced Data. VLDB Journal (2012)
10. Hore, B., Mehrotra, S., Tsudik, G.: A Privacy-Preserving Index for Range Queries. In: VLDB (2004)
11. Krauthgamer, R., Mehta, A., Raman, V., Rudra, A.: Greedy list intersection. In: ICDE (2008)
12. Li, J., Omiecinski, E.: Efficiency and Security Trade-Off in Supporting Range Queries on Encrypted Databases. In: DBSec (2005)
13. Raman, V., Qiao, L., Han, W., Narang, I., Chen, Y.: Lazy, adaptive rid-list intersection, and its application to index anding. In: SIGMOD (2007)
14. Shi, E., Bethencourt, J., Chan, H.T.-H., Song, D.X., Perrig, A.: Multi-Dimensional Range Query over Encrypted Data. In: IEEE S&P (2007)
15. Song, D.X., Wagner, D., Perrig, A.: Practical techniques for searches on encrypted data. In: IEEE S&P (2000)
16. Waters, B., Balfanz, D., Durfee, G., Smetters, D.: Building and encrypted and searchable audit log. In: NDSS (2004)

Appendix

Document-Document Relationship

We also present some insights into how the adversary may try to glean information about the Document-Document relationships. This corresponds to the popular "ciphertext-only" analysis in cryptanalysis. Here, the goal is to analyse what the adversary is able to determine regarding the overlap (common words) between two documents by simply looking at their color indexes. However, we provide no metric for measuring the security of our scheme against such an attack.

Let us consider this adversary's task: Given an index structure I that is generated from a dataset sampled from a distribution D, a set of encrypted documents $\langle I, \widetilde{D} \rangle$, a sequence of observed queries Q, and two document indices i_1, i_2, an adversary decides whether the plaintext of the encrypted documents $\widetilde{d}_{i_1}, \widetilde{d}_{i_2}$ have at least one common word. Let us write the strategy employed by the adversary as

$$Adv(I, \langle i_1, i_2 \rangle, Q)$$

where the output is in $\{\text{Yes}, \text{No}\}$.

We quantify the effectiveness of *Adv* through the following game between *Adv* and an challenger:

GAME_GENERIC: *The challenger obtains a randomly generated database, preprocesses it with a random secret key, and outputs an index structure I. Next, the challenger flips a coin b. If head, he selects a pair of indices $\langle i_1, i_2 \rangle$, randomly and uniformly among all possible pairs of documents sharing at least one common word. Otherwise, the pair are selected uniformly selected among all possible pairs of documents that do not have common word. The challenger next sends I, i_1, i_2 to the adversary, and the adversary guesses the value of b.*

We call the probability that the adversary give the correct guess its *effectiveness*. A dishonest server wants a strategy that maximizes its effectiveness. Note that the randomness involved include how the dataset, the secret key, the observed query and the pairs of indices are chosen. Let us call the probability the adversary gives the wrong guess given that b is head, its *false reject*. Likewise, let us call and the probability the adversary gives the wrong guess given that b is tail, its *false accept*. It is easy to see that,

$$effectiveness = 1 - (false\ accept + false\ reject)/2 \qquad (5)$$

Hence, equivalently, a dishonest server wants to minimize the sum of its false accept and false reject.

Information Utilized by the Adversary: Let us first consider the case where the server has full view of the index-structure. From the index structure, the server can determine the colors assigned to each document by bucketization. Let us consider an adversary who makes decision based on (1) c, the number of common colors assigned to both documents, and (2) c_{d_1} and c_{d_2}, the total number of colors assigned to documents d_1 and d_2 respectively. Essentially, the adversary determines a threshold T and decides the two documents have common words iff $c \geq T$. The technical challenge now is in deriving the threshold, given that we know the distribution $\mathcal{D}$, and color sets c, c_{d_1} and c_{d_2}.

The above strategies do not use any information of the observed queries. The observed set of queries $\mathbf{Q}$ is useful (from the dishonest server's viewpoint) as it reveals the index structure if the linked list is provided using cryptographic mean. However, we assume that the server already has the full view of the index structure, and hence $\mathbf{Q}$ plays a negligible role. Nevertheless, $\mathbf{Q}$ could provide other information, for instance, how many words being allocated a particular color etc. However, we will not discuss the possible role of $\mathbf{Q}$ in the remainder of this paper.

Threshold for Naive Randomized Algorithm: Recall that the adversary, given the two indices (i_1, i_2), is able to derive c_{d_1} and c_{d_2}, i.e., the number of colors assigned to d_{i_1} and d_{i_2} respectively, and also c, the number of common colors. Let us consider this variant of GAME_GENERIC described earlier:

GAME(D-D): *The challenger tosses a coin b. If b is head, the challenger carries out process P1 as described below, otherwise, the challenger carries out the process P2. The colors assigned to the two documents are passed to the adversary. The adversary guesses the outcome of the coin toss.*

P1: Randomly pick c_{d_1} (without replacement) colors for d_{i_1} and c_{d_2} colors for d_{i_2}.
P2: Randomly pick a color for d_{i_1} and d_{i_2}. Randomly pick $c_{d_1} - 1$ (without replacement) colors for d_{i_1} and $c_{d_2} - 1$ colors for d_{i_2}.

Note that P1 corresponds to the case where the two documents have a common word, while P2 corresponds to the case where they do not have common word. The effectiveness of the adversary can be defined as before (equation 5). To maximize his effectiveness, the optimal adversary picks the choice that is most likely given the observed number of common colors, similar to the *ideal observer decoding* in coding theory. Consider the two following probabilities:

$$Prob(\mathbf{B} = \text{head} | \mathbf{C} = c) \tag{6}$$

$$Prob(\mathbf{B} = \text{tail} \mid \mathbf{C} = c) \tag{7}$$

The adversary decides that the coin tossed is head (i.e. there is a common word) if and only if the probability (6) is larger than proability (7). Since the prior probability of $b = $ head is same as the prior probability of $b = $ tail, it is equivalent to comparing the two likelihoods:

$$Prob(\mathbf{C} = c | \mathbf{B} = \text{head})$$

$$Prob(\mathbf{C} = c | \mathbf{B} = \text{tail})$$

It can be shown that

$$\frac{Prob(\mathbf{C} = c | \mathbf{B} = \text{tail})}{Prob(\mathbf{C} = c | \mathbf{B} = \text{head})} = \frac{cC}{c_{d_1} c_{d_2}}$$

where C is the total number of colors. Thus, if $\frac{cC}{c_{d_1}c_{d_2}} < 1$, the adversary decides that there is a common word. In other words, the threshold is set to be:

$$T = \frac{c_{d_1}c_{d_2}}{C} \tag{8}$$

Role of k in Enhanced Randomized Algorithm: Recall, k (out of possible s colors in the code) is the number of colors used for indexing a word in the document. If two documents indeed have exactly one common word, the probability that this word is assigned to different colors in the two document is $1 - \frac{1}{k}$. In other words, the false reject is at least $1 - \frac{1}{k}$. As an approximation, assuming that there is no false accept, the effectiveness of the adversary can be approximated by

$$0.5 + \frac{1}{2k}.$$

Therefore, security clearly increases (effectiveness decreases) as the value of k increases, i.e., the number of colors used for each word increases.

Secure Quasi-Realtime Collaborative Editing over Low-Cost Storage Services

Chunwang Zhang[1], Junjie Jin[1], Ee-Chien Chang[1], and Sharad Mehrotra[2]

[1] School of Computing, National University of Singapore, Singapore
{chunwang,jin89,changec}@comp.nus.edu.sg
[2] Department of Computer Science, University of California, Irvine, CA, USA
sharad@ics.uci.edu

Abstract. A realtime collaborative editor facilitates concurrent editing of a document by multiple authors. It is desired that the document be shared only among the authors, and protected from the potentially curious server. Existing approaches have taken two distinct paths – centralized server based approaches that achieve high concurrency and meet real-time requirement but compromise on security and incur high server cost, and peer-to-peer based approaches that support security but compromise on users' convenience and mobility. In this paper, we observe that by relaxing the realtime requirement, we can achieve security, reduce server cost and yet exploit the conveniences of the centralized setting. In particular, we consider generic low-cost storage servers in the cloud that provide storage integrity but do not guarantee low-latency. Essentially, our method breaks the document into small encrypted regions that are stored on the server and coordinates the authors' access. Although two authors are unable to concurrently modify a same region, the system is able to provide "quasi-realtime" experience. By relaxing the requirement to quasi-realtime, the difficulties in achieving document consistency, and the requirement on resources are significantly reduced. We give a proof-of-concept implementation on top of Dropbox, a commercial cloud storage service. Preliminary user studies show that the system is effective.

1 Introduction

A realtime collaborative editing system facilitates concurrent editing of a document shared by a few authors. While such systems improve productivity, it is desired that the document confidentiality be preserved. In particular, if the systems are hosted in the cloud, we want to protect the documents from the potentially curious servers.

There are many realtime collaborative editing systems with centralized public servers such as Google Docs [8] and the now discontinued Google Wave [9]. The centralized setting has a few advantages. With a centralized server, synchronization among the authors and techniques of *operational transformation* [6] can be efficiently and easily carried out, addressing the main technical challenge on concurrency faced by collaborative editing systems. Moreover, reliable storage can

W. Jonker and M. Petković (Eds.): SDM 2012, LNCS 7482, pp. 111–129, 2012.
© Springer-Verlag Berlin Heidelberg 2012

be hosted by the servers. With such reliable storage, authors can readily edit the document from different devices and at different time, and thus facilitate mobility.

A main drawback of the centralized setting is the difficulty in achieving document confidentiality against the potentially curious servers. There are incentives, for example, business competitions, for the centralized servers to actively look into users' sensitive data [15]. In addition, the centralization of data also makes the servers high-value targets for attacks [1,26]. To guide against the potential security risks, documents and operations must be carefully protected using, for example, proper encryption techniques, before being stored on the servers. However, for techniques of operational transformation, the servers need to know the contents of the operations in order to transform them. Without knowing the actual operations which contain certain information about the documents, it is very difficult for the servers to carry out the transformations.

On the other hand, a peer-to-peer (P2P) collaborative editing system naturally alleviates the above-mentioned issues since no server is involved. For the security requirement, as long as secure channels can be established among the authors, document confidentiality can be achieved. There are also many P2P collaborative editing systems such as SubEthaEdit [28] and CoWord [21]. Although no server is required, resolution of conflicts are now "pushed" to the peers and thus increases the computation load on the peers. Moreover, since there is no reliable storage keeping the latest version of the document, mobility is cumbersome to achieve. For example, consider the situation where Alice and other authors are concurrently editing a document using their desktops under a P2P setting, and later Alice goes offline for a few minutes and then resumes editing on her mobile device. Although possible, it is cumbersome for Alice's mobile device to retrieve the latest version of the document, locate and establish connection with other authors and then carry out collaborative editing.

A centralized system can be adopted in the P2P setting in the following way: after secure communication channels have been set up among the peers, one of the peer takes the role of the server and thus realtime collaborative editing can be carried out. In such adoption, the "super-peer" has to be present throughout the session. This leads to the difficulty in getting seamless recovery when the super-peer fails. It is also possible to have a hybrid setting where the peers employ a storage server to keep the latest version, while collaborative editing is done in the P2P setting. Nevertheless, this requires frequent uploading of the whole file and thus consumes large bandwidth. A recently proposed system SPORC [7] can be treated as a P2P system but with their communications going via a centralized server. The centralized server plays the role of establishing an ordering of the issued operations, which can be easily carried out on the encrypted operations. Such consistent ordering helps to simplify the designs of concurrency control. Nevertheless, it also inherits the requirement of low latency on the server of the centralized system, and high computing cost on the clients of the P2P system.

A main driving force of cloud computing is cost-saving. We know that there are already many commercial file hosting and sharing services in the cloud such as

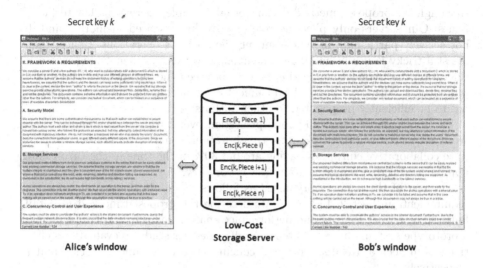

Fig. 1. An illustration of the scenario where there are two authors collaboratively editing a document using our system

Dropbox[12], SugarSync [13] and Box [3]. With such services, users can reliably store their files there and easily share the files with anyone they like across the Internet. These storage services are low-cost in the sense that they do not guarantee low-latency, provide only low bandwidth, and/or allow limited number of access. Nevertheless, they are reliable in providing storage-integrity. Instead of having a fully trusted dedicated server, we want to leverage such existing storage services to provide a low-cost collaborative editing system where the document confidentiality is preserved. Hence, preferably, no additional new services are required on the servers to facilitate collaborative editing, and no processes are required to keep track the state of an editing session.

We take security, mobility, cost and user experience as the main design criteria. While it is difficult to achieve all of them simultaneously, we observe that by relaxing the realtime requirement to "quasi-realtime", we can have both the conveniences provided by the centralized setting and yet achieve document confidentiality over a generic cloud storage service. While a "true" realtime collaborative editor allows multiple users to edit a same sentence, or even a same word concurrently, in contrast, we do not allow multiple editing in a same *viewport*, but support concurrent editing in different viewports. Such design choice is based on the assumption that users seldom concurrently modify a small region of interest so as to avoid confusion, but yet want to concurrently edit the same document.

Essentially, our proposed method automatically breaks the document into pieces which are encrypted and stored in the server, and ensures that only one author can modify a piece at any given time. Figure 1 illustrates the scenario where there are two authors collaboratively editing a document using our system.

Although the proposed method is conceptually simple, there are a few technical issues. Our servers only play the role of providing "shared memory", and do not actively participate in synchronizing the author's operations. Hence, there are still tricky issues in handling concurrency, especially when taking into consideration the frequent connection failures between the authors and the server. Moreover, localized editing to the document may affect global information, which has to be efficiently propagated to other authors .

We implemented a proof-of-concept system over Dropbox. Preliminary user study shows that, in the two-author collaboration scenario, our system can facilitate collaborative editing by saving around 30% of the time of the turn-taking approach, and the communication cost is very low.

The rest of the paper is organized as follows. We state the assumptions and requirements in Sect. 2. In Sect. 3, we describe the proposed method in detail, followed by a brief security and performance analysis in Sect. 4. We implemented a prototype system and conducted a small-scale user study to evaluate its effectiveness in Sect. 5. Related work and conclusion can be found in Sect. 6 and 7, respectively.

2   Framework and Requirements

We consider a server S and a group of authors $A_1, \ldots, A_t$, who want to collaboratively edit a document D which is stored in S in one form or another. The authors are mobile and may use different devices at different time, so the devices are stateless in the sense that they do not keep the record of editing operations after the end of the editing session. Nevertheless, the authors and/or the devices can keep some sufficiently long secret keys. For simplicity, we consider only textual document, which can be treated as a sequence of lines of readable characters and each character is associated with different attributes. An example of such documents is shown in Fig. 1.

2.1   Security Model

We assume that there are some authentication mechanisms so that each author can establish a secure channel (e.g., SSL/TLS) with the server. The authors trust each other and share a key k which is kept secret from the server. We consider a *honest-but-curious* server that follows the protocols as expected, but may attempt to collect information from the document with malicious intentions. The server must not be able to learn the document's content. Since the server is honest, it will not delete the document, deny connections from particular authors, or give authors inconsistent copies of the document. Nevertheless, we believe that it is possible to extend our proposed method to achieve authenticity against a malicious server without incurring large amount of resources. This extension would be an interesting future work.

2.2   Storage Services

Our system relies on a reliable existing storage service to host the shared document. The service is reliable in the sense that the file system integrity is maintained and it provides a consistent view of the file system under the shared environment. As mentioned in the introduction, we do not require high bandwidth or low-latency guarantees. The servers support the following *atomic operations* over the network.

1. *getFile(name)*: Retrieve the file "*name*" from the server.
2. *deleteFile(name)*: Delete the file "*name*" on the server.
3. *putFile(content, name)*: Upload the file "*name*" with the given content. If there is already a file "*name*" on the server, overwrite it.
4. *rename(oldname, newname)*: Rename the file "*oldname*" to "*newname*". If two clients happen to rename a same file concurrently, only one of them can succeed.
5. *listDir()*: List the metadata for all files in the directory. The metadata for each file must include at least its filename and last modified time.

Each atomic operation is to be completed over the network in one round-trip: the request, followed by the reply. Note that communication may fail during the operations. Actual storage services may provide different operations. The above set of atomic operations is minimal required for our system.

2.3   Mobility and Cost

Consider the scenario described in the introduction. When Alice switches the editing session from one device to another device, such transition should be easy and convenient for her. In particular, the new device should be easy to obtain the latest version of the document and establish communication with the relevant entities. Note that with the centralized storage server, such requirements on ease-of-use can be easily achieved. Since we consider light-weight mobile devices such as PDAs and smartphones, computations on the client side must not be overly intensive. Furthermore, communications between the clients and the server should not consume large bandwidth.

2.4   Concurrency Control and User Experience

Collaborative editing systems need concurrency control mechanisms to keep all the clients' local copies consistent. While with a centralized server, consistency is not difficult to achieve, it is important to ensure that the control mechanisms do not weaken usability of the system. In particular, below are some situations that the concurrency control mechanism should minimize:

1. The number of *roll-backs*. A roll-back occurs when a few operations issued by an author are deemed to conflict and have to be discarded, and thus already modified document has to be rolled back. The length of a roll-back should also be minimized.

2. The number of user interventions. Certain concurrency control mechanisms (for e.g., some optimistic locking mechanisms) require users' feedback in resolving conflicts. This should be avoided. Furthermore, users' effort in concurrency control (for e.g., button clicks) should also be minimized.
3. Waiting time to modify a region. Clearly, the time to withhold an author from editing the document should be minimized.

3   Proposed Method

A common "manual" practice to concurrently edit a document is to have the authors divide the document into large pieces according to the structure of the document, where each piece can only be edited by a single author at any given time. The authors coordinate with each other by communicating through some real-time channels like using phone calls or even via email systems, to lock and unlock a piece. Our system essentially automates this process with the coordination and management of the pieces transparent to the authors.

Essentially, our system automatically breaks the large document into small pieces which are encrypted and stored on the server, and ensures that a piece can only be modified by one author at any given time so as to avoid conflicts. Modified pieces are periodically re-encrypted on the client side and pushed back to the server, overwriting the original ones there. Due to the automation, frequent switches among the pieces can be carried out in a seamless manner, and thus the authors can enjoy "quasi-realtime" experiences by concurrently working on different pieces.

3.1   System Overview

The proposed system has the following components: it (1) employs a simple pessimistic locking mechanism (with timeout) to achieve concurrency; (2) manages the pieces in a smart way by automatically dividing (merging) a piece if it is getting too large (small) as the result of edit, and keeps the document intact even if failures happen during the dividing/merging process; (3) maintains global information in an efficient way, and (4) provides a user-friendly editing experience. As mentioned before, the server is not actively involved in the collaborative session, in the sense that there is no server-side process that is dedicated to keep track of the editing operations and push information back to the authors. The application logic, therefore, must be enforced on the client side.

3.2   Internal Representation

The system breaks the document into a sequence of *sub-files* $F_1, F_2, \ldots, F_n$ which are to be encrypted and stored as individual files in the same directory on the server. The name of each subfile is also encrypted using format preserving encryptions to produce valid filenames. The filename (in plaintext form) is a 4-tuple (p, i, g, s), where

1. p: A string identifying the document.
2. i: The index indicating the position of the subfile in the sequence. Here, i is a decimal real number (for e.g. "12.15"). A subfile with index i appears before the subfile with index j iff $i < j$.
3. g: The global information. This indicates changes made in the subfile that could affect some global states, like total number of lines. Note that although such information can be derived from the subfile, having it in the filename could potentially reduce communication cost.
4. s: Status of the subfile, that is, whether the subfile is *locked* or *unlocked*. If it is locked, we also include the identity of the author who has locked it.

We use total number of lines as an example to illustrate how global information can be efficiently maintained. Note that (p, i, g, s) is the minimal required information for our system. For example, the subfile (*"part"*, 2.0, 100, *"unlocked"*) means that it contains 100 lines of content and it is currently not being locked by anyone, while the subfile (*"part"*, 3.5, 150, *"(Alice)locked"*) contains 150 lines of content, and it is currently being locked by Alice. More information might have to be included when extending the system to richer text format.

3.3 Concurrency Control

A successful *listDir* operation will give the information (p, i, g, s) and the last modified time for each subfile in the directory. With such information, together with the atomic operations defined in Sect. 2.2, we can have a simple pessimistic locking mechanism. In this mechanism, the atomic operation *rename* plays the role of locking and unlocking a subfile. In particular, locking (unlocking) a subfile is carried out by changing its name to the *locked* (*unlocked*) status through a *rename* request. Authors can continue to read a locked subfile while it is being updated, but they are not allowed to modify it. They will be continuously notified about the updates.

However, due to frequent network failures, a subfile may be locked forever, if for instance, the author holding the lock is unable to unlock due to such failures. We need a lock timeout to release those subfiles. Let the length of the timeout be T_u. The clock for timeout starts immediately when a subfile is locked and restarts whenever it is updated. If a subfile with its name in the locked status has not been modified for a time period T_u, it is no longer considered as being locked and thus any one can re-lock it. As the authors' time are not synchronized, we further extend the timeout to $T_u + \sigma$ where σ is a bound on the time differences of the authors.

Note that in this locking mechanism, we do not have to explicitly unlock a subfile as anyone can re-lock it after a certain amount of time (i.e., $T_u + \sigma$). However, for better user experience, if it is clear that a user is not working on a piece, the piece will be unlocked immediately.

3.4   Piece Management and Failure Recovery

As a subfile is being edited, it may become extremely large or small. Note that the size of subfiles affects the performance dramatically. While a small piece size will facilitate collaborative editing as the authors can now work on finer pieces, it will generate large network overhead. Our system employs a simple piece management policy: whenever a subfile is getting too large (small), the system will automatically divide it into smaller pieces (merge it into other pieces). In our current implementation, the piece size is controlled by a range $[S_{min}, S_{max}]$ that is setable by the authors.

Dividing/merging a subfile involves a sequence of *deleteFile* and *putFile* operations. Network may fail during this process, leaving certain operations not being carried out. For example, consider the case where Alice wants to divide a large subfile by first deleting the original one on the server and then uploading the divided subfiles. Suppose that the network gets disconnected just after she has carried out the deleting operation. Since the new divided subfiles are not uploaded yet, some contents of the document are thus lost. Note that other authors cannot distinguish whether such contents are disappeared due to Alice's deletion or due to network failures, as there is no server side process that is monitoring the connections of the authors. We say that the document is not intact if some of its content are lost or replicated.

Algorithm 1. MERGE(F_1, F_2): Merge two subfiles F_1 and F_2

Input: Subfiles F_1 and F_2, with name (p, n_1, g_1, s_1) and (p, n_2, g_2, s_2) respectively.
1: Create a new subfile F' with name (p, n', g', s') where
   $n' = n_2$, $g' = g_1 + g_2$ and $s' = s_2$;
2: Copy the contents of F_1 and F_2 to F';
3: $rename((p, n_2, g_2, s_2), (p, n_2, g_2, "(n')D"))$;
4: $rename((p, n_1, g_1, s_1), (p, n_1, g_1, "(n')D"))$;
5: $putFile(F', (p, n', g', s'))$;
6: $delete((p, n_1, g_1, "(n')D"))$;
7: $delete((p, n_2, g_2, "(n')D"))$;

Algorithm 1 describes a merging process that ensures intactness. The dividing process is similar and thus it is omitted. The key idea here is to first rename the subfile to be divided/merged in a proper way rather than deleting it directly from the server. Subfiles ending with "$(n')D$" are called the temporary *indicating* subfiles which provide necessary information for failure recovery in case any error happens during the dividing/merging process. Whenever an indicating subfile is found stayed on the server for a long time (e.g., $T_u + \sigma$), the subfile will be either deleted or renamed to the unlocked status depending on whether the target subfile (i.e., the subfile with index n') is already on the server or not, keeping the document always in an intact state.

3.5   Management of Global Information

Localized edit to a piece may affect global information. In our editor, there is a status bar that displays the position of the current cursor w.r.t the start of the document (see Fig. 1, at the bottom of the window). This cursor position, in term of "line number", is global information: if an author deletes or inserts one line in her viewport, the coordinate of the cursor in other authors' viewports should be updated accordingly. For example, suppose that Alice is working on the 5th line of the document while Bob is working on the 1000th line. If Alice deletes one line in her viewport, the coordinate of Bob's cursor should be updated to 999 accordingly. Although such information can be always derived from the subfile by downloading the latest version from the server, doing that, however, will consume the limited network bandwidth.

We address this efficiency issue by adding the required information, that is, the total number of lines of a subfile, into the subfile's name. When a subfile is updated, such information must be updated accordingly. Other authors, by reading only the filename (through the periodical *listDir* request), can know easily how the subfile has been changed. This gives an efficient way to maintain the global information. More data might have to be included when extending the system to support more global information.

However, the filename length restrictions must be taken into consideration. For file systems that limit the length of the filename (e.g., Windows has some odd behaviors with length over 260 characters, including path), information that can be included in the filename could be limited. In such a case, we can have each subfile associate with a small metadata file recording all the necessary global information that we want to maintain, and ensure that each update to the subfile must update the metadata file as well. We would like to explore this possibility in the future.

3.6   User Interface

It would be troublesome to require the authors to manually lock and unlock a piece, especially when the pieces are small and switches between the pieces are frequent. Indeed, in our system, there is no GUI control, like clickable buttons, for them to do so. The authors can start to edit any regions of interest immediately, while the system takes care of the underlying layer locking and unlocking operations. To edit a particular location in the document, the author moves the cursor to that location and then starts editing. Let us denote T_e as the time where the author's editing action (implicitly) generates an locking request, and T_r as the time where the server's response to the locking request reaches the author. In the event where the locking is unsuccessful, whatever editing operations issued by the author during the period T_e to T_r have to be discarded, and we call such event a roll-back. Clearly, from users' point of view, the number of roll-backs, and their period have to be minimized. In our system, fairly intuitive color information is provided for the authors to distinguish between regions with different locking status. By trying not to modify a region that is shown being used by others, they can significantly reduce the chance of roll-backs (although not totally avoid them). Furthermore, even when a roll-back happens, operations involved between T_e and T_r are usually few, because the *rename* operation typically completes in just a few seconds. In our informal test, most of the *rename* operations complete within 3 seconds. Thus, we totally relieve the authors from the tedious tasks of locking and unlocking a subfile by only paying a price for seldom and short-time roll-backs.

For cases where the authors' devices do not have sufficient resources, for instance, when they are using light-weight mobile devices, they can work on a small part of the total document. When a client is just started, it downloads only the first few (for e.g., 3) subfiles from the server. Whenever an author requires for new contents during her editing, the next subfile will be retrieved and the current first subfile will be removed from the editor. In such a way, large documents are supported even with resource-limited devices.

4   Analysis

With a centralized server, the system design is much simplified. Although the server does not actively help in synchronizing the authors and pushing updates back to them, having it essentially facilitates mobility, and makes it possible to support light-weight mobile devices. Furthermore, as the server is generic, the system can be implemented on a variety of existing storage services most of which provide a certain amount of free storage space. Thus, the cost of having a server is lower as compared to other centralized systems which require dedicated servers.

4.1   Security Analysis

Like SPORC [7], our system bases its security and privacy guarantees on the presence of secure encryption schemes and the security of the authors' cryptographic keys, and not on a trusted or invulnerable server. Since the curious server sees only the encrypted version of the document, it cannot collect any information about the document's content. Furthermore, individual editing operations generated by each author stay only in the client itself, and are invisible to the server. So it is also impossible for the server to perform operation analysis. The document confidentiality is hence achieved.

However, there are still some information that the server can deduce. One particular example is the size of the shared document, since the server is already storing the (albeit encrypted) document. The server also knows how many pieces the document has been cut into. More importantly, the server knows the identities of the authors involved in the collaborative editing session as they must login first to the server, and their action sequences (i.e., who has modified which piece at what time). By comparing the differences in size between two successive updates to a same subfile, the server is able to guess overall what kinds of operations (e.g., insertion, deletion) have been performed, although the precise operation contents and editing positions are not clear. Although, intuitively, such information may not be useful to an adversary, users of this system should be aware of such possible leakages.

Unlike SPORC, we do not consider a malicious server that may intentionally modify, delete or re-order particular subfiles. We argue that there is little incentive for commercial storage services to perform such malicious actions. Nevertheless, as mentioned before, we believe that it is possible to extend our system to achieve authenticity and integrity against a malicious server without incurring high overhead to the storage services. We leave this for future work.

4.2   Performance-Critical Parameters

The performance of our system can be affected by many parameters, as summarized in Table 1. By performance, we are referring to user editing experience and network overhead. One interesting work is to investigate, comprehensively, how these parameters will affect the system, and to determine the optimal values through, for example, system modeling or large-scale user studies. That could be a separate paper. In this paper, we just discuss the tradeoff between them.

Table 1. Summary of the performance-critical parameters

S_{min}	Minimum size of a sub-file;
S_{max}	Maximum size of a sub-file;
T_u	Lock timeout;
T_o	Connection timeout;
T_s	Auto update saving period;
T_k	Auto update checking period.

1. S_{min} and S_{max}: The minimum and maximum size of a subfile. Subfiles out of this range will be divided or merged. Thus, in a sufficiently long-term usage, the average size is $(S_{min} + S_{max})/2$ (i.e., assumed a uniform distribution). A small average size facilitates collaborative editing as authors can now work on finer pieces and switches between them are less possible to trigger conflicts, but leads to higher network overhead as more information has to be returned by the periodical *listDir* request and more frequent locking (and unlocking) requests have to be sent. The distance between S_{min} and S_{max} should be reasonably large; otherwise, file dividing and merging may happen too often which wastes a lot of bandwidth. On the other hand, S_{min} (S_{max}) cannot be too small (large) in order to avoid the cases of extremely small (large) subfiles.

2. T_u: The lock timeout, that is, after how much time the lock for a subfile is no longer considered as valid. A larger T_u increases the waiting time for a subfile to be released, while a smaller T_u increases the number of locking requests. In particular, T_u should be sufficiently larger than the connection timeout T_o in order to tolerate the network delay.

3. T_o: The connection timeout. The larger the average network delay is, the larger the T_o should be. In particular, if T_o is not large enough, an atomic operation may be indeed carried out on the server while the author is unaware of it (and considers the operation as failed). Although this will not cause any problem in concurrency, it frustrates the authors and increases the network overhead (e.g., the author may issue a same operation quickly).

4. T_s: The update saving period. Every T_s seconds, the modified subfile is automatically encrypted and uploaded to the server, replacing the original one there. A smaller T_s can push changes more quickly and reduce the loss when a failure happens. However, it will increase the network overhead and the number of requests. In particular, T_s should be smaller than $T_u - T_o$ so that an active author can work on a subfile steadily without being disrupted.

5. T_k: The update checking period. Every T_k seconds, each client will check the server for new updates through a *listDir* request. Like T_s, a smaller T_k will improve the "realtime" experience but increase the network cost. Note that T_s and T_k together determine the modification propagation time T, that is, the time between a change is made and the change reaches other authors' devices. In particular, $0 < T < T_s + T_k + T_o$.

In real applications, these parameters must be determined according to, for instance, the real network conditions and possible constraints from the storage services. As an example, if the storage services do not limit the bandwidth usage and/or the number of accesses, we can have a small piece size and small T_s and T_k which in turn improves the authors' editing experience. The best way is to conduct formal experiments to decide the optimal values.

5   Implementation and User Study

We implemented a proof-of-concept system over Dropbox using its API v1.2 (in Java). The API provides all the atomic operations we defined in Sect. 2.2, and functionalities for clients to do authentications. The document is broke into many small files according to its structure. Both the name and content of each file are encrypted using AES-256 (with CBC mode) and the shared secret key. Authors login to the Dropbox server using valid username and password pairs they have, locate the directory and then open the document for editing. The corresponding files are then downloaded to the clients, decrypted and displayed as a single document to them. We provide a simple interface for the authors to edit the document, as shown in Fig. 1. Basic editing operations such as insertion, deletion, copy, cut and paste are provided. Authors can also change the style of any particular characters. Note that there are no control buttons for them to lock and unlock any files. Regions with red background indicate that they are currently being updated by others.

We want to study the effectiveness of the system, that is, whether users can save a significant amount of time by using our system in collaborative editing, and the communication cost. We conducted a few small-scale user studies to achieve such goals. The performance-critical parameters are set as follows: S_{min}=10 and S_{max}=100 (lines), $T_o = 30$, $T_u = 120$ and T_s=T_k=10 (seconds).

5.1 Scenarios and Participants

We simulated a scenario where there were two authors collaboratively editing a document. In this scenario, each author had to complete a list of editing tasks that were provided by us. We used a thesis paper (80 pages) as the base document, and created 4 different task lists from it, denoted as T_1, T_2, T_3 and T_4. Each task list contains 25 editing tasks, for example, *"Insert the sentence "Centralized systems are easier to build as compared to distributed systems." at position {1}"*, *"Delete the word "collaborative editor" at the first paragraph in section 2.1"*, and *"Set the font size of the heading "Chapter 1 Introduction" to 18 and make it bold"*. The task lists are carefully designed in a way such that the two authors have to edit some same regions so as to trigger conflicts (and thus roll-backs). Each task list takes around 15 minutes to complete. Due to the space limit, details of the task lists are omitted here. 8 participants took part in the study, denoted as $A_1, A_2, \ldots, A_8$. 4 of them are male, and 4 are female. All of them are undergraduate students from the CS department of the first author's university. All use computers on a regular basis, and have experience in editing various kinds of documents. We randomly grouped them into 4 groups.

5.2 Effectiveness

We compared the effectiveness of our system with the basic *turn-taking* approach: after one author finishes, she passes the document to the other author for editing. While a more natural approach that allows the participants to freely communicate with each other and edit the document in any ways they like could be more interesting, the turn-taking approach is much easier to conduct and control in practice.

The experimental procedure is summarized in Table 2. Each group was required to complete two rounds of tasks, and in each round, they had to complete a given task list in the two-author collaboration scenario using either our system or the turn-taking approach. Group 1 and 3 started with our system in the first round while Group 2 and 4 used it in the second round so as to avoid the possible bias on any particular systems due to the training effect. Note that for each participant, a different task list was used in the second round. Participants in each group sat back-to-back so that they could not see directly each other's screen. We provided WordPad as the editor (i.e., when not using our system) because WordPad is common in Windows and it provides basic editing functionalities which are very close to our editor. We recorded the time that the participants spent in each round.

The experiment result is summarized in Table 3. We define total editing time as the sum of the time spent by the two participants for turn-taking approach, and the time spent by the participant who finished late for our system. The result of total editing time is also shown in Table 3 (i.e., the 6th and 10th columns) and illustrated in Fig. 2. It is clear that our system can facilitate collaborative editing. Consider Group 1 and 3 where our system was used in the first round. The time spent is only 77.52% (i.e., $(22{:}05+23{:}06)/(28{:}10+30{:}07)$)

Table 2. Summary of the experimental procedure

Participants		1st round		2nd round	
	Task	Editing system	Task	Editing system	
Group 1	A1	T1	Our system	T3	Turn-taking
	A2	T2		T4	
Group 2	A3	T1	Turn-taking	T3	Our system
	A4	T2		T4	
Group 3	A5	T3	Our system	T1	Turn-taking
	A6	T4		T2	
Group 4	A7	T3	Turn-taking	T1	Our system
	A8	T4		T2	

of that of the turn-taking approach. Consider the results of Group 2 and 4, the time reduction is even more: participants in our system used only 61.47% (i.e., (18:54+19:04)/(30:53+30:53)) of the time of the turn-taking approach. Thus, to summarize, our system is effective in the sense that, in the two-author collaboration scenario, our system can clearly improve productivity by saving around 30% (i.e., 1–(77.52%+61.47%)/2) of the time, as compared to the case where they take turns to edit the document.

There are some other observations. First, with our system, each participant spent more time in completing the required tasks: the average time is 20 minutes, while that is 15 minutes in the turn-taking approach. This is partially because of the roll-backs where some already made changes have to be discarded due to conflicts and the participants have to move back sometime later to continue the failed tasks. Note that our task lists were intentionally designed in such a way so as to trigger conflicts. Another reason is the familiarity with editing tools and the "search" function provided by WordPad. Most of the participants have used WordPad before, and we indeed noticed some of them use keyword search to help in finding the locations of particular tasks. A second observation is that, with a same editing system, participants typically spent less time in their second rounds which indicates that the training effect is still present.

Table 3. Summary of the experiment results

Participants		The 1st round				The 2nd round			
	Task	Editing system	Time (m:s)	Total time (m:s)	Task	Editing system	Time (m:s)	Total time (m:s)	
Group 1	A1	T1	Our system	21:17	22:05	T3	Turn-taking	14:01	28:10
	A2	T2		22:05		T4		14:09	
Group 2	A3	T1	Turn-taking	16:04	30:53	T3	Our system	18:54	18:54
	A4	T2		14:49		T4		15:34	
Group 3	A5	T3	Our system	20:42	23:06	T1	Turn-taking	14:45	30:07
	A6	T4		23:06		T2		15:22	
Group 4	A7	T3	Turn-taking	14:45	30:53	T1	Our system	16:14	19:04
	A8	T4		16:08		T2		19:04	

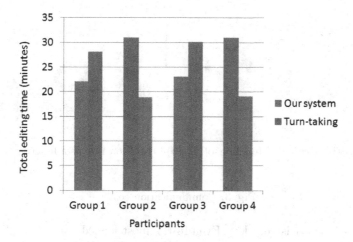

Fig. 2. Total editing time

Given that conflicts are rare in practice when the document is large, we expect our approach to continue to perform well when the number of collaborating users increases. In contrast, the turn-taking approach would sequentialize the process of editing preventing individuals from accessing the file concurrently.

5.3   Communication Cost

We measure the communication cost in terms of the bandwidth usage and the operation rate (i.e., number of operations per minute). While the communication cost could also be affected by parameters like average piece size and the lock timeout T_o, in this small experiment, we only consider it as a function of T_s and T_k (i.e., the update saving and checking period, respectively). The parameters are set as follows: S_{min}=10, S_{max}=100 (lines), $T_o = 30$ and $T_u = 120$ (seconds). We change T_s and T_k from 5 to 60 (i.e., 5, 10, 30 and 60, in seconds). For each combination, we asked the participants in each group to complete a given task list under the two-author collaboration scenario using our system, and recorded the amount of data and the number of requests transferred during this period. The task lists here are much shorter, and each takes around 5 minutes to complete.

The results are computed as an average of the 4 groups. Figure 3(a) shows the bandwidth usage as a function of T_s and T_k. As expected, the bandwidth usage decreases when T_s and T_k increase, because data has to be less frequently exchanged between the clients and the server. The figure also shows that the update saving period T_s plays a more important role in the overall cost. For a fixed T_k, when the value of T_s doubles, the communication cost can be reduced by nearly a half. In contrast, the checking period T_k has only limited effect. For example, for a fixed T_s of 30s, the bandwidth usage only decreases from 1.81 to 1.56 (KB/s) when we increase T_k from 5s to 60s. Figure 3(a) also shows that the

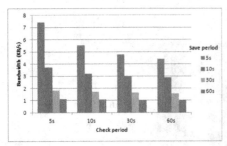 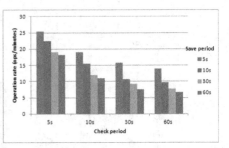

(a) Bandwidth usage as a function of T_s and T_k

(b) Operation rate as a function of T_s and T_k

Fig. 3. Communication cost

communication cost is very low. Even in the most loaded case ($T_s = T_k = 5\text{s}$), the overall bandwidth usage is only around 7.5 KB/s. While in the least loaded case ($T_s = T_k = 60\text{s}$), the bandwidth usage decreases to only 1.0 KB/s.

Figure 3(b) shows the operation rate (ops/minute) as a function of T_s and T_k. Like the bandwidth, the operation rate also decreases when T_s and T_k increase, but the downward trend is more gently. The overall operation rate changes from 25.5 to 6.75 (ops/minute) from the most loaded case to the least case. For storage services like Dropbox that limit the number of accesses per day, these parameters must be carefully set in order not to exceed to maximum values.

6 Related Work

Many real-time collaborative editing systems with centralized servers have been proposed over the past two decades [17,20,18,8,9]. Early systems like ShrEdit [17] employ simple concurrency control mechanisms such as locking and require the servers to manage the locks. The lock granularity could be a whole document, a section, a sentence or any selected texts. While we also employ a similar locking mechanism, servers in our system are not required to maintain any locking information. Many recent systems, for example, Google Wave [9], employ operational transformation (OT) [24,6] for consistency maintenance and concurrency control in an intention-preserving manner [20,9]. With a centralized server, OT can be carried out in the server and thus reduces the clients' workload. There are also systems that leverage transactional techniques in database to ensure concurrency [29]. However, all these systems are designed based on the assumption of dedicated and trusted servers.

On the other hand, there are also many peer-to-peer collaborative editing systems [6,14,27,28,21] and research efforts on improving the concurrency control in the P2P setting [19,10,22,25,24]. Typically, P2P systems require the documents to be replicated on each involved device and are sometimes cumbersome for session switches when the authors are mobile. Although it is also possible to have a hybrid setting [2,30], such systems still require active involvements of the servers.

A recent system SPORC [7] proposed a generic group collaboration framework using untrusted cloud servers where the document confidentiality and integrity are preserved. The centralized server plays the role of assigning a total ordering for the submitted operations, which can be easily carried out on encrypted operations. Although simple, there are still requirements of a dedicated server and resources on the server to keep track of the editing session. Moreover, since the workload of performing operational transformation are now pushed to the clients, the computation cost on clients is high and thus this approach is not suitable for mobile applications. In contrast, our system can be applied on any existing cloud storage services and we require no control of the servers. Our system is also carefully designed to support light-weight mobile devices.

Gabriele et al. [5] and Huang et al. [11] proposed methods to protect document privacy in Web-based (collaborative) editing applications such as Google Docs [8] and Microsoft Office Live [4]. The general idea is to encrypt the document contents before uploading them to the cloud server. Although these solutions can achieve certain degree of document privacy, applying them to the current Web-based document editing applications will partially disable the collaborative editing feature. In addition, two very recent systems, Venus [23] and Depot [16], allow clients to use cloud resources without having to trust them. Venus provides strong consistency in the face of a potentially malicious server, but requires the majority of a "core set" of clients to be online in order to achieve most of its consistency guarantees, and does not support applications other than key-value storage. Depot, on the other hand, does not rely on the availability of a "core set" and supports varied applications. Moreover, it allows clients to recover from malicious forks. However, unlike our system, Depot is not designed for real-time collaborative applications.

7   Conclusion

Many existing real-time collaborative editing systems employ operation transformations to achieve consistency. However, supporting such techniques with the additional goals on security, mobility and low services cost is difficult. In this paper, we argue that a relaxed quasi-realtime requirement could significantly simplify the system design. Preliminary user-studies on our proof-of-concept implementation showed that that such system is effective.

Acknowledgments. The authors would like to thank Veronica Hu He, National University of Singapore, for her help in implementing the system and conducting the user studies. Chang and Zhang are partially supported by grant TDSI/09-003/1A.

References

1. Debian investigation report after server compromises (December 2003), http://www.debian.org/News/2003/20031202
2. Baecker, R.M., Nastos, D., Posner, I.R., Mawby, K.L.: The user-centered iterative design of collaborative writing software. In: Proceedings of the ACM CHI 1993 Human Factors in Computing Systems, pp. 399–405. ACM (1993)
3. Box. Box: Simple Online Collaboration, http://www.box.com/
4. Microsoft Corporation. Microsoft Office Live, http://www.officelive.com/
5. D'Angelo, G., Vitali, F., Zacchiroli, S.: Content cloaking: preserving privacy with google docs and other web applications. In: Proceedings of the 2010 ACM Symposium on Applied Computing, pp. 826–830. ACM (2010)
6. Ellis, C.A., Gibbs, S.J.: Concurrency control in groupware systems. ACM SIGMOD Record 18(2), 399–407 (1989)
7. Feldman, A.J., Zeller, W.P., Freedman, M.J., Felten, E.W.: Sporc: group collaboration using untrusted cloud resources. In: Proceedings of the 9th USENIX Conference on Operating Systems Design and Implementation, p. 1 (2010)
8. Google. Google Docs, https://docs.google.com
9. Google. Google Wave, https://wave.google.com/wave
10. Greenberg, S., Marwood, D.: Real time groupware as a distributed system: concurrency control and its effect on the interface. In: 1994 ACM Conference on Computer Supported Cooperative Work, pp. 207–217. ACM (1994)
11. Huang, Y., Evans, D.: Private editing using untrusted cloud services. In: The 31st International Conference on Distributed Computing Systems (ICDCS 2011), pp. 263–272. IEEE (2011)
12. Dropbox Inc. Dropbox: Simplify your life, https://www.dropbox.com/
13. SugarSync Inc. SugarSync, https://www.sugarsync.com/
14. Koch, M.: The collaborative multi-user editor project iris. Technical Report (1995)
15. Li, J., Krohn, M., Mazières, D., Shasha, D.: Secure untrusted data repository (sundr). In: Proceedings of the 6th Conference on Symposium on Opearting Systems Design & Implementation, vol. 6, p. 9. USENIX Association (2004)
16. Mahajan, P., Setty, S., Lee, S., Clement, A., Alvisi, L., Dahlin, M., Walfish, M.: Depot: Cloud storage with minimal trust. ACM Transactions on Computer Systems (TOCS) 29, 12 (2011)
17. McGuffin, L.J., Olson, G.M.: ShrEdit: A Shared Electronic Work Space. University of Michigan, Cognitive Science and Machine Intelligence Laboratory (1992)
18. Finkel, R.A.: Mullick, S. MUSE: A Collaborative editor. Masters Project. University of Kentucky (1998), http://www.cs.engr.uky.edu/~raphael/studentWork/muse.html
19. Neuwirth, C.M., Kaufer, D.S., Chandhok, R., Morris, J.H.: Issues in the design of computer support for co-authoring and commenting. In: 1990 ACM Conference on Computer Supported Cooperative Work, pp. 183–195. ACM (1990)
20. Nichols, D.A., Curtis, P., Dixon, M., Lamping, J.: High-latency, low-bandwidth windowing in the jupiter collaboration system. In: Proceedings of the 8th Annual Symposium on User Interface Software and Technology (UIST 1995), pp. 111–120. ACM (1995)
21. Advanced Collaborative Technology Research. Codoxware: Connecting people and documents, http://www.codoxware.com/

22. Ressel, M., Nitsche-Ruhland, D., Gunzenhäuser, R.: An integrating, transformation-oriented approach to concurrency control and undo in group editors. In: 1996 ACM Conference on Computer Supported Cooperative Work, pp. 288–297. ACM (1996)
23. Shraer, A., Cachin, C., Cidon, A., Keidar, I., Michalevsky, Y., Shaket, D.: Venus: Verification for untrusted cloud storage. In: Proceedings of the 2010 ACM Workshop on Cloud Computing Security Workshop, pp. 19–30. ACM (2010)
24. Sun, C., Jia, X., Zhang, Y., Yang, Y., Chen, D.: Achieving convergence, causality preservation, and intention preservation in real-time cooperative editing systems. ACM Transactions on Computer-Human Interaction (TOCHI) 5, 63–108 (1998)
25. Sun, C., Maheshwari, P.: An efficient distributed single-phase protocol for total and causal ordering of group operations. In: 3rd International Conference on High-Performance Computing (HiPC 1996), p. 295. IEEE Computer Society (1996)
26. Taylor, O.: Intrusion on www.gnome.org (2004), http://mail.gnome.org/archives/gnome-announce-list/2004-March/msg00114.html
27. ter Hofte, G.H., van der Lugt, H.J.: Cocodoc: a framework for collaborative compound document editing based on opendoc and corba. In: Proceedings of the IFIP/IEEE International Conference on Open Distributed Processing and Distributed Platforms, pp. 15–33. Chapman & Hall, Ltd. (1997)
28. TheCodingMonkeys. SubEthaEdit: Collaborative text editing., http://www.codingmonkeys.de/subethaedit/
29. Wu, Q., Pu, C.: Modeling and implementing collaborative editing systems with transactional techniques. In: Proceedings of the 6th International Conference on Collaborative Computing: Networking, Applications and Worksharing, pp. 1–10. IEEE (2010)
30. Zafer, A.A.: Netedit: A collaborative editor. Master's thesis, Master of Science. University de Virginia, USA (2001)

Secure Metric-Based Index for Similarity Cloud

Stepan Kozak, David Novak, and Pavel Zezula

Masaryk University, Brno, Czech Republic
{xkozak1,david.novak,zezula}@fi.muni.cz

Abstract. We propose a similarity index that ensures data privacy and thus is suitable for search systems outsourced in a cloud. The proposed solution can exploit existing efficient metric indexes based on a fixed set of reference points. The method has been fully implemented as a security extension of an existing established approach called M-Index. This Encrypted M-Index supports evaluation of standard range and nearest neighbors queries both in precise and approximate manner. In the first part of this work, we analyze various levels of privacy in existing or future similarity search systems; the proposed solution tries to keep a reasonable privacy level while relocating only the necessary amount of work from server to an authorized client. The Encrypted M-Index has been tested on three real data sets with focus on various cost components.

1 Introduction

With more and more data being collected in all kinds of scientific processes (medicine, astronomy, etc.) or commercial applications such as social networking and on-line marketing, searching in large data sets became one of the key tasks performed these days. Such data often does not provide sufficient meta-data description, therefore in many applications similarity search is more important than an exact match or keyword search.

Since similarity search itself is a very resource demanding process, the trend is to outsource such services to 3rd party cloud providers. Outsourcing to a cloud provides many advantages such as low initial investments, low storage costs and a very good scalability (more storage or computational power can be added on the fly, when it's needed – so called pay-as-you-go principle).

We can see two possible scenarios of outsourcing similarity search. In the first case, user has their similarity search technology and wants to use the hardare of a cloud infrastructure provider. In the second scenario, a similarity search service provider makes the technology available for end users so they can use the engine without an actual knowledge of the technology. We observe an increasing trend of the latter case and we will refer to this as *similarity cloud*.

In both scenarios, users might not want to expose all their data which might be sensitive (e.g. medicine data) or valuable (e.g. data collected from a scientific research), to a 3rd party provider, which is, in general, untrusted. In these cases, privacy of the data is of high importance. Hence the similarity cloud has to provide mechanisms which allow applying privacy requirements of the end users.

W. Jonker and M. Petković (Eds.): SDM 2012, LNCS 7482, pp. 130–147, 2012.

The general objective of outsourcing is to move all the resource-demanding process to the cloud and allow authorized clients to run search queries and get answers. Intuitively, involving an encryption will negatively influence the efficiency of the service. The less the cloud servers know about the data, the less efficient indexing techniques can be used on the server side. A suitable balance between sufficient level of privacy and performance has to be found.

The topic of secured similarity search has been studied recently [1–4]. Some of these works focus on keyword similarity indexing [1–3] and the work of Yiu et al. [4] studies the indexing based on general metric principles. We consider the paper pioneering in the area that we expect to become more important and we consider this research direction promising.

In this work, we try to specify more precisely the application scenarios and goals of the secure similarity search; our analysis results in a taxonomy of privacy in similarity search services. We propose a novel metric-based technique that ensures reasonable level of privacy while relocating only the necessary amount of work from server to an authorized client. The proposed approach can exploit existing efficient metric indexes that are based on a fixed set of reference objects (pivots). Our method has been implemented utilizing M-Index [5, 6], an established indexing and searching approach that is currently being used in several real applications.

The M-Index and other similar approaches treat the data space as a *metric space* $(\mathcal{D}, d)$, where $\mathcal{D}$ is a *domain* of objects and d is a total *distance function* $d : \mathcal{D} \times \mathcal{D} \longrightarrow \mathbb{R}$ satisfying metric postulates (non-negativity, identity, symmetry, and triangle inequality) [7]. The set of indexed objects $X \subseteq \mathcal{D}$ is typically searched by the *query-by-example* paradigm, for instance by the *range query* $R(q, r) = \{o \in X \mid d(q, o) \leq r\}$, $q \in \mathcal{D}$ or by the *nearest neighbors query* $k\text{-NN}(q)$ covering the k objects from X with the smallest distances to given $q \in \mathcal{D}$.

Contribution and Structure of This Paper

- In Section 2, we describe the goals of secure similarity search and we define the taxonomy of privacy in similarity clouds. In Section 3, we describe some of the existing approaches.
- We propose a mechanism for ensuring privacy in the M-Index and similar approaches in Section 4. Further, we discuss privacy and efficiency of the proposed solution and describe its prototype implementation.
- We performed experiments on three real-life datasets in order to measure the efficiency degradation caused by our privacy ensuring approach; we also analyzed individual cost components in real client-server environment (Section 5). The paper concludes in Section 6 with suggestions for future work.

2 Problem Definition

In this section, we establish the terminology used throughout this paper and define the main objectives of secured similarity search in an outsourced (client-server) setting.

2.1   Terminology

Raw Data. The original (sensitive) data objects to be indexed and searched. For example binary files of images or any other data collection.

Metric Space Objects (MS Objects). Metric space descriptors extracted from the raw data, each descriptor has a reference to the corresponding raw object; they are compared by a metric function. In some cases, the raw data and the MS objects are identical (for instance, gene sequences or other biomedical data); in other cases, several MS objects are extracted from one raw object.

Secret Key. Encryption key used to encrypt the raw data and/or MS objects. Encryption key is also used for authorized querying of the data.

Data Owner. Subject outsourcing the search service, owner of the data.

Server. Server(s) of the 3rd party similarity cloud. From the data owner's point of view, server is not trusted because it is not fully controlled by the data owner (server can be attacked and data from it leaks to an attacker). Therefore server should not have the access to the original (unencrypted) data and should have as less as possible information about the MS objects.

Authorized Client. Client authorized by the data owner to use the search service (i.e. client having the secret key).

Attacker. Any potential malicious user with purpose of getting the data.

2.2   Objectives

In general, the process of outsourcing is the following: In the construction phase, the data owner creates the MS objects from the original raw data, sends these MS objects to a similarity cloud for indexing and the raw data to a data storage. In the search phase, any authorized client can query the similarity cloud to obtain IDs of the relevant objects referring to original data objects, that can be subsequently retrieved from the raw data storage. Scheme of such outsourced similarity system is depicted in Figure 1. General objectives of outsourced secure similarity search can be formulated as follows:

- Resource demanding process (the search itself) should be performed on the server side as much as possible (clients that query the server might be simple devices without big computational power).
- Communication cost between the client and the server should be as low as possible (in optimal case, client sends only initial search request and then receives result from the server).
- Data should be stored on the server in a secure way so that a potential attacker can gain as little information about the data as possible.

Intuitively, the security requirement goes against the efficiency objective. If most of the computations should be performed on server side, the server has to have enough information about the data to process such task efficiently. Hence, the right balance between the security and efficiency should be found for each specific application setting.

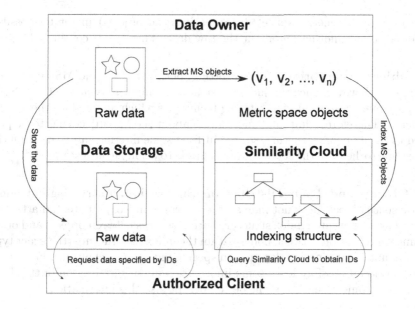

Fig. 1. General scheme of outsourced similarity search

2.3   Levels of Privacy

In this section, we introduce and discuss several general approaches to a (secure) outsourced similarity search as we see it.

No Encryption. This is the fundamental setting suitable for not sensitive data or data stored in a completely trusted environment (own servers, etc.). It is also the most efficient solution, because all the work can be done on the server and no additional encryption/decryption processes have to be employed. All advanced indexing techniques can be applied on the server side without loss of efficiency.

Raw Data Encryption. Another approach is to extract the MS objects from the raw data and build a standard indexing structure on these MS objects; then the raw data can be encrypted with some symmetric cryptosystem (AES or any other) and uploaded to the cloud data storage. The similarity search itself can be performed without any change, the whole search process can be done on the server (the index and MS objects are kept unencrypted). After the search, the raw data storage returns encrypted result data to the client for decryption.

This approach is good from the performance point of view, because the resource demanding process (similarity search with expensive distance computations) is done on the server side, while the client decrypts the final result (which can also be a time consuming process, but this can be hardly omitted since the authorized client is naturally the only party having the decryption key).

From the security point of view, this approach is not applicable if the MS objects are also sensitive or identical to the raw data. And even if not, the knowledge of the metric space (distances between objects) might be possibly exploited to get information about the raw data. This case is considered below.

MS Objects Encryption. In this setting, both raw data and MS objects are encrypted. However, once the indexing structure cannot fully access the MS objects, it cannot use pruning or filtering techniques which may reduce the system efficiency. Therefore, additional information about the MS objects has to be provided to the indexing structure, so that at least some filtering can be done on the server side (otherwise the server would degrade to a simple data storage).

MS Objects and Their Distribution Encryption. Encrypting individual metric space objects does not hide all the information from a potential attacker. Server has unencrypted index structure with distances between objects and other distance information between nodes within the indexing structure (the exact type and amount of information depends on specific indexing mechanism). From this, an attacker can possibly learn some information about distribution of the data. The aim in some scenarios might be to encrypt also this information.

Note: Since raw data can be stored (and encrypted) separately and indexing structures can only contain MS objects with a reference to the original resource, we further consider the raw data always encrypted and discuss only the process of securing MS objects within the indexing structures (therefore we focus on the last two approaches of the above list).

3   Existing Approaches

The topic of secured similarity search is being studied and there are several results in this field. Several techniques for the similarity (keyword) search in the text data has been proposed and analyzed [1–3]. However, all the solutions were designed only for specific type of data with specific distance function to measure the similarity. There is also a recent work concerning secure multidimensional interval queries in over outsourced attribute data [8]. On the other hand, general metric secure similarity search, where no additional information about the data or the distance function is known, is a relatively new research area.

Naturally, there exists a straightforward solution: The data owner can encrypt every object and send only the encrypted objects to the server without any additional information. During the search phase, an authorized client downloads all the objects from the server, decrypts them and performs the search. This solution achieves perfect security, however it is clear that it cannot be used in real applications because it has extremely high communication cost and it loses all the advantages of cloud environment (especially scalability).

Few advanced techniques for outsourcing similarity search (with general metric space approach) have been proposed. In this section, we provide brief overview of two of the techniques of Yiu et al. [4]. Both these solutions encrypt the MS objects and hide the data distribution (see Section 2.3).

3.1   Encrypted Hierarchical Index Technique

First approach is called Encrypted hierarchical index search (EHI) and it works as follows. Efficient indexing structure is build upon the MS objects, all the nodes of the indexing structure are encrypted with an arbitrary symmetric cipher, address of the root node is public. The search procedure logic is implemented on the client, which requests nodes of the structure from the server, decrypts the node, processes the objects stored in this node and requests other node until it completes the operation.

This approach has obvious advantage in its security, because a potential attacker cannot gain any information either about the data itself or about the metric space, since everything is stored encrypted. Another advantage is a straightforward implementation and robust design, because we can use many indexing structures practically without change of its internal structure.

However, there is a cost we have to pay for this high security level: communication costs (a lot of traffic is between client and the server) and efficiency of the search procedure. Since all the nodes of the indexing structure are encrypted, server cannot traverse through the structure and can only serve as a storage, sending the client what was requested. All the time-consuming search operations have to be implemented on the client side, and the client has to perform a lot of encryption/decryption operations which (in general) might be very resource demanding as well. This approach seems to be only slightly better than the trivial solution described above.

3.2   Metric-Preserving Transformation

EHI with the drawbacks mentioned above might not be applicable in some scenarios, because the client can be a device with limited resources (e.g. smart phone or even simpler device with less computational resources). Yiu et al. [4] propose Metric-Preserving Transformation (MPT) technique which uses an order-preserving encryption function. For details see the paper [4]. The goal of MPT was to reduce communication cost of EHI and pass part of the search work to the server while preserving sufficient privacy of the data.

However, to achieve sufficient security level, one has to have a representative sample of the data collection before the indexing structure is built and sent to the server (it is necessary for the order-preserving encryption function to work properly). This could be a problem in dynamic data sets where the collection is often changing.

4   Encrypted Metric-Based Index

In this section, we propose an approach that can add privacy to metric indexes that are based on distance permutations of a fixed set of reference objects [9–11, 6]. Our approach is introduced as an extension of a structure called M-Index [5, 6] (because it enables both precise and approximate similarity search and has other advantages) but it can be generalized straightforwardly to any

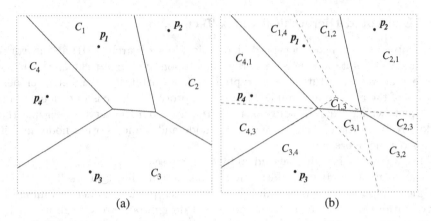

Fig. 2. Principle of recursive Voronoi partitioning: first level (a), second level (b)

other member of this class of metric indexes. Let us first briefly introduce the standard M-Index.

4.1 M-Index

The M-Index [5, 6] is a dynamic disk-efficient metric-based index that uses a set of reference objects (pivots) $p_1, \ldots, p_n \in \mathcal{D}$ in order to partition the indexed set $X \subseteq \mathcal{D}$. Namely, the *recursive Voronoi partitioning* is used: at the first level, each object $o \in X$ is assigned to its closest pivot p_i creating Voronoi cell C_i; at the second level, data from C_i are partitioned further using pivots $p_1, \ldots, p_{i-1}, p_{i+1}, \ldots, p_n$ forming cells $C_{i,j}$, etc. Figure 2 depicts an example of such partitioning with four pivots to the first and second level, respectively. This approach can also be formalized as *pivot permutations* [12, 13]: For each object $o \in X$, let $(\cdot)_o$ be permutation of indexes $\{1, \ldots, n\}$ such that $\forall i, j \in \{1, \ldots, n\}$:

$$(i)_o < (j)_o \Leftrightarrow d(p_{(i)_o}, o) < d(p_{(j)_o}, o) \vee d(p_{(i)_o}, o) = d(p_{(j)_o}, o) \wedge i < j.$$

Sequence $p_{(1)_o}, \ldots, p_{(n)_o}$ is then ordered with respect to distances between the pivots and o. The M-Index uses prefixes of this permutation to index o.

Since neither this space partitioning nor the data distribution are uniform, the M-Index has a *dynamic* variant that further partitions only the cells that exceed certain data volume limit. The M-Index then maintains a dynamic *Voronoi cell tree* to keep track of actual depth for individual cells. The schema of this tree is sketched in Figure 3.

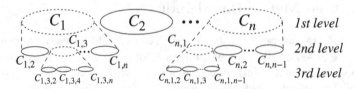

Fig. 3. M-Index Voronoi cell tree

The M-Index can evaluate the range and k-NN queries using several space pruning and filtering mechanisms [5] – only part of the Voronoi cells has to be accessed to ensure returning of all the required objects. Beside this *precise* query evaluation strategies that returns the precise answer A^P, the M-Index can also evaluate k-NN(q) queries in *approximate* manner [6] (not all objects from A^P are always returned while the search costs can be significantly reduced). In this case, the algorithm heuristically specifies a candidate set $S_C \subseteq X$ of the objects that are "close" to query q; this set S_C is then refined by evaluating distances $d(q, o)$, $\forall o \in S_C$ and selecting the k closest objects that form the approximate search result A. The size of the candidate set S_C can be parametrized. The *recall* is a common measure to quantify the quality of the result A with respect to precise answer A^P: $recall(A) = \frac{|A \cap A^P|}{|A^P|} \cdot 100\%$.

4.2   Encrypted M-Index

Our solution exploits the fact that only the prefix of the pivot permutation is used for indexing any object $o \in \mathcal{D}$ within M-Index. No additional distances need to be computed during insertion of o into the index. The M-Index search algorithms also need only query-pivot distances (or their permutation) in order to form the candidate set S_C. Therefore, the set of pivots can be part of the private information known only by the data owner (and shared with authorized clients). The final refining has to be done on the client, but S_C (created on the server) is supposed to be significantly smaller than the whole collection X and it can be pre-ranked. These operations are formalized in the following paragraphs and schematically depicted in Figures 4 and 5.

Data Insertion. In the construction phase, for each object $o \in X$, the data owner calculates pivot permutation, encrypts the object o (using arbitrary symmetric cipher) and sends encrypted object e along with its pivot permutation to the server. The server-side M-Index locates the leaf node of the dynamic cell tree that corresponds to given pivot permutation (see Figure 3); object e together with the pivot permutation is stored in this node and, if necessary, this leaf node is split (again, only the permutations stored with the objects are necessary for the split). This insert procedure is sketched in Figure 4 and its client part is formalized in Algorithm 1.

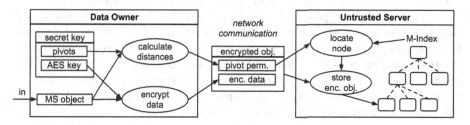

Fig. 4. Schema of the insert operation into encrypted M-Index

---

Algorithm 1. Encrypted M-Index insert algorithm

Input: $o \in \mathcal{D}$, secretKey containing pivots $p_1, \ldots, p_n$ and cipher key

1 calculate $d(o, \text{secretKey}.p_i)$, $\forall i \in \{1, \ldots, n\}$;
2 init new enc. object e;   `/* e := struct {distances, permutation, data} */`
3 **if** *precise strategy is used* **then**
4      $e.distances \leftarrow d(o, \text{secretKey}.p_1), \ldots, d(o, \text{secretKey}.p_n)$;
5 **else**
6   sort the distances to find permutation $(1)_o, \ldots, (n)_o$;
7      $e.permutation \leftarrow (1)_o, \ldots, (n)_o$;
8 $e.data \leftarrow \text{secretKey}.encrypt(o)$;   `/* store encrypted data only */`
9 $\text{server}.insert(e)$;

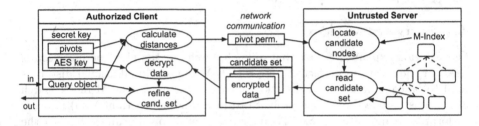

Fig. 5. Schema of the search operation in encrypted M-Index

Query Evaluation. Once the index is constructed, the data owner provides the clients with the private information (set of pivots and key for the symmetric cipher) and any client possessing this *secret key* can perform the search. To execute any search query, authorized client first computes distances to pivots (part of the secret key) and sends the search request to the M-Index on the server side (the search request consists of query object pivot permutation or distances to pivots, the query object itself is not a part of the request). Please, follow the diagram of this procedure in Figure 5. The server determines and sends back the candidate set S_C (set of encrypted objects), the client then decrypts the objects from S_C and finalizes the result (computes the distances of decrypted candidate objects to the query object). In this way, all basic types of search queries mentioned above can be evaluated (precise range and k-NN as well as the approximate k-NN). From the client point of view, the algorithm is very similar for all these types of queries and it is formalized in Algorithm 2.

Depending on the type of the search in Algorithm 2, either the query-pivot distances (line 5) or only the pivot permutations (line 9) are sent to the server. In either case, the candidate set is refined after decrypting the retrieved objects. For the approximate k-NN search, the client can choose the size CandSize of the candidate set S_C (line 10); S_C retrieved from the server is pre-ranked, therefore the client can choose to decrypt and compute distances only for candidates with the highest rank to speed up the search process.

Algorithm 2. Encrypted M-Index search algorithm (client)

Input: range $R(q, r)$ or k-NN(q), *secretKey* with $p_1, \ldots, p_n$ and cipher key
Output: Answer set A
1 calculate $d(q, secretKey.p_i)$, $\forall i \in \{1, \ldots, n\}$;
2 init new encrypted object e ;   /* e := struct {distances, permutation} */
3 initialize new encrypted object e;
4 **if** *precise range query is used* **then**
5      $e.distances \leftarrow d(q, secretKey.p_1), \ldots, d(q, secretKey.p_n)$;
6      $S_C \leftarrow$ server.*rangeSearch*(e, r) ;   /* candidate set of enc. obj. */
7 **else**
8   sort the distances to find permutation $(1)_q, \ldots, (n)_q$;
9      $e.permutation \leftarrow (1)_q, \ldots, (n)_q$;
10     $S_C \leftarrow$ server.*approxKNN*$(e, \text{CandSize})$ /* candidate set of enc. obj. */
11 $A \leftarrow \emptyset$;
12 **foreach** *object c in S_C* **do**
13     $o \leftarrow$ secretKey.*decrypt*(c);
14   compute distance $d(q, o)$;
15   **if** *o satisfies the query constraint* **then**
16         $A \leftarrow A \cup \{o\}$;

Algorithm 3 formalizes the range search algorithm on the server side. It uses the precomputed query-pivot distances and the query radius r to prune the index tree using several metric-based constraints [6] (line 3 of Alg. 3). Furthermore, because each indexed object contains distances to the pivots, the server can use *pivot filtering* [7, 6] to further reduce the candidate set size (lines 5–7).

Algorithm 4 describes the server-side procedure for the approximate k-NN search. As mentioned in Section 4.1, the candidate set of a given size can be determined only based on query pivot permutation or query-pivot distances: The M-Index can order the Voronoi cells by some "promise value" (line 3). The precise k-NN search can be realized as an approximate k-NN search, that determines distance ρ_k to the k-th nearest neighbor of q, and then subsequent precise range query $R(q, \rho_k)$ is executed [7].

Algorithm 3. Range query algorithm (server.*rangeSearch*)

Input: encrypted query object q with distances $q.distances$, radius r
Output: Candidate set $S_C \subseteq X$
1 $S_C \leftarrow \emptyset$;
2 **foreach** *Voronoi cell C traversing the M-Index* **do**
3   **if** *C cannot be pruned using q.distances and radius r* **then**
4          $S_C \leftarrow S_C \cup C$;
5 **foreach** *object o in S_C* **do**
6   **if** $\max\limits_{i=1}^{n} |q.distances[i] - o.distances[i]| > r$ **then**
7          $S_C \leftarrow S_C \setminus \{o\}$;

Algorithm 4. Approximate k-NN algorithm (server.*approxKNN*)

   Input: encrypted q with $q.permutation$, candidate set size CandSize
   Output: Pre-ranked candidate set S_C
1   $S_C \leftarrow \emptyset$;
2   **while** $|S_C| <$ CandSize **do**
3      $C \leftarrow$ next promising Voronoi cell from the index;
4      $S_C \leftarrow S_C \cup C$;
5   trim S_C to required size CandSize;

4.3 Security Analysis

The secret key of authorized clients consist of the set of pivots and key for symmetric cipher used to encrypt the data. The information which is stored on the server (and can possibly leak to an attacker) are the pivot permutations (or object-pivot distances) and the encrypted MS objects. Since the pivots are part of the private key and only authorized clients know them, only they can query the server by "meaningful" queries. An attacker can query the server index using an arbitrarily chosen pivot permutation not knowing to which query object(s) this permutation belongs; the received candidate objects are encrypted and without any similarity distances or other meta-data. If the server is compromised, the attacker could learn the index structure and thus the sets of clustered MS objects (encrypted); nevertheless, not knowing the pivots and the metric function, it would be difficult to learn specifics about the data set. Clearly, this approach belongs to the third privacy level defined in Section 2.3.

In order to even better hide information about the data set distribution, we would like to apply certain distance transformations that would preserve the utmost pruning and filtering efficiency of the server-side index. The aim is to provide the security level described in the forth paragraph of Section 2.3 and this belongs to our future work.

4.4 Implementation

The M-Index is implemented with the aid of MESSIF, a general and robust framework that supports the task of building prototypes of similarity search algorithms [14]. Encrypted M-Index is implemented as an encryption layer in MESSIF. Even though the algorithm was designed for the M-Index as the server algorithm, the architecture of encryption layer is general and robust. Therefore it can be used with any MESSIF-based algorithm.

Core of the encryption layer is an encryption client which can (if supplied with a secret key) provide a communication interface (layer) for a remote server running a similarity search algorithm (indexing structure running in a distributed cloud environment for example). Both client and server are Java processes communicating via TCP/IP.

5   Experimental Evaluation

The main objective of the experimental evaluation is to measure the price paid for ensuring privacy in terms of the efficiency loss – the computation demands placed upon the client due to the privacy protection and the client-server communication costs (volume of exchanged data and communication time). The client computations consist principally of (1) data encryption/decryption and (2) the search algorithm fragments relocated from the server (mainly computation of the distance function). All these cost components are quantified and their significance is compared for different types of data sets (small vs. large, simple distance function vs. complex distance function). In every experiment, the performance of the proposed secure M-Index is compared with the basic (non-encrypted) version of M-Index in order to properly quantify the cost paid for the security.

5.1   Data Sets and Settings

The Encrypted M-Index was tested on three real data sets, whose properties are summarized in Table 1.

YEAST [1] A gene expression data matrix obtained from a Microarray experiment on yeast. Each entry indicates the expression level of a specific gene (row/tuple) at a specific condition (column/attribute) [4].

HUMAN [2] A gene expression data matrix obtained from a Lymphoma/Leukemia Molecular Profiling Project.

CoPhIR [3] Collection of one million images downloaded from Flicker photo site. From each image, five MPEG-7 visual descriptors were extracted and the distance combines them [15]. We test scalability of our solution on this set.

Table 1. Data sets summary

Name	# of records	Data type	Distance function
YEAST	2,882	17-dim. num. vectors	L_1
HUMAN	4,026	96-dim. num. vectors	L_1
CoPhIR	1,000,000	280-dim num. vectors	combination of L_p

We performed all the experimental evaluations on a machine with 8 CPU cores (double quad core) with 8GB RAM, 4 high-speed disks in RAID-5. To reduce an influence of network communication time, both encryption client and M-Index server were running on the same machine communicating via loopback interface. Standard symmetric cipher AES with 128 bit key was used for encryption.

---

[1] http://arep.med.harvard.edu/biclustering/
[2] http://arep.med.harvard.edu/biclustering/
[3] http://cophir.isti.cnr.it/

Evaluation parameters of the M-Index running on the server side for each data set are summarized in Table 2. The pivots used were chosen at random from within the data set. The experimental evaluation is divided into two phases: the construction phase (data insertion) and the search phase.

Table 2. M-Index parameters

Name	Bucket capacity	Storage type	# of pivots
YEAST	200	Memory storage	30
HUMAN	250	Memory storage	50
CoPhIR	1,000	Disk storage	100

5.2 Index Construction

For the construction phase, we used bulk insert operations to insert the data into M-Index running as the server via encryption client. The size of each bulk was 1,000. Measures taken for each data set are the following (they are used for both construction and search phases):

client time the overall client computation time: data encryption/decryption, distance computations (object-pivot distances), and processing overhead,

server time the time to store objects in the M-Index (and to build the M-Index cell tree) or, in the search phase, to prepare the candidate set,

communication time time spent on communication between server and client,

overall time sum of client, server and communication times.

Results for the construction phase are summarized in Table 3. We can see that the relative importance of the client, server and communication times differs for the three data sets: for the small YEAST and HUMAN data sets, the server time is more than 50 % of the client time and the communication time is very important, and, for CoPhIR, the server and communication times are marginal in comparison with the time spent by client-side computations. This is caused by the fact that the CoPhIR distance function is more demanding than the YEAST and HUMAN and the distances are computed on client. By analogy, the encryption time is relatively more important for YEAST and HUMAN.

Table 3. Index construction of encrypted M-Index

	YEAST	HUMAN	CoPhIR
Client time [s]	0.208	0.324	1,584.5
Encryption time [s]	0.117	0.155	32.2
Dist. comp. time [s]	0.026	0.101	1,541.4
Server time [s]	0.116	0.188	70.2
Communication time [s]	0.182	0.288	52.9
Overall time [s]	0.506	0.800	1,707.7

Let us compare these results with the basic non-encrypted M-Index. All the settings (computational power, network, M-Index parameters, client-server architecture, etc.) were the same, the only difference was the absence of the encryption layer. The index construction results for non-encrypted M-Index are summarized in Table 4. For the small YEAST and HUMAN data sets, we can see that the overall time increase caused by the encryption (Table 3) was about 60 % (e.g. 0.315 s vs 0.506 s, for YEAST). In the case of CoPhIR, the overall time is practically the same for both variants because the encryption time is marginal comparing to the distance computation time.

Table 4. Index construction of the basic (non-encrypted) M-Index

	YEAST	HUMAN	CoPhIR
Client time [s]	0.001	0.009	0.300
Server time [s]	0.144	0.216	1,563.4
Dist. comp. time [s]	0.026	0.101	1,541.4
Communication time [s]	0.170	0.265	141.4
Overall time [s]	0.315	0.490	1,705.2

5.3 Approximate Search

For the evaluation of the search efficiency, we used the approximate k-NN search algorithm on one hundred query objects randomly chosen from the data set. We varied the parameter k but the results were similar and we present only results for $k = 30$. All presented results are averaged over the 100 queries. For each data set, we varied the size of the candidate set provided by the server (see Section 9) which influences the quality of the result and efficiency. Besides the measures introduced in the previous section, the following values are presented:

decryption time time spent on deserialization and decryption of the candidate objects received from the server,
recall quality of the result (see Section 4.1),
communication cost amount of data sent between the server and client.

The search results for the Encrypted M-Index are summarized in Table 5 (YEAST) and Table 6 (CoPhIR). Results for the HUMAN data set are not presented – the trends do not differ from YEAST (the sizes of the collections are very similar and the character of data and distance function is the same).

For the two small data sets (YEAST and HUMAN) with a simple distance function, server time is approximately 50% of the client time. For the CoPhIR data set, the ratio of server/client time is approximately 1/5 due to resource demanding distance computations on client side. The relative significance of decryption time (which includes also deserialization of the objects) is the same for all the data sets (and candidate sizes) and it is relatively high; this cost component can be hardly moved from the client, provided the system is secure (decryption can be done only by an authorized client having a secret key).

Table 5. Approximate 30-NN evaluation using the Encrypted M-Index (YEAST)

Candidate set size	150	300	600	1,500
Client time [s]	0.002	0.003	0.006	0.014
Decryption time [s]	0.001	0.002	0.004	0.010
Dist. comp. time [s]	0.001	0.001	0.002	0.003
Server time [s]	0.001	0.002	0.004	0.009
Communication time [s]	0.003	0.003	0.004	0.008
Overall time [s]	0.006	0.008	0.014	0.031
Recall [%]	59.80	82.87	91.3	91.6
Communication cost [kB]	25.805	51.643	103.308	258.314

Naturally, the decryption, distance computation and communication time values are linearly proportional to the size of the candidate set S_C, which also influences the recall. For the YEAST data set, we can observe that the $|S_C| = 600$ (about 20 % of the collection size) results in recall over 90 % and further increase of the S_C size does not lead to a significant recall improvement. For CoPhIR, we can achieve almost 90% recall with the S_C size of 50,000 (5 % of the collection).

Table 6. Approximate 30-NN evaluation using the Encrypted M-Index (CoPhIR)

Candidate set size	500	1,000	5,000	10,000	20,000	50,000
Client time [s]	0.034	0.047	0.224	0.446	0.899	2.429
Decryption time [s]	0.019	0.026	0.132	0.264	0.534	1.451
Dist. comp. time [s]	0.009	0.018	0.082	0.180	0.356	0.969
Server time [s]	0.005	0.016	0.059	0.110	0.207	0.498
Communication time [s]	0.006	0.008	0.029	0.054	0.106	0.290
Overall time [s]	0.045	0.071	0.312	0.610	1.212	3.217
Recall [%]	7.619	10.952	36.667	55.238	71.905	87.143
Communication cost [kB]	460	921	4,605	9,211	18,423	46,058

For comparison, we present the results of the search procedure on the basic (non-encrypted) M-Index – see Table 7 (YEAST) and Table 8 (CoPhIR). In this setting, practically all the work is done on the server side. The most significant difference between encrypted and non-encrypted M-Index is in the communication cost and time, because the non-encrypted variant directly returns the answer set with 30 objects, not the candidate set (which can have up to 50,000 objects in case of CoPhIR). The fixed set of 30 objects transferred between sever and client implies same communication time for all S_C sizes. The amount of work on the client is negligible, therefore there are no values in the search result tables.

To summarize this section, the price paid for privacy in the search phase on Encrypted M-Index is mainly the communication cost (which grows linearly with the candidate set size) and the time of decrypting the candidate objects. This results in approximately three times longer overall search time measured on the encrypted variant. The distance computations, performed during the necessary candidate set refinement on the client, constitute between 1/10 and 1/3 of the overall search time, depending on the complexity of the distance function.

Table 7. Approx. 30-NN evaluation using basic (non-encrypted) M-Index (YEAST)

Candidate set size	150	300	600	1,500
Client time [s]	–	–	–	–
Server time [s]	0.001	0.001	0.002	0.003
Dist. comp. time [s]	0.001	0.001	0.002	0.003
Communication time [s]	0.002	0.002	0.002	0.002
Overall time [s]	0.003	0.003	0.004	0.005
Communication cost [kB]	5.161	5.164	5.162	5.161

Table 8. Approx. 30-NN evaluation using basic (non-encrypted) M-Index (CoPhIR)

Candidate set size	500	1,000	5,000	10,000	20,000	50,000
Client time [s]	–	–	–	–	–	–
Server time [s]	0.023	0.032	0.116	0.215	0.416	1.029
Dist. comp. time [s]	0.009	0.018	0.082	0.180	0.356	0.969
Communication time [s]	0.006	0.006	0.005	0.005	0.005	0.006
Overall time [s]	0.029	0.038	0.121	0.220	0.421	1.023
Communication cost [kB]	26.421	26.174	26.403	26.325	26.196	26.254

5.4 Comparison with Other Solutions

In order to compare our solution with the referenced approaches, we evaluated 1-NN queries on the YEAST data set, which corresponds with the setting of Yiu et al. [4]. To be more specific, we adjusted the approximate 1-NN strategy so that the server-side M-Index was limited to access only one M-Index Voronoi cell which then forms the candidate set (this leads to candidate sets of average size 42). Again, we ran these 1-NN queries for 100 randomly chosen query objects (they were excluded from the indexed set). In Table 9, we report average values of the collected measures. The recall value says how many queries (out of 100) resulted in the actual nearest neighbor.

In comparison with results presented by Yiu et al. [4], the Encpryted M-Index outperformed all the techniques in the communication cost. It also outperformed FDH [4] (technique which uses also approximate search) in CPU time. On the other hand, it takes more time to construct the index (the Encrypted M-Index was approximately twice slower than FDH).

However, it is always difficult to compare the wall-clock CPU times, as they strongly depend on specific implementation and hardware. Moreover, the referenced paper does not specify technical details about the symmetric cipher used (and its key length), the computational power and network setting. Also, the referenced approaches [4] modify the distance function for indexing, therefore they belong to the fourth privacy level whereas our approach fulfills conditions of the third level (see Section 2.3).

Table 9. Approximate 1-NN search evaluation results for the YEAST data set

Client time [ms]	0.509
Decryption time [ms]	0.160
Dist. comp. time [ms]	0.210
Server time [ms]	1.001
Communication time [ms]	1.180
Overall time [ms]	2.690
Recall [%]	94.0
Communication cost [kB]	2.368

6   Conclusions and Future Work

We proposed a method that can be used to ensure data privacy in similarity search systems outsourced in a cloud. The proposed solution exploits existing efficient metric indexes based on a fixed set of pivots. This set is part of the secret key controlled by authorized clients, while the server itself cannot compute the similarity distance function, nor it can access any data in an unencrypted form. A potential attacker can only learn encrypted object data and pivot permutations.

Our approach has been implemented as a real client-server "similarity cloud" system exploiting an existing mature implementation of the M-Index (disk-efficient, parallel, potentially distributed). The performance of the system was experimentally evaluated on several real data sets focusing on individual components of the search time (server, communication, data decryption, client data operations). The Encrypted M-Index has the intention of providing required privacy while preserving the server-side efficiency as much as possible and relocate only the necessary computations to the client (data decryption and computation of query-data distances).

In the future, we would like to analyze the precise range and k-NN evaluation strategies of Encrypted M-Index in comparison to the approximate strategy and to other possible solutions. Further, we would like to study various types of distance transformations (i.e. transform the distances to pivots stored on the server for precise strategies); such transformation could better hide information about the data set distribution and thus further restrict possible attacks.

Acknowledgments. This work was supported by national Czech Research Foundation project GACR P103/12/G084.

References

1. Park, H.A., Kim, B.H., Lee, D.H., Chung, Y.D., Zhan, J.: Secure similarity search. In: 2007 IEEE International Conference on Granular Computing (GRC 2007), pp. 598–598. IEEE (2007)
2. Li, J., Wang, Q., Wang, C., Cao, N., Ren, K., Lou, W.: Fuzzy keyword search over encrypted data in cloud computing. In: Proceeding of the 29th Conference on Information Communications, pp. 441–445 (2010)
3. Cao, N., Wang, C., Li, M., Ren, K., Lou, W.: Privacy-preserving multi-keyword ranked search over encrypted cloud data. In: 2011 Proceedings IEEE INFOCOM, pp. 829–837. IEEE (2011)
4. Yiu, M.L., Assent, I., Jensen, C.S., Kalnis, P.: Outsourced Similarity Search on Metric Data Assets. IEEE Transactions on Knowledge and Data Engineering 24(2), 338–352 (2012)
5. Novak, D., Batko, M.: Metric index: an efficient and scalable solution for similarity search. In: Second International Workshop on Similarity Search and Applications (SISAP 2009), pp. 65–73. IEEE (2009)
6. Novak, D., Batko, M., Zezula, P.: Metric Index: An Efficient and Scalable Solution for Precise and Approximate Similarity Search. Information Systems 36(4), 721–733 (2011)
7. Zezula, P., Amato, G., Dohnal, V., Batko, M.: Similarity Search: The Metric Space Approach. In: Advanced Database Systems, vol. 32. Springer (2006)
8. Hore, B., Mehrotra, S., Canim, M., Kantarcioglu, M.: Secure multidimensional range queries over outsourced data. The VLDB Journal 21(3), 333–358 (2011)
9. Chávez, E., Figueroa, K., Navarro, G.: Effective Proximity Retrieval by Ordering Permutations. IEEE Transactions on Pattern Analalysis and Machine Intelligence 30(9), 1647–1658 (2008)
10. Amato, G., Savino, P.: Approximate similarity search in metric spaces using inverted files. In: Proceedings of the 3rd International Conference on Scalable Information Systems (2008)
11. Esuli, A.: PP-Index: Using permutation prefixes for efficient and scalable approximate similarity search. In: Proceedings of LSDS-IR 2009 (2009)
12. Chávez, E., Navarro, G., Baeza-Yates, R., Marroquín, J.L.: Searching in metric spaces. ACM Computing Surveys 33(3), 273–321 (2001)
13. Skala, M.: Counting distance permutations. Journal of Discrete Algorithms 7(1), 49–61 (2009)
14. Batko, M., Novak, D., Zezula, P.: MESSIF: Metric similarity search implementation framework. Digital Libraries Research and Development 4877(102), 1–10 (2007)
15. Bolettieri, P., Esuli, A., Falchi, F., Lucchese, C., Perego, R., Piccioli, T., Rabitti, F.: CoPhIR: A Test Collection for Content-Based Image Retrieval. CoRR abs/0905.4 (2009)

Provenance for Web 2.0 Data

Meghyn Bienvenu[1], Daniel Deutch[2], and Fabian M. Suchanek[3]

[1] CNRS and Université Paris-Sud
[2] Ben Gurion University of the Negev
[3] Max-Planck-Institute for Informatics

Abstract. In this paper, we look at Web data that comes from multiple sources, as in the Web 2.0. We argue that Web data is more than just its content. Rather, a piece of Web data carries along different facets, such the *transformations* that data underwent, the different *perspectives* that users have on the content, and the *context* in which a statement is made. We put forward the idea that *provenance*, i.e. the tracing of where data comes from, can help us model these phenomena. We study how far existing approaches address the issue of provenance for Web data, and identify gaps and open problems.

1 Introduction

With the arrival of the Web 2.0, virtually everyone can publish and disseminate data on the Web. This phenomenon contributes to the richness and diversity of content on the Web. At the same time, it gives Web data dimensions that go beyond its pure content: Every piece of information carries a history of where it was first produced, by whom it was first produced, and in which context it was first stated. In this article, we shed light on these attributes of Web data, and we make first steps towards a formal model for these phenomena. We start by exemplifying some of the key properties of Web data.

Data Transformation. Consider a social network such as Facebook or Twitter: users can publish their own opinions and knowledge, but they can also refer to data posted by other users. Such references typically propagate further, through friends of friends. This phenomenon applies also to other medias such as blogs, emails, and collaborative resources like Wikipedia. Transformations on the Web may be diverse and complex, and "copying" or referring to an existing piece of data is only one example. For instance, there are many services that *aggregate* different feeds into a single piece of data, e.g. Facebook notifications on the number of friends attending an event, or the number of friends "liking" a particular fact. Any given piece of information can carry along an entire history of such transformations.

User Perspectives. People may have different views and opinions on the same thing (e.g. on politicians, or the quality of restaurants or hotels). Statements made by one content provider do not necessarily coincide with statements made

W. Jonker and M. Petković (Eds.): SDM 2012, LNCS 7482, pp. 148–155, 2012.
© Springer-Verlag Berlin Heidelberg 2012

by another provider. A consumer of data might prefer some providers to others. Thus, the origin or *perspective* of the data is an essential meta-property of Web data.

Data Context. The correctness of data (and the trust of users in it) may also depend on the *context* in which this data was published. As a simple example, the statement "Sarkozy is the president of France" is interpreted as true if published in 2008, but is incorrect if published in late 2012. In this simple example, the context of a fact is a timestamp; however, in general, it may be any metadata, such as authorship or location, affecting the trust in facts. We observe that the context metadata is typically not an inherent part of the fact itself. However, it is an essential attribute of any piece of information.

The landscape becomes more intricate when transformation, perspectives, and context are combined: authors may cite other content, and the context of the data should capture both the original and the citing author. This requires the management of context for *propagated* content.

A Proposed Tool: Provenance. We propose to model the different aspects of pieces of information by *provenance*. The provenance of a piece of data is a record of meta-information, which is attached to the piece of data, and which indicates where the piece of data comes from. In particular, this meta-information can record the context in which the data was created. In the setting of relational and semi-structured databases, provenance [1–5] was shown to be an extremely useful technique for managing both the original context of data and the ways in which it was manipulated and transformed. We believe that provenance can be used with similar success for Web data, but one of the main challenges here lies in capturing context, perspectives and transformations in a mathematical provenance model.

Applications of Provenance. A formal framework for the provenance for Web data can have far-reaching applications. First, it can establish the **authorship** of a certain piece of information. This is useful, e.g., for the protection of intellectual property rights. Provenance can also help guarantee the **privacy** of information (as shown in the context of relational databases by e.g. [1]), e.g in social networks. Finally, provenance is essential for determining the **trust** in a given piece of data.

Desiderata. To realize the great potential of provenance for Web data, two main challenges should be addressed. First, one must devise an expressive provenance **model**. This model should account for different types of Web data (Web 2.0, social networks, weblogs, etc.), different kinds of provenance (privacy, location, time, etc.) under different kinds of transformations (references, aggregation, negation, etc.). Principled and generic models for provenance have proven to be highly effective in the context of relational and semi-structured databases; we believe they could play a similarly central role for Web data.

Second, the provenance model should be accompanied by a **reasoning** mechanism. Inspired by [6], we propose that such a mechanism should handle (at least) the following two archetypical questions: (1) *Given a provenance annotation,* *which statements hold for it?* This would allow queries such as "What happened in 2012?" or "What is the set of statements that both Alice and Bob can access?". (2) *Given a statement, what are the provenance annotations for which the statement holds?* This would allow questions such as "How did this statement come about?", or "Who has sufficient credentials to see this statement?". Note that provenance annotations could be arbitrarily complex: the answer to the question could be "Either Alice or David and Charles together", or "Everybody who is in Unix group X and is friends or relatives with Alice".

2   Modeling Provenance and Context

Provenance in Databases. Several different provenance management techniques have been introduced in e.g. [3–5]. A general framework for provenance management was proposed in [1]. It uses the mathematical structure of *semirings* to capture provenance of various kinds (including those mentioned above [7]). The model applies to a wide range of applications, in a manner that corresponds exactly to the operations of the positive relational algebra. Extensions of the framework to XML query languages [8] and Datalog [1] have also been defined. Recent work [9] has shown that if the set of available data transformations includes an *aggregate* construct (a common type of Web data transformation), then the semiring framework no longer suffices to capture all possible transformations; an alternative construction based on semi-modules was proposed.

Provenance in the Semantic Web. The Semantic Web captures provenance by Named Graphs [10]. Named Graphs equip every triple statement on the Semantic Web with a 4th component, the graph identifier, which can be used for grouping triples into sets. Newer versions of the query language SPARQL allow targeting triples of specific sets or asking for sets with specific properties. The Named Graph model is very useful for the Semantic Web, but is, by itself, far from being a universally applicable provenance model for Web data. It provides no sophisticated reasoning capabilities, nor any support for transformations beyond simple inclusion. The work of [11, 12] devises provenance for SPARQL queries on linked Web data, and [13] studies algebras of provenance annotations for RDFS. However, a general model of provenance would need to support also the data transformations that happen in social networks or in collaborative platforms such as Wikipedia. The work on watermarking ontologies [14, 15] serves to prove the provenance of Semantic Web data. However, it does not provide a model of provenance in general, let alone means to reason on it.

Provenance on the Web. A large amount of data on the Web already comes naturally with provenance information. The content of every Web page is trivially associated with its URL. Information quoted from or taken from other pages often comes with an indication of the source. Social networks know the concept of authorship, which translates directly into provenance in our setting. Information that has been extracted automatically from Web pages provides another source of provenance data. Many extraction systems [16–19] note from which source a piece of information was extracted. In a similar spirit, automatically generated ontologies [20, 21] can often trace the source of every one of their statements. The YAGO ontology [20], for example, has systematically attached provenance meta-data to its triples. YAGO stores the source, the confidence of extraction, and the extraction technique with every single one of its facts – totaling 80 million for the entire ontology. Recently, YAGO's facts have been annotated with a temporal and a geo-spatial component [22], indicating when and where an event took place. This yields hundreds of thousands of statements with attached meta information, making it an ontology that is anchored in time and space. This work can serve as a use-case for the model of Web data provenance.

Context and Viewpoints in Artificial Intelligence. J. McCarthy was among the first to highlight the need for a formal treatment of context [23]. He proposed [24] to annotate formulas with the context in which they hold, i.e., to use formulas of the form $ist(c, \varphi)$, which mean that φ is true in the context c. He argued that contexts should be first-class citizens in the logic, enabling statements about the properties of particular contexts and the relationships between them, e.g. "If someone is the president of a country, then that person is president in all geographic subcontexts". McCarthy's ideas inspired several concrete logics of context [25–28]. An alternative framework, called multi-context systems [29, 30], treats contexts as local theories which can be interrelated by means of bridge rules, which specify how information can be transferred between contexts.

Epistemic logics [31, 32] have long been studied as a means for representing and reasoning about the viewpoints of different agents. Such logics augment a standard logic, most commonly propositional logic, with a set of *epistemic operators* which can be used to make complex statements about the viewpoints of a group of agents, such as: "Alex does not know that Sue and Bob are dating, but Mary believes that Alex knows that they are dating". Various extensions [33] have been proposed to capture the dynamics of knowledge and belief (e.g. that once Bob tells Alex that he dates Sue, Alex now knows this).

Context logics and epistemic logics were not designed to handle large amounts of *data* and do not offer database-style querying capabilities. Moreover, in the case of multi-agent epistemic logics, the basic reasoning tasks are PSPACE-hard [34], making them ill-suited for querying vast quantities of Web data.

Challenges. While the different provenance models described above have proven useful in their respective fields, none is able to address all the desiderata for Web data provenance. If we take the models used in databases as a starting point, we notice that the transformations of provenance are mirrored in the operations on the data (e.g. semiring operations correspond exactly to the operations of the positive relational algebra). In order to extend this idea to the realm of Web data, the following challenges must be addressed: (1) Identify a set of Web data transformations that is expressive enough to capture common features of Web data; (2) Design a mathematical model that captures these transformations; and (3) Design an automated mechanism that identifies real-life transformations, and outputs an instance of the model. The envisioned model should allow complex inference on contexts and viewpoints, as is done in AI, and it should be semantic, large-scale, and distributed - issues addressed in (Semantic) Web research. We believe that a holistic approach bridging these different research areas can yield a model for Web data provenance that is both expressive and tractable.

3   Reasoning about Context

A Simple Model. To illustrate possible reasoning tasks on provenance, we present a simple model for contexts and propagation. We define a *context-annotated database* as a pair (D, A), where D is a database, and A is a mapping from the facts of D to a positive Boolean expression over a fixed set C of context variables. The semantics is given in terms of valuations of the context variables. Given a valuation V of C, we denote by $V(D, A)$ the (standard) database which contains exactly those facts $f \in D$ such that the Boolean expression $A(f)$ evaluates to true under V. In addition, we allow a *background theory*. This is a propositional formula (including negation) over C that captures basic relationships between contexts. Finally, the user may be interested only in certain contexts, which may be the conjunction or disjunction of atomic contexts from C (e.g., all facts that hold in 1990 or 2000). We thus define the notion of a *viewer context*, as a positive propositional theory over C.

Data Transformations. We add a simple model for data transformations, captured by positive relational algebra transformations of the data; these correspond to positive Boolean algebra on annotations. For example, if the same rumor is sent to Alice by two friends Bob and Carol, then it is associated with a Boolean expression Bob ∨ Carol (where Bob and Carol are context variables standing for trust in Bob and Carol respectively), expressing that it is enough for Alice to trust one of them in order to trust the fact.

Reasoning Tasks. In Section 1, we introduced two general reasoning questions for provenance In our toy model, the decision problems corresponding to these questions can be formalized as follows:

Definition 1 (POSS Problem). *Given an annotated database (D, A), a propositional formula F (comprising the background theory and viewer context), and a Boolean positive relational algebra query Q, decide whether there exists a valuation V of C which satisfies F and is such that Q holds in $V(D, A)$.*

Theorem 1. POSS *is PTIME if F is positive, and NP-complete in general.*

Definition 2 (CERT Problem). *Given an annotated database (D, A), a propositional formula F (comprising the background theory and viewer context), and a Boolean positive relational algebra query Q, decide whether it is the case that Q holds in $V(D, A)$ holds for every valuation V which satisfies F.*

Theorem 2. CERT *is PTIME if F is Horn, coNP-complete in general.*

Challenges. The above model is merely a toy model designed to illustrate the concept of reasoning on provenance. When moving to more intricate data transformations, notably aggregates, Boolean formulas may not be enough to represent the context [9]. Other transformations (like re-tweeting) might require nesting of annotations, in the spirit of nested modalities from context and epistemic logics, and of provenance for the nested relational calculus [35]. Also, from a usability point-of-view, it may prove more natural to express the annotations and background theory using (a suitable fragment of) first-order logic, rather than propositional logic. Moving to a richer logical language will likely affect the complexity of reasoning, and it might also open up more reasoning tasks beyond the two that we considered. Finally, there are important practical challenges in the implementation of a reasoning engine for provenance; optimizations will be crucial in order to ensure scalability.

4 Conclusions

In this paper, we have emphasized the need for a model of provenance for Web data and for reasoning capabilities. We have given an overview of different approaches in the areas of the Semantic Web, in the Database domain, and in Artificial Intelligence. However, we have come to the conclusion that none of the existing approaches addresses the problem of provenance for Web data in its entirety. Thus, we believe that the exploration of the issues of provenance, data transformation, and data perspectives will be a fertile ground for future research.

References

1. Green, T.J., Karvounarakis, G., Tannen, V.: Provenance semirings. In: PODS (2007)
2. Cui, Y., Widom, J., Wiener, J.L.: Tracing the lineage of view data in a warehousing environment. ACM Transactions on Database Systems 25(2) (2000)
3. Buneman, P., Cheney, J., Vansummeren, S.: On the expressiveness of implicit provenance in query and update languages. ACM Trans. Database Syst. 33(4) (2008)
4. Buneman, P., Khanna, S., Tan, W.-C.: Why and Where: A Characterization of Data Provenance. In: Van den Bussche, J., Vianu, V. (eds.) ICDT 2001. LNCS, vol. 1973, pp. 316–330. Springer, Heidelberg (2000)
5. Benjelloun, O., Sarma, A., Halevy, A., Theobald, M., Widom, J.: Databases with uncertainty and lineage. VLDB J. 17, 243–264 (2008)
6. Abiteboul, S., Duschka, O.M.: Complexity of answering queries using materialized views. In: Mendelzon, A.O., Paredaens, J. (eds.) PODS, pp. 254–263 (1998)
7. Green, T.: Containment of conjunctive queries on annotated relations. In: ICDT (2009)
8. Foster, J., Green, T., Tannen, V.: Annotated XML: queries and provenance. In: PODS (2008)
9. Amsterdamer, Y., Deutch, D., Tannen, V.: Provenance for aggregate queries. In: PODS (2011)
10. Carroll, J.J., Bizer, C., Hayes, P., Stickler, P.: Named graphs, provenance and trust. In: WWW 2005: Proceedings of the 14th International Conference on World Wide Web, pp. 613–622. ACM, New York (2005)

11. Theoharis, Y., Fundulaki, I., Karvounarakis, G., Christophides, V.: On provenance of queries on semantic web data. IEEE Internet Computing 15(1), 31–39 (2011)
12. Cheney, J., Chong, S., Foster, N., Seltzer, M.I., Vansummeren, S.: Provenance: a future history. In: Proc. of OOPSLA (2009)
13. Theoharis, Y., Fundulaki, I., Karvounarakis, G., Christophides, V.: On provenance of queries on semantic web data. IEEE Internet Computing 99(preprints) (2010)
14. Suchanek, F.M., Gross-Amblard, D.: Adding fake facts to ontologies. In: Demo at the International World Wide Web Conference. ACM (2010)
15. Suchanek, F.M., Gross-Amblard, D., Abiteboul, S.: Watermarking for Ontologies. In: Aroyo, L., Welty, C., Alani, H., Taylor, J., Bernstein, A., Kagal, L., Noy, N., Blomqvist, E. (eds.) ISWC 2011, Part I. LNCS, vol. 7031, pp. 697–713. Springer, Heidelberg (2011)
16. Etzioni, O., Cafarella, M., Downey, D., Kok, S., Popescu, A.M., Shaked, T., Soderland, S., Weld, D.S., Yates, A.: Web-scale information extraction in knowitall (preliminary results). In: World Wide Web Conference (2004)
17. Suchanek, F.M., Sozio, M., Weikum, G.: SOFIE: A Self-Organizing Framework for Information Extraction. In: International World Wide Web conference (WWW 2009). ACM Press, New York (2009)
18. Nakashole, N., Theobald, M., Weikum, G.: Scalable knowledge harvesting with high precision and high recall. In: WSDM (2011)
19. Carlson, A., Betteridge, J., Wang, R.C., Hruschka Jr., E.R., Mitchell, T.M.: Coupled semi-supervised learning for information extraction. In: Proceedings of the Third ACM International Conference on Web Search and Data Mining, WSDM 2010 (2010)
20. Suchanek, F.M., Kasneci, G., Weikum, G.: YAGO: A core of semantic knowledge - unifying WordNet and Wikipedia. In: Williamson, C.L., Zurko, M.E., Patel-Schneider, P.F., Shenoy, P.J. (eds.) World Wide Web Conference, Banff, Canada, pp. 697–706. ACM (2007)
21. Auer, S., Bizer, C., Kobilarov, G., Lehmann, J., Cyganiak, R., Ives, Z.G.: DBpedia: A Nucleus for a Web of Open Data. In: Aberer, K., Choi, K.-S., Noy, N., Allemang, D., Lee, K.-I., Nixon, L.J.B., Golbeck, J., Mika, P., Maynard, D., Mizoguchi, R., Schreiber, G., Cudré-Mauroux, P. (eds.) ASWC 2007 and ISWC 2007. LNCS, vol. 4825, pp. 722–735. Springer, Heidelberg (2007)
22. Hoffart, J., Suchanek, F.M., Berberich, K., Weikum, G.: Yago2: a spatially and temporally enhanced knowledge base from wikipedia. Artificial Intelligence Journal (2012)
23. McCarthy, J.: Generality in artificial intelligence. Communications of the ACM 30(12), 1029–1035 (1987)
24. McCarthy, J.: Notes on formalizing context. In: IJCAI, pp. 555–562 (1993)
25. Buvac, S., Mason, I.A.: Propositional logic of context. In: Proc. of AAAI, pp. 412–419 (1993)
26. Buvac, S.: Quantificational logic of context. In: Proc. of AAAI, pp. 600–606 (1996)
27. Nossum, R.: A decidable multi-modal logic of context. J. Applied Logic 1(1-2), 119–133 (2003)
28. Klarman, S., Gutiérrez-Basulto, V.: Two-dimensional description logics for context-based semantic interoperability. In: AAAI (2011)
29. Giunchiglia, F., Serafini, L.: Multilanguage hierarchical logics, or: How we can do without modal logics. Artificial Intelligence 65(1), 29–70 (1994)
30. Serafini, L., Bouquet, P.: Comparing formal theories of context in ai. Artificial Intelligence 155(1-2), 41–67 (2004)

31. Hintikka, J.: Knowledge and Belief. Cornell University Press (1962)
32. Fagin, R., Halpern, J.Y., Moses, Y., Vardi, M.Y.: Reasoning About Knowledge. MIT Press (1995)
33. van Ditmarsch, H., van der Hoek, W., Kooi, B.: Dynamic Epistemic Logic. Springer (2007)
34. Halpern, J.Y., Moses, Y.: A guide to completeness and complexity for modal logics of knowledge and belief. Artif. Intell. 54(2), 319–379 (1992)
35. Foster, J.N., Green, T.J., Tannen, V.: Annotated xml: queries and provenance. In: PODS, pp. 271–280 (2008)

Towards Enabling Behavioral Trust among Participating Cloud Forensic Data Center Agencies

Sean Thorpe[1], Tyrone Grandison[2], Indrajit Ray[3], and Abbie Barbir[4]

[1] University of Technology, Kingston, Jamaica
[2] IBM Research, York Town Heights, NY, USA
[3] Colorado State University, Fort Collins, USA
[4] Bank of America
thorpe.sean@gmail.com,
tyroneg@us.ibm.com,
indrajit@cs.colostate.edu,
abbie.barbir@bankofamerica.com

Abstract. In this position paper, the authors present some of the concerns with respect to monitoring and managing the behavioral trust of participants in a forensic cloud data center environment. The basic idea of the approach is to view the interaction process of collaborating forensic cloud data centers overseeing an existing investigation or a set of such investigations across distinct jurisdictions. This work is an important first step to support the need for enabling trustable cloud digital investigations among participating law enforcement agencies.

1 Introduction

While cloud forensics is a field that is still in its infancy, it is gaining traction in the face of proliferate criminal actors taking advantage of the insecurity of these abstract domains. By definition a virtual cloud domain represents the service oriented architecture (SOA) based technology that unlocks the economies of scale gained from leveraging traditional web hosted services. In other words, the cloud as a service model offers on-demand, elastic and scalable provisions to its networked end users.

The cloud deployment model is categorized using networked communities of public, private and hybrid domains of users. Underlining these cloud service deployment models is the fact that each deployment has a generic set of service layers, namely the Infrastructure as a Service (IAAS), Platform as a Service (PAAS) and Software as a Service (SAAS) layers. To date, vendors like Amazon with its Elastic Cloud Provisions (EC2) and Google are major IAAS providers. Windows Azure, VMWare and Xen Citrix represent the major PAAS and SAAS providers [1]. These service layer designs however inherently lack any trusted Forensics and Security constructs within the existing virtualization stack, and this has unfortunately become an urgent need by law enforcement.

W. Jonker and M. Petković (Eds.): SDM 2012, LNCS 7482, pp. 156–161, 2012.

Cloud forensics at this point still does not have a universally accepted definition, but current practices borrow heavily from the existing digital forensics literature in how information retrieval can be supported within these logical domains [15]. To ground the theories that this paper puts forward, a suitable definition for cloud forensics would be one based on Casey's definition of forensics as "a characteristic of evidence that satisfies its suitability for admission as fact and its ability to persuade based upon proof (or high statistical confidence)" [2].

As an elastic service model, cloud computing environments are ideally open distributed domains similar to Grid computing and main frame environments [3]. These data clouds are composed of autonomously participating groups that interact with each other using specific mechanisms and protocols to offer and/or use services (e.g. computation, storage, and bandwidth). The difference between the grid and the cloud however is in the elastic, on-demand nature of the resources available across private, as well as public, domains. For the purposes of managing a trustable cloud forensic investigation where participating forensic cloud data centers can be located in any independent set of geographic jurisdictions, one realizes that such participation may not have sufficient knowledge about their interaction partners in the environment; particularly those in a public cloud domain setting. As a result, the authors see trust management mechanisms as a promising solution for strengthening the confidence quality of the interaction between forensic cloud data centers established to act as oversight agencies in the daily operations of large scale cloud computing investigations. We define trust in a Cloud Forensics environment as "the extent to which every participating digital investigative datacenter is willing to interact with each other, at a specific moment in time, with evidence of relative security regarding the identity and the behavior of their counterparts"; even though unexpected negative outcomes could result from the entire interaction process.

This definition extends on the views by Papalilo et.al. [3] and we adopt that this trust permeates all layers of the virtualization stack. We extend the principles in [3] to suggest the need to have a probabilistic cloud forensic data center trust model for both the identity and the behavior of the interaction parties. In this paper, we present the conceptual views for managing the trust of these participatory cloud forensic data centers. Ideas of quality assurance for identifying the "real" behavior of a participant during an interaction and for "keeping" the behavior of the participants "in control" are also presented. If the behavior of a cloud forensic data center participant is "out of control", then this participant's reliability and dependability are called into question, which translates to either:

- The participant not being used as an interaction partner for certain applications, because the expected behavior and trust requirements were not met but the participant could still be considered for other applications with moderate trust requirements OR.
- The participant not being considered anymore for further interactions, independent of the expected behavior and trust requirements of applications.

The rest of the paper is organized as follows. In section 2, an explanation of the trust behavior of cloud forensic data center participants is provided. In section 3, our view on how behavior trust can be established and managed among cloud participants is given. Section 4 presents the considerations for managing (behavioral) trust in cloud forensic environments. In Section 5 concludes and provides discussion on future work.

2   Behavioral Trust of Cloud Forensic Participants

2.1   The Problem of Behavior Definition in Clouds

In the literature, the behavior of collaborative parties in cloud environments remains an abstract notion. Participants can be listed either in a "trust list" or "distrust list" [11]. In most cases, "trust list" behavior reflects the expectations of a participant to simply receive a response from another participant involved in an interaction or sometimes to get accurate results. If an interaction party behaves differently from "normal" expectations, it moves to the "distrust list". Participants within a "trust list" exhibit behavior that is considered a part of trusted zones and are thus eligible for future interactions. Participants within a "distrust list" exhibit behavior which may have only minor or no possibility to be considered for further interactions within the participating group. These claims become particularly important to a cloud digital investigation team who may have to be collaborating in participant groups across different geographic jurisdictions and must cooperate with the collaborating parties to unearth potential evidence required in completing a case for court.

To support a flexible behavioral management and classification system of trust for the cloud forensic data center, additional mechanisms are necessary, e.g. splitting behavior into detailed elements, observing them continuously and offering the possibility for evolving behavior classification.

2.2   Behavior Trust and Quality of Service for the Cloud Forensic Data Center

The use of system based logs for a cloud investigation[12,13] in our prior work demonstrates that the forensic data center users must recognize the need for different aspects of Quality of Service(QoS). In the forensic cloud data center environment, usability of data is an important factor as adopted from work done in [5]. Hence, it is meaningful to investigate the relationship between the QoS and the behavior of participants in a cloud forensic investigation, where the participating forensic data center trust groups are from different jurisdictional cloud environments.

QoS refers to the ability of a cloud forensic data center participant to provide network and computation services such that each user's expectations for timeliness, quality and performance are met. There are several dimensions of QoS described in the literature [6], e.g. accuracy, precision and performance. To support a QoS dimension, the cloud forensic investigator request must specify a level of service for one or more of these dimensions, and the underlying control mechanisms should be capable of delivering these services at the requested QoS levels. QoS deals with a range of expected behavior of an individual cloud forensic data center participant, which as a whole defines the completion of the service a forensic team (or forensic application service) demands. In this context, it is important to map the forensic user's expectations and preferences to the system parameters and capabilities. Hence if the QoS levels are high this can directly influence the trust levels within the data center environments, and the reciprocal is equally true.

From the standpoint of the authors, trust is the most important social element in policing these Internet-supported cloud data systems, as motivated by the earlier work of Grandison and Sloman[14].

3   Establishing Trust among Forensic Cloud Participants

A high degree of trust in a cloud forensic data center participant means that they are likely to be chosen as an interaction partner. Conversely, a low degree of trust suggests that the participant cannot be selected anymore, especially in the case when other, more trusted interaction partners are available. In this way, the trust model aims to guide a participant's decision making process regarding how, when, and who to interact with the others. When an interaction with a new forensic data center is started, i.e. when no information on previous behavior exists, it can use its beliefs about different characteristics of these interaction partners and reason by learning the behavior over a number of interactions. This will act as an enabler in deciding how much trust should be put in each of them. Furthermore, the participant could ask others in the environment about their experiences with the target forensic data center participant(s). If sufficient information is obtained and if this information can be trusted, the participant can reliably choose its interaction partners.

4   Behavioral Trust and Statistical Methods of QOS within a Forensic Cloud

Considering different sources for gathering trust information from (self experience, indirect experience, user/application trust requirements), each forensic cloud data center participant sorts out the collaboration partners and starts interacting only with the "most trusted" of them. During the collaboration experiments, the behavioral trust elements are verified either with 100% or with a certain verification frequency. By verification frequency we mean the number of confirmed recommendations issued over time for a party joining the forensic cloud data center trust list or group. We posit that a verification result, assumes that the trust values are updated and influence the decision making process as to whether the collaboration with a certain participant will continue or will be interrupted. The problems start once any deviation from the expected behavior of a collaboration partner is recognized. We can seek to measure behavior deviation in two ways-: either by deviation with the current collaborating cloud forensic data centers, or an observed deviation over time.

The first type of deviation has a more immediate effect on the current collaboration and the validity of the data being processed. If a 100% verification strategy is applied, it is easy to tell that until that specific moment, no other deviation has happened. On the contrary, if a verification frequency is applied, it is not possible to tell that no more deviations occurred except those verified and where confirmed to have existed.

5   Conclusions

In this position paper, the authors have presented some of the concerns with respect to monitoring and managing the behavioral trust of participants in a forensic cloud data center environment. The basic idea of the approach is to view the interaction process of collaborating forensic cloud data centers overseeing an existing investigation or a set of such investigations across distinct jurisdictions. Ongoing work explores the hardening and verification of a suitable family of trust formalisms and the development of a proof of concept simulation. This cloud simulator environment is similar to Gridsim [4] and explores the use of four (4) enterprise cloud service providers (CSP) including the University of Technology - Jamaica as the participatory cloud forensic groups. We expect to achieve from this ongoing work a qualification of the identifiable trust elements that should be considered, together with more complex scenarios. The aim is to evaluate the effects that trust has in determining how forensic cloud data center groups collaborate as well as to ascertain the performance of every single participant within the groups as a function of the efficiency of designing a sustainable trust model. We believe this is very important, in the face of elevated and intensive threats that inadvertently could compromise the security of forensics within these logical domains.

References

1. Mell, P., Grance, T.: NIST Definition of Cloud Computing, http://csrc.nist.gov/publications/nistpubs/800-145/SP800-145.pdf (retrieved from: September 2009)
2. Casey, E.: Digital Evidence and Computer Crime, 2nd edn. Academic Press, San Diego (2004)
3. Papalilo, E., Friese, T., Smith, M., Freisleben, B.: Trust Shaping: Adapting Trust Establishment and Management to Application Requirements in a Service-Oriented Grid Environment. In: Zhuge, H., Fox, G.C. (eds.) GCC 2005. LNCS, vol. 3795, pp. 47–58. Springer, Heidelberg (2005)
4. GridSim, http://www.gridbus.org/gridsim
5. Foster, I., Kesselman, C.: The Grid2: Blueprint for a New Computing Infrastructure. Morgan Kaufmann (2004)
6. Ali, A.S., Rana, O., Walker, D.W.: WS-QoC: Measuring Quality of Service Compliance. In: Proceeding of the Second International Conference on Service-Oriented Computing Short Papers (ICSOC), New York, USA, pp. 16–25 (2004)
7. Lindstrom, P.: Attacking and Defending Web Service (2004), http://www.forumsystems.com/papers/AttackingandDefending_WS.pdf
8. De Roure, D., Jennings, N., Shadbolt, N.: Research Agenda for the Semantic Grid: A Future E-Science Infrastructure (2001), http://www.semanticgrid.org/v1.9/semgrid.pdf
9. Foster, I., Kishimoto, H., Savva, A., Berry, D., Djaoui, A., Grimshaw, A., Horn, B., Maciel, F., Siebenlist, F., Subramaniam, R., Treadwell, J., Von Reich, J.: The Open Grid Services Architecture (2005), http://www.gridforum.org/documents/GWD-I-E/GFDI.030.pdf
10. Papalilo, E., Freisleben, B.: Combining Incomparable Public Session Keys and Certificateless Public Key Cryptography for Securing the Communication Between Grid Participants. In: Meersman, R., Tari, Z. (eds.) OTM 2007, Part II. LNCS, vol. 4804, pp. 1264–1279. Springer, Heidelberg (2007)
11. Thorpe, S.: Modeling Trust in a Cloud Computing Context. In: Proceedings of the ACM CIKM/PIKM (October 2010)

12. Thorpe, S., Ray, I.: Detecting Temporal Inconsistency in Virtual Machine Activity Timelines. Proceedings of Journal of Information Assurance and Security (JIAS) 7(1) (May 2012)
13. Thorpe, S., Ray, I.: File Timestamps in a Cloud Digital Investigation. Journal of Information Assurance and Security 6(2), 495–502 (2011) ISSN1554-1010
14. Grandison, T., Sloman, M.: A survey of trust in Internet applications. IEEE Communications Surveys& Tutorials 3(4) (2000)
15. Riley, D., Wren, C., Berry, T.: Cloud Forensic Challenges for Law Enforcement proceedings. In: Proceedings of the International Conference for Internet Technology and Secured Transactions, London, UK (November 2010)

Towards Trustworthy Health Platform Cloud

Mina Deng[1], Marco Nalin[3], Milan Petković[1,2], Ilaria Baroni[3], and Abitabile Marco[3]

[1] Philips Research, The Netherlands
[2] Eindhoven University of Technology
[3] Scientific Institute Hospital San Raffaele, Italy
{mina.deng,milan.petkovic}@philips.com,
{nalin.marco,baroni.ilaria,abitabile.marco}@hsr.it

Abstract. To address today's major concerns of health service providers regarding security, resilience and data protection when moving on the cloud, we propose an approach to build a trustworthy healthcare platform cloud, based on a trustworthy cloud infrastructure. This paper first highlights the main security and privacy risks of market available commodity clouds, and outlines security and privacy requirements of a trustworthy health platform cloud, on top of which to deploy various health applications, in compliance with EU data protection legislation. Results from the recent EU TClouds project will be described as a possible solution towards trustworthy cloud architecture, based on a federated cloud-of-clouds, while enforcing security, resilience and data protection in various cloud layers for provisioning trustworthy IaaS, PaaS and SaaS healthcare services.

Keywords: Health Platform as a Service, trustworthy cloud architecture, security, resilience, data protection.

1 Introduction

Attracted by significant benefits of cloud computing, which include improved performance at lower cost and global coverage providing ubiquitous access to healthcare data/applications, many vendors in the healthcare space are seriously considering to go "on the cloud". At the same time there are several other reasons, especially for critical infrastructures applications (e.g., life-threatening), to stay with their legacy systems [16]. Providers of services operating in critical situations (such as patient monitoring or personal emergency response system) are concerned with resilience. They cannot afford any downtime. Another concern in the healthcare domain is related to security and data protection, as many of these applications deal with sensitive health data. When it comes to the use of public clouds, data management outsourcing becomes the biggest concern: being dependent on someone else availability, trustworthiness and ability to protect the data forces the healthcare service providers to undertake and guarantee to their customers responsibilities, which actually belong to the Cloud provider. This includes the threats of malicious insiders, which has been always one of the most dangerous attacks to protected data. Cloud providers need to have a trustworthy, self-managed middleware services that can automatically manage cloud infrastructural resources. Furthermore, nowadays users have very limited control over the service deployment on

W. Jonker and M. Petković (Eds.): SDM 2012, LNCS 7482, pp. 162–175, 2012.

the cloud and have no control over the exact location of the provided services. Besides these technical aspects, to build reliable and trustworthy infrastructures, cloud providers have to face legal issues in data protection in a flexible infrastructure that is usually spread across different countries, raising privacy problems of cross-border data transfer and storage. Therefore methods and techniques to offer trustful services and to build legislation-proof infrastructure to protect customers' data is of utmost importance. Finally, many healthcare providers see the porting and development cost to switch to cloud-based solutions as an important barrier.

In this paper, we propose a design for a trustworthy healthcare platform as a service that addresses the aforementioned concerns. As the platform is expected to manage sensitive health data and be used even in critical applications, it specifically addresses the issues of resilience, security and data protection. It is built on top of a trusted cloud infrastructure that addresses these technical issues and provides users with control over their personal data in compliance with the legal requirements imposed by EU legislation. Next to that, the platform addresses the needs to further decrease development and porting costs, while supporting rapid development of healthcare applications.

The rest of this paper is organized as follows. Section 2 describes the most important risks and consequently derives the requirements. Our trustworthy healthcare platform as a service is presented in Section 3. Trustworthy cloud infrastructure which is the basis on which the platform is build is described in Section 4. Section 5 focuses on middleware and security components. Finally, the use cases and our applications are presented in Section 6.

2   Requirements and the Rationale

The rationale behind this paper is to propose a trustworthy healthcare platform cloud that is built by deploying a trustworthy healthcare platform on top of a trustworthy cloud infrastructure. A healthcare platform is proposed to host numerous healthcare applications, and also provide storage for medical data such as PHR (Personal Health Records). The underlying trustworthy cloud infrastructure is designed to increase the level of trust both for storage and computing, in order to enable security, privacy, and resilience against cloud network failures. This section highlights security threats to commonly available commodity clouds, and security and privacy requirements for building a trustworthy health cloud. We also introduce the TClouds project, which is initiated in the EU providing trustworthy cloud infrastructures to support critical healthcare ICT systems.

2.1   Security and Privacy Risks to Commodity Cloud

Security and privacy risks of cloud computing have been identified by a number of studies, such as Cloud Security Alliance's top threats of cloud computing [9]), ENISAs Cloud risk assessment [11], and Gartners Cloud risk assessment [13]. Key risks include abuse and nefarious use, insecure interfaces and APIs, malicious insiders, shared technology, data loss or leakage, account or service hijacking, lock-in, isolation failure, compliance risks, insecure or incomplete data deletion, data location, availability, and investigative support. In a recent study, crucial security and privacy vulnerabilities of commodity cloud such as Amazons Elastic Compute Cloud (EC2) [7] have been investigated. These vulnerabilities were caused by inappropriate use of Amazon Machine Images (AMIs) management by cloud subscribers. The attacks were able to extract highly sensitive information (including passwords, keys, and credentials) automatically from a variety of publicly available AMIs. Security analysis of OpenStack [17] was performed, identifying a number of security shortcomings [5] of the individual OpenStack component of Nova, Swift, and Glance. Moreover, Microsoft's Azure experienced a major outage on Feb. 29th 2012, due to an incorrect time calculation for the leap year [15].

2.2 Requirements for a Trustworthy Health Cloud

We employ the *Security and Privacy by Design* principle to build a trustworthy Health Cloud to enhance security, privacy and resilience. Requirements for the trustworthy healthcare cloud were analyzed from perspectives of applications and the cloud architecture (i.e., platform and infrastructure layers).

We identified core requirements for building trusted cloud architecture [3] as: (1) *Separation of duties*: cloud providers are responsible for setting up and managing cloud resources (servers and storage), while cloud subscribers are responsible for managing the virtual infrastructure and security policies of end users. (2) *Isolation*: isolation of the multiple tenants on the virtual infrastructure of the different subscribers is of utmost importance, and data isolation from the cloud provider should also be achieved. (3) *Verifiability of trustworthiness*: a technically enforceable level of trust shall be established beyond audits, certification or service level agreements, to ensure integrity of the remote platform such that cloud resources (storage and computing) are in a trustworthy environment. (4) *Integration into subscriber's IT infrastructure*: to provide reliable end-to-end security, we need to have a seamless integration of the cloud resources into subscribers' infrastructure, and maintain a consistent security level among all resources.

Taking the healthcare application perspective, security and privacy requirements of trustworthy health cloud have been analyzed based on the service-logic and the architecture-driven requirement engineering metrologies [10], while considering EU data protection and privacy legislation. These requirements are summarized, alongside an estimate of the provision in different layers of the cloud services. First, there are requirements for *PaaS, also SaaS and IaaS*, layers: log service and integrity of log files (i.e., events on data or virtual machine are securely logged); access control and data security; and confidentiality and integrity of communication channels. In addition, there are requirements to be realized at *SaaS* layer: authentication and authorization for users (developer, end user and administrator) and client-side device; patient's consent and user-centric policy management; legislation compliance via contract and legal enforcements; identity management; (revocable) anonymity of patients; and user data anonymization/pseudonymization according to patient's policy. Moreover, requirements for the *IaaS* layer include: isolation between virtual machines (VMs), to ensure VM's administrative part is inaccessible to unauthorized parties (outsider) or cloud administrators (insider); data confidentiality and integrity via secure data storage (protected by internal security policies); authentication for virtual machine image installation and instance instantiation; and proof of trustworthiness of environment and integrity of virtual machines. The latter can be achieved either by verifying trust levels of commodity cloud environments, or by own trustworthy IaaS cloud with secure hypervisors [19].

2.3 TClouds Approach

TClouds (Trustworthy Clouds) project[1], from the European Commission, aims to address the concerns on security, privacy and resilience in cloud computing, and increase the current understanding of the potential for commodity cloud-based services to host Internet-scale ICT (e.g. healthcare) infrastructures. TClouds is built upon a set of principles: (1) *Flexible trust models*: cloud consumers shall be able to determine their individual security and privacy preferences to provision user-centric protection. (2) *Federated ecosystem of independent cloud providers*: it prevents cloud services depending on any individual provider. Benefits include reduced cloud lock-in and switching cost, simplified migration and standardized APIs, and to avoid monopolistic structures. (3) *Scalable security mechanisms*: the security architecture does not break the underlying cloud principles, and is scalable, transparent, and resilient against failures of the underlying virtual infrastructure. (4) *EU legislation compliance*: TClouds provides a European regulatory framework to address legal and business implications for privacy-enhanced cross-border infrastructure clouds.

3 Trustworthy Health Platform Cloud

3.1 Description of the Health Platform

This section outlines the functionalities of the TClouds healthcare platform, mainly offering *Health Trusted PaaS* (or *Health T-PaaS*) services. Indeed, as end users will have means to manage their personal data as well, we consider the platform also offers SaaS services towards end users in this regard. The healthcare platform is a trustworthy cloud-based multilevel platform providing novel services that:

1) Store trustworthily health data (with trusted IaaS);
2) Provide API for the 3rd party apps to access patient's health data, in a privacy-preserving manner (PaaS);
3) Provide API for the 3rd party apps to use identity/role management services (PaaS);
4) Provide an interface to allow developers to register their apps and access patients' data;
5) Allow end users to manage their data, and specify policies on which data an application/user can access (SaaS).
6) Provide log service and auditing mechanism for authorization requests, user's data access, apps and data management, policy administration.

A first draft architecture of this platform has been developed in the TClouds project, shown in Fig. 1.

[1] http://www.tclouds-project.eu/

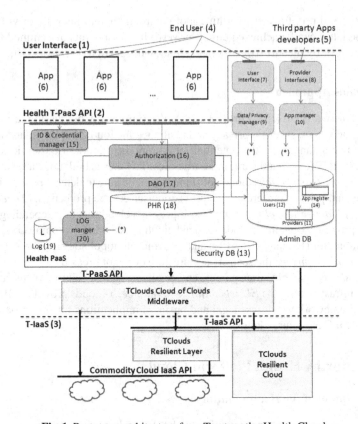

Fig. 1. Prototype architecture for a Trustworthy Health Cloud

Even if the picture is of high level, it shows the boundaries of the Health T-PaaS, with its interfaces both toward users (being actual end users or developers of third parties applications); and toward applications deployed on the platform; as well as toward the lower infrastructure layers, offered by a trustworthy IaaS cloud (to be described in Sec 4).

3.2   Application Interfaces to the Platform

It is expected that many different external 3rd party applications (#6 in Fig. 1) will be deployed on the platform, developed by different service providers using their own resources (or the TClouds trusted IaaS cloud, but not mandatory). The middleware part of the platform (#11 to #20) is the core of the Health T-PaaS. Basically it provides:

1) An interface for applications to retrieve roles and IDs of the platform users (i.e., OpenID-like APIs with improved privacy protection, in which minimum required set of attributes of user's ID will be provided for authentication).

2) An interface for applications to perform CRUD (Create, Read, Update, Delete) operations over the users' personal data. The web services to access users' data will

require an authentication protocol, e.g. based on OAuth, and specific CRUD operations will be granted only depending on users' privacy settings.

Several data bases are represented: an *administration database* (to store #11 apps developers/providers and #12 end users administrative information, and #14 for registration of apps), an *access log database* (#19), a *security database* (#13) and the *PHR database* (#18). Every service developer/provider can deploy one or more apps (#6) on the platform. All health information hosted by the platform are stored in the PHR database (#18) and its integrity is preserved and maintained by the DAO component (#17). The security database (#13) contains privacy policies and data access rights specified by end users. Not to forget the log functionalities (by #19 and #20 – note that some connections has been replaced by asterisks), to save all the accesses to personal data for auditing purposes. An interesting functionality of the Health T-PaaS is indeed the possibility to provide logs both of applications and of end users.

3.3 User Interfaces to the Platform

Users are able to access the health platform directly via user interfaces. There are in particular two types of users:

Application Developers. These are the developers working for the 3rd party service providers (e.g. EHR provider for a hospital). They can access the platform, register themselves with their affiliations and register new applications to be hosted on the platform. We offer a flexible approach to register applications, by allowing developers to specify the security requirement and creating an access profile (e.g. which data need to be accessed) for a particular application, which should be compliant with patient's consent and policy. It will be enforced by the authorization component (#16).

End Users. End users are patients/customers and healthcare and wellbeing professionals (e.g. GP, doctors, nutritionists, or personal trainers). End users are able to manage their data by CRUD operations and control security and privacy policies. End users shall have full control over their personal data and decide the access policy (read, write, delete, etc.), empowering other users or applications to access their data. They can also monitor the logs at any time on who, when and how have accessed their data. Should end users lose confidence in certain service provider, user or application, they would consequently update their policies to prohibit this party from accessing their data. Moreover, if a particular application changes its access profile (e.g. asking for more access rights than originally planned and authorized), the user would be immediately notified; and the application cannot access the data until the user explicitly authorizes it.

4   Building Trustworthy Cloud Infrastructure

The aforementioned healthcare platform will be deployed upon a trusted cloud architecture, which is composed of *TClouds Trustworthy Platform (T-PaaS)* and *Trustworthy Infrastructure (T-IaaS)* clouds (or generally referred as TClouds). By *trust* we refer to security, privacy, and resilience. This section describes the TClouds integrated architecture and its ecosystem.

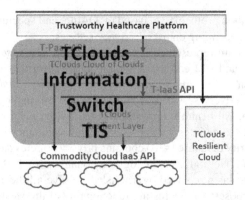

Fig. 2. Building blocks of trustworthy cloud architecture and the TClouds Information Switch (TIS)

In short, TClouds offers a resilient cloud-of-clouds infrastructure providing automated computing resilience against attacks and accidents, in complement or in addition to commodity clouds. This enhanced functionality will be achieved through specialized middleware standing between basic multi-cloud untrustworthy services and the applications requiring security and dependability. The TClouds architecture, in the lower part of Fig. 1, provides service interfaces to produce multilevel trust services with single or multiple clouds.

The *TClouds T-IaaS* services can be realized through a resilient cloud, or a resilient layer on top of a commodity cloud, such as Amazon cloud. It provides trustworthy infrastructure services (*T-IaaS API*) to users at the platform layer. In short, the T-IaaS services provide trustworthy versions of IaaS services, regarding storage and computation. The idea is to provide resilient object storage and virtual machines (VMs), by combinations of fault/intrusion prevention and tolerance mechanisms that build a resilience layer on top of the corresponding untrustworthy storage and processing systems. Examples of security mechanisms will be discussed in Sec 5.3, such as Virtual Trusted Domain and Secure Block Storage.

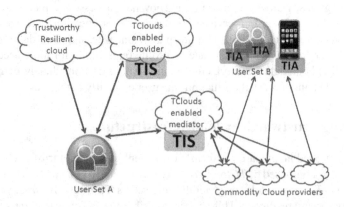

Fig. 3. Trustworthy cloud ecosystem

The *TClouds T-PaaS* services enable adaptive resilience from cloud-of-clouds by extending the T-IaaS API or being built directly on top of commodity clouds. The trustworthy platform services (*T-PaaS API*) are at a higher level of abstraction and are useful to build complex reliable and distributed applications. Examples of underlying security components include resilient object storage, resilient workflow execution, etc. These services are implemented by combinations of fault/intrusion prevention and tolerance mechanisms and protocols, to be discussed in Sec 5.2.

TClouds can be deployed with a number of alternative strategies, with the notions of *TClouds Information Switch (TIS)* and *TClouds Information Agent (TIA)* [3]. The TIS in Fig. 2 is a conceptual block implementing trusted components and protocols in the middleware layer between commodity infrastructure clouds and cloud-supported services (e.g. the health platform). It offers all or part of trustworthy IaaS and PaaS services that are defined in the TClouds architecture, ranging from dedicated VMs to fault tolerant blocks with several TIS replicas. The TIS can build in incremental levels of security, privacy and resilience, depending on its criticality. The TIA is a particular instantiation of the TIS, as a software client residing with cloud users. To mitigate potential security threats, trusted hardware platform can be used to improve resilience of the TIA.

Fig. 3 presents the ecosystem that is capable of offering trustworthy cloud services, from providers to users. A set of users (in set A) can either access services from the TClouds-enabled cloud (enabled with TIA) or the trustworthy resilient cloud directly. The same users can also access trustworthy cloud services implemented on top of commodity clouds through a TClouds-enabled mediator. An alternative way to achieve trustworthy services from commodity cloud is via the TClouds-enabled software (TIA) at the client side of users in set B (or on mobile phones).

5   Middleware and Security Components

Security and privacy requirements for building a trustworthy health cloud, discussed in Sec 2.2, will be addressed on the TClouds security middleware embedded in the architecture. The design and implementation of a set of middleware components that enable users to decide on their trust requirements, encouraging user-centric deployment of appropriate security. This section selects a number of security mechanisms for provisioning trust incrementally in various layers of the cloud services (IaaS, PaaS and SaaS). These deployed security extensions do not break the underlying cloud principles, and are scalable, transparent, and resilient to failures of the cloud virtual infrastructure.

5.1   Security Components in the Health Platform

The proposed healthcare platform in Fig. 1 provides security functionalities including identity management (#15), authorization (#16), and the log service (#20). Apart from this, an access control mechanism and an automatic security auditing tool can also be employed into the platform.

Identity Management and Authorization. The identity management, authentication and authorization mechanism is depicted in Fig. 4. Roles and identities of platform users are managed by the Identity and Credential manager (#15), implemented with OpenID or OAuth 2.0; and the authorization mechanism (#16) employs OAuth (compilable with versions 1.0 and 2.0), enabling end users to allow the 3rd providers (applications) to access the user's personal data stored on the healthcare platform (e.g., PHR in #18). A use scenario is: Each time an application sets up its data access policy (e.g. to read a patient's data), the application would be authorized by the patient (via #16) with an access token, as a sandbox composed of a set of necessary attributes specifying the limited scope of the patient's personal data that the application is allowed to access, according to the patient's policy. If the patient modifies the policy (stored in #13), the platform would consequently deny the following requests of the application to access the patient's data.

Log Service. Log Service (#20) will be deployed to log events originated in the health cloud [20]. Moreover, the Log Service shall ensure integrity, privacy, access control and availability of log entries (stored in #19). Primarily, the Log Service track events at the Cloud infrastructure layer, such as creation, destruction or migration of Virtual Machines (VMs), or allocation and deletion of a bucket of storage. It could also be used by the healthcare platform and applications deployed on the TClouds infrastructure to provide accountability and auditability, for instance as basis for auditing or reporting the Service Level Agreement (SLA) and patient's consent compliance. This Log Service is mainly based on secure logging schemes [14, 18], providing integrity of logs, privacy-aware and access control mechanisms. Moreover, Log Service relies on a resilient storage to guarantee availability and logging of cloud of clouds events.

Access Control. The platform deploys an access control mechanism [1] acting as a policy decision point to manage the hosting of VM instances at an appropriate computing node that satisfies user requirements, during normal operations as well as in incidents. User requirements are technical properties identified from healthcare applications include, QoS/SLA requirements (e.g. system availability, reliability measures, and lower/upper resource limits), and security and privacy requirements (e.g. location of data distribution and processing). This component will take two forms of input: Infrastructure properties and policies, and User properties defining application components dependencies. It assumes that the ACaaS is controlled by the set of trusted Cloud Admin, and the hardware of Computing Node is secure and trusted, incorporating a Trusted Platform Module chip (TPM).

Automatic Audit Tool. Another mechanism deployed is an automatic audit tool, called SAVE (Security Assurance for Virtual Environment) [6]. This automated audit mechanism empowers the healthcare platform and applications to validate isolation of multitenants (such as various service providers) in the cloud. It extracts configuration data from multiple virtualization environments, transforming the data into a normalized graph representation, and subsequent analysis of its security properties. The assumption is that the automated validation requires access to the configuration information on the physical nodes or through a central management interface. The current technology is integrated and adapted based on OpenStack.

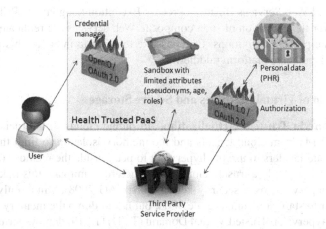

Fig. 4. Identity management, authentication and authorization mechanism is the health platform

5.2 Cloud of Clouds Middleware for Adaptive Resilience

One of the TClouds research challenges is to demonstrate how to build trusted cloud services using resources from a diverse set of commodity public clouds, employing a paradigm known as distributed trust to implement a Cloud of Clouds to tolerate faults and intrusions on up to a certain number of providers. The rationale is to prevent from both accidental and malicious cloud failures by exploiting replication in diverse and uncorrelated infrastructures.

Resilient Object Storage. A cloud-of-cloud service mechanism developed at TClouds T-PaaS is the Resilient Object Storage [4, 8], which provides reliable and secure storage through a federation of object storage services from multiple providers. The system builds on so-called Byzantine fault-tolerant replication that stores data on several providers. Multiple clients may concurrently access the same remote storage provider and operate on the same objects, through an interface that contains the basic and most common operations of object cloud storage. The system can be used to store medical data, and provide confidentiality through encryption, integrity through cryptographic data authentication, and reliability through data replication and erasure coding. Key management for encryption and authentication keys is integrated. Moreover, the data can be shared by multiple (trusted) parties that access the healthcare platform using the untrustworthy clouds as coordination media. An object storage (called DepSky [4]) was implemented on four commercial storage clouds (Amazon S3, Rackspace Files, Windows Azure Blob Service, Nirvanix CDN) forming a cloud-of-clouds trusted storage system.

Fault-Tolerant Workflow Execution. Resilience of Web-service-based workflows of the platform and applications is enhanced by Fault-tolerant Workflow Execution (or Resilient BPEL) [2], by active replications to tolerate web service crashes and provide high availability for the trustworthy healthcare platform. Workflows of Composite Web Services (Web services that are composed of other Web services) are described in an XML-based Web Services Business Process Execution Language (BPEL). Engines responsible for the execution of such composite Web services are replicated, in transparency to the process definitions. One possible location to integrate this mechanism could be the healthcare platform middleware.

5.3   Isolation of Virtual Machines and Secure Storage

VM Isolation via Trusted Virtualization. In public clouds, it is crucial to ensure isolation of VMs from cloud tenants and the memory isolation to limit the power of malicious cloud insiders to use the hypervisor to peek inside the memory of the VMs. Our approach is to build a trusted cloud infrastructure to mitigate this risk – a secure hypervisor, supervised by a security kernel (Sirrix AG 2008), which only allows an administrator to start, stop and migrate VMs, but not to dump the memory. Controlled with secure hypervisor, Trusted Virtual Domain (TVD) [12, 19] deploys virtual domains on shared resources (including computing, storage and networks) with a single security policy, which is strictly isolated from the virtual networks of other TVDs. In our trustworthy healthcare cloud, TVD can be deployed to ensure isolation of stakeholders of the healthcare applications, transparent data protection, and enforcement of access control policies. In the current implementation, the complete healthcare platform (possibly several VMs) are deployed within the same TVD. Major benefits of this approach are separation from other customers on the cloud, and encryption of data and of the communication between our virtual machines. In the next development phase, different VMs of healthcare platform and applications will be separated into different TVDs (e.g. one for each stakeholder), and define the allowed information flows between the TVDs. In this approach, an information flow manager would be needed to support communication between TVDs. For instance, the challenge would be to develop proxies that intercept the communication at the boundaries of a TVD, such that the TVD manager can take control and govern the communication.

Secure Block Storage. In contrast to constructing a trusted cloud infrastructure from stretch, an alternative is to build a security middleware on top of commodity clouds. In current commodity clouds offerings, subscribers need to trust cloud providers when processing sensitive health data. In this case, plaintext data processed inside VM instances is temporarily stored in the memory. This relies on the assumption that cloud providers have limited privileges and cannot inspect memory. One alternative is to ensure confidentiality by computation in the encrypted domain, such as with Full Homomorphic Encryptions or Garbled Circuits. However, this approach is not yet efficient in practical implementations. Secure Block Storage (SBS) provide solution to protect data at rest in the cloud, as a non-linear raw memory attached to virtual machine (VM) instances as block device (virtual hard disk, e.g. iSCSI). It is a secure transparent layer, transparent to the application or platform layer, to provide confidentiality, integrity and authenticity for block devices, and is also responsible for user-centric key management. SBS relies on a trusted platform (TPM) as secure and attestable hypervisor. Data stored on block device, mounted as a file system inside the VM, are transparently encrypted (e.g. with AES) and integrity-protected (e.g. with Message Authentication Codes) by the hypervisor. SBS also provides Version Control (or Replay Attacks Prevention) for encrypted data chunks, via hardware/virtual counters (e.g. provided by the TPM).

6   Benchmark Applications and Benefits

A prototype of the health platform is under development, and two applications are created to be deployed on the platform to demonstrate provisioned services including home monitoring data collection from client to cloud, virtualized data storage, cloud based processing and analysis, data sharing between different healthcare service providers and privacy management for patients.

The Home Monitoring application offers SaaS services for end users (e.g. depressed patients in our scenario) to monitor sleep, physical activity and light data via a mobile device (e.g. Philips-Respironics Actiwatch). The data are uploaded via a client side interface to the cloud, and the cloud performs data analysis to generate graph-based presentation to provide personalized coaching. The data are stored in a virtualized secure storage and periodically shared with healthcare professionals from hospital, in order to support the clinical decision and treatment process.

The Wellbeing Portal application supports cloud self-managed PHR services for depressed patients, with graphical analysis of trends of sleep activities, light exposure and real-time mood variations. It allows patients to specify their privacy policies to control the information that should be accessible to a particular doctor (psychiatrist). The PHR data can be updated in two ways: data are collected from the 3rd party service providers (e.g. the home monitoring application described above) or from manual update by patients. These two applications are to be accessible via client side interfaces such as PC, iPad, or smart phone.

Main benefits for end users: The Health T-PaaS offers three principal benefits for end users. 1) *Global coverage and ubiquitous access*: The health platform makes it easy for end users to share data with other service providers and access various applications deployed on the platform on the Internet scale. 2) *Trustworthy platform*: Compared with the current market offerings for cloud based healthcare solutions, the platform enforces security, privacy and resilience, and facilitates a trustworthy environment to allow end users to access the 3rd party healthcare applications. 3) *Full control over personal data*: Users personal data and their privacy rights are protected in compliance with the EU data protection legislation. Users are able to modify their security and privacy policies to permit particular service providers to access whole or part of their data.

Main benefits for Service Providers: 1) *Deduced cost*: Compared to traditional healthcare IT services, the cloud based health platform brings advantages on lower infrastructure investment cost, lower hardware and software maintenance cost. It also minimizes revenue loss from datacenter outage and network intrusion/failure with a reduced recovery time, by making a resilient workflow execution and data storage affordable and easy to use. 2) *Reduced provisioning time and higher productivity*: Instead of developing own IT infrastructure for repository or network, the platform provides off-the-shelf services for health providers to develop applications with reduced service provisioning time and thereafter higher productivity per application. 3) *Trustworthy – security, resilience and data protection*: Security middleware components are integrated into the health platform and the underlying cloud infrastructure, facilitating a trustworthy environment for developing and deploying healthcare applications. Various security features are offered including log service, authorization and single sign-on, access control, automatic audit, cloud-of-clouds adaptive resilient storage, resilient workflow execution, trusted virtualization domain, etc. 4) *Dynamic service composition*: The health platform supports connectivity between different service providers, allowing a more dynamic service composition, flexible business model and marketing strategy. This makes it easier for a provider to change the commercial partner if needed, without impacting the development process.

7   Conclusion

Cloud computing offers significant business benefits, in terms of cost reduction and improved productivity with consolidated resources, and global coverage for ubiquitous access to healthcare services. On the other hand, concerns regarding security, data protection, and resilience have kept many life-critical healthcare service providers staying off the cloud. Besides, legislation required sufficient levels of privacy and data protection in a cross-border cloud environment have become another barrier. Moreover, current health cloud services offerings require full trust to cloud providers, where threats of malicious insiders have become one of the most dangerous attacks to protected data and applications in the cloud. This paper attempts to address the aforementioned issues by introducing a trustworthy cloud platform that is built by deploying on top of trustworthy cloud architecture. The healthcare platform is proposed to host numerous healthcare applications, and also provide storage for medical data such as personal health records. The underlying trustworthy cloud infrastructure is designed to increase the level of trust both for storage and computing, while taking EU data protection and privacy legislation into consideration. Various techniques are employed to provision security, data protection and resilience against data center outage and cloud network failures. Two benchmark applications are implemented as a proof of concept to demonstrate features of the proposed the health platform. Finally, major benefits for both end users and service providers are discussed.

Acknowledgements. This research has been supported by the TClouds project, funded by the European Commission's FP7 under grant agreement number ICT-257243.

References

1. Abbadi, I.M., Alawneh, M., Martin, A.: Secure virtual layer management in clouds. In: International Joint Conference of IEEE TrustCom/IEEE ICESS/FCST, pp. 99–110 (2011)
2. Behl, J., Distler, T., Heisig, F., Kapitza, R., Schunter, M.: Providing Fault-tolerant Execution of Web-service-based Workflows within Clouds. In: Proceedings of the 2nd International Workshop on Cloud Computing Platforms, CloudCP 2012 (2012)

3. Bessani, A., Abbadi, I.M., Bugiel, S., Cesena, E., Deng, M., Gröne, M., Marnau, N., Nürnberger, S., Pasin, M., Schirmer, N.: Tclouds: Privacy and resilience for internet-scale critical infrastructures. In: Petcu, D., Poletti, J.V. (eds.) European Research Activities in Cloud Computing, ch. 6, pp. 160–186. Cambridge Scholars Publishing (March 2012)
4. Bessani, A.N., Correia, M.P., Quaresma, B., André, F., Sousa, P.: Depsky: dependable and secure storage in a cloud-of-clouds. In: Proceedings of the Sixth European Conference on Computer Systems, pp. 31–46 (2011)
5. Bleikertz, S., Bugiel, S., Nagy, Z.A., Nürnberger, S., Kurmus, A., Schunter, M.: Chapter 4 security analysis of openstack, technical requirements and architecture for privacyenhanced and resilient trusted clouds. Technical report, TClouds (2011)
6. Bleikertz, S., Schunter, M., Probst, C.W., Pendarakis, D., Eriksson, K.: Security audits of multi-tier virtual infrastructures in public infrastructure clouds. In: Proceedings of the 2010 ACM Workshop on Cloud Computing Security Workshop, CCSW 2010, pp. 93–102. ACM (2010)
7. Bugiel, S., Nürnberger, S., Pöppelmann, T., Sadeghi, A.-R., Schneider, T.: Amazonia: when elasticity snaps back. In: ACM Conference on Computer and Communications Security, pp. 389–400 (2011)
8. Cachin, C., Keidar, I., Shraer, A.: Fail-aware untrusted storage. SIAM J. Comput. 40(2), 493–533 (2011)
9. CSA. Cloud security alliance: Top threats to cloud computing (2010), https://cloudsecurityalliance.org/topthreats/csathreats.v1.0.pdf
10. Deng, M., Petkovic, M., Nalin, M., Baroni, I.: A home healthcare system in the cloud-addressing security and privacy challenges. In: IEEE International Conference on Cloud Computing, pp. 549–556 (2011)
11. ENISA. Cloud computing risk assessment (2009), http://www.enisa.europa.eu/act/rm/files/deliverables/cloud-computing-risk-assessment
12. Griffin, J.L., Jaeger, T., Perez, R., Sailer, R., Van Doorn, L., Caceres, R.: Trusted virtual domains: Toward secure distributed services. In: Proc. of 1st IEEE Workshop on Hot Topics in System Dependability, HotDep (2005)
13. Heiser, J., Nicolett, M.: Gartner's assessing the security risks of cloud computing (2008), http://www.gartner.com/DisplayDocument?id=685308
14. Ma, D., Tsudik, G.: A new approach to secure logging. TOS 5(1) (2009)
15. Microsoft. Windows azure service disruption update (2012), http://blogs.msdn.com/b/windowsazure/archive/2012/03/01/windows-azure-service-disruption-update.aspx
16. Nalin, M., Baroni, I., Sanna, A.: E-health drivers and barriers for cloud computing adoption. In: CLOSER 2011, pp. 385–390 (2011)
17. OpenStack. OpenStack Open Source Cloud Computing Software, http://www.openstack.org/ (retrieved in 2012)
18. Schneier, B., Kelsey, J.: Secure audit logs to support computer forensics. ACM Trans. Inf. Syst. Secur. 2(2), 159–176 (1999)
19. Sirrix. High-assurance security kernel protection profile (eal5), according to the common criteria v3.1 r2, 2007, certified by german federal office for information security, bsi (2008)
20. Vernizzi, D., Cesena, E., Ramunno, G., Smiraglia, P.: Chapter 11 logging, tclouds d2.2.1, preliminary architecture of middleware for adaptive resilience. Technical report, TClouds (2011)

Author Index